THE SPORTING 2005 YEAR

THE
SPORTING 2005 YEAR

COMPILED AND EDITED BY TIM HILL
INTRODUCED BY EAMONN HOLMES

BBC RADIO FIVE LIVE

HarperSport
An Imprint of HarperCollins*Publishers*

First published in UK in 2005 by
HarperSport
an imprint of HarperCollinsPublishers
London

© British Broadcasting Corporation 2005

A CIP catalogue record for this book is available
from the British Library

Published by arrangement with the BBC
The BBC and Five Live Mark logos are trademarks of the
British Broadcasting Corporation and used under license

BBC logo © BBC 1996
Five Live logo © BBC 2005

All images © Getty images

ISBN 0 00 721598 3

Produced by Atlantic Publishing

Printed and bound in Italy by Lego Spa

The HarperCollins website address is
www.harpercollins.co.uk

BBC Radio FiveLive website address is
www.bbc.co.uk/fivelive

ACKNOWLEDGEMENTS
Particular thanks to
Alison Gauntlett, Jane Benn,
Melanie Cox, Helen Grimes, Sarah Rickayzen, Cliff Salter
Design by John Dunne

Introduction	7
Athletics	**8**
World Championships	10
London Marathon	13
Badminton	**14**
Boxing	**16**
Cricket	**20**
The Npower Ashes Series	22
First Test: Lord's	24
Second Test: Edgbaston	32
Third Test: Old Trafford	42
Fourth Test: Trent Bridge	50
Fifth Test: The Oval	58
Bangladesh Tests	74
Twenty20	75
Natwest Series	76
Natwest Challenge	78
C&G Trophy	80
Twenty20 Cup	84
Totesport League	87
County Championship	88
Cycling: Tour de France	**90**
Darts	**94**
Football	**96**
The Premiership	98
Jose Mourinho	102
Premiership 2005–2006	111
Carling Cup	112
FA Cup	114
Des meets: Alan Hansen	122
UEFA Champions League	124
UEFA Cup	138
UEFA Super Cup	140
Community Shield	142
Des meets: Arsène Wenger	144
World Cup Qualifying	148
Golf	**154**
The Open	156
The Masters	159
US Open	160
US PGA	161
Horse Racing	**162**
The Grand National	164
The Derby	166
The Oaks	167
2000 Guineas	168
1000 Guineas	168
King George	168
Cesarewitch	168
Lincoln Heritage Cup	168
St Leger	168
Irish Derby	169
Prix de l'Arc de Triomphe	169
Hennessey Gold Cup	169
Cheltenham Gold Cup	169
Des meets: Frankie Dettori	170
Motor Sport	**174**
Formula One	176
Des meets: Bernie Ecclestone	184
Motorcycling	188
Rowing	**194**
The Boat Race	196
Rugby	**198**
The Six Nations	200
The British Lions Tour	206
Des meets: Clive Woodward	212
Zurich Premiership	218
Rugby Super League	224
Powergen Challenge Cup	226
Snooker	**232**
Swimming	**236**
Tennis	**238**
Wimbledon	240
Australian Open	250
French Open	252
US Open	254
London Olympics 2012	**256**

Contents

BBC RADIO FIVE LIVE

INTRODUCED BY EAMONN HOLMES

In some ways 2005 was just like Groundhog Day:
Valentino Rossi made it five in a row, Lance Armstrong seven;
Tiger and Federer ruled the roost in the Slams; Johnny Murtagh rode the
Derby winner; Ricky Hatton's 39th opponent went the way of the
previous 38; Paula Radcliffe added to her marathon haul…

But it was also a year of shocks and surprises.
Wales went from wooden spoon zeros to Grand Slam heroes
in two seasons; Hull gatecrashed the Challenge Cup party,
the annual outing hosted by the Big Four; 150–1 shot Shaun Murphy
was crowned King of the Crucible. And Murphy's odds seemed positively
miserly compared with what the bookies were offering when
Liverpool trailed AC Milan 3–0 in Istanbul.

On some sporting fronts we seemed to be
witnessing not a temporary blip but a changing of the guard.
Jose Mourinho masterminded the overthrow of the
Old Trafford–Highbury Premiership duopoly; Fernando Alonso
became F1's youngest champion as Schumacher and Ferrari were
reduced to bit-part players; Andrew Murray was the new darling of
SW19, outside the top 400 at the start of the year, knocking on
the door of the top 50 at the end of it. And, of course, it was the year
in which Freddie and Co. took possession of the coveted urn for the first
time since Mrs T. was in No.10 and *Reet Petite* was at No.1.

The popping of the champagne corks at the Oval encapsulated
the whole sporting year. Vintage stuff.

Athletics

WORLD CHAMPIONSHIPS

Paula races to gold

Paula Radcliffe finally achieved her dream of winning a world title when she took the gold medal in the women's marathon at the World Athletics Championships in Helsinki.

Positioning herself at the front early in the race and constantly fending off pressure from Kenya's defending champion Catherine Ndereba and Romania's Constantina Dita, Paula Radcliffe was finally able to stretch away from fellow runners at the 18.5 mile mark, crossing the finishing line 64 seconds ahead of Ndereba, much to the delight of the vocal British contingent who had come to support her. Although five minutes slower than the

world record she set in 2003 Radcliffe was at last able to wipe away the memories of the Athens Olympics in 2004 when she failed to finish both her races. In the same event fellow British runner Mara Yamauchi achieved a personal best after crossing the line in 2:31.26 to finish 18th while teammate Hayley Haining was 25th, also clocking a personal best of 2:34.41.

The problem last year was that I knew things were falling apart in the last two weeks before and I didn't trust that my body was strong. This year I did and I knew that everything had gone well and it was just a case of getting out there today and executing it.

Paula Radcliffe

I had to run out of my skin. I've not been in the best shape this year, suffering from injuries. I felt my leg all the way home so to get a medal was an achievement.

Mark Lewis-Francis

I had to run out of my skin

Bronze medals for relay teams

A jubilant women's 4 x 400 metres team won a surprise bronze on the last day of the championships after a strong start from Lee McConnell who took the first leg. At the end of the race there was a protest from the Polish team who claimed that Ohuruogu had cut across their runner on the final leg. It proved unsuccessful with the 21-year-old fully defending her tactics as she achieved a clear run home. Meanwhile, in the men's track events the 4 x 100 metres team also gained a bronze despite the squad being dogged by injury and illness before the championships. Olympic gold medal holder Darren Campbell was unable to compete because of a virus and Christian Malcolm had received treatment for a pelvic injury, arriving late in Finland, giving him little time to train with the squad. Devonish later admitted his disappointment with the result having been a member of the squad that won gold in this event in Athens last year.

Outstanding performers

Welshman Tim Benjamin was one of several athletes to show a very professional performance. In the men's 400 metres the 23-year-old came a creditable fifth showing his world-class abilitiles by achieving a finishing time of 44.93 sec. despite running in the challenging lane one. Heptathlete Kelly Sotherton produced a stunning performance in the high jump, finishing in fifth position and keeping medal winners Carolina Kluft and Eunice Barber well within her sights.

Above: A jubilant Paula Radcliffe wins gold in Helsinki, banishing thoughts of her disappointment at the Athens Olympic Games in 2004.

Top: The Great Britain and N.I. 4 x 400 metres team celebrate the first medal for the British team at the Championships. (l-r) Mark Lewis-Francis, Christian Malcolm, Jason Gardener and Marlon Devonish.

Opposite: The women's 4 x 400 metres relay team after their bronze medal run. (l-r) Donna Fraser, Lee McConnell, Christine Ohuruogu and Nicola Sanders.

I'm not sure there are enough coaches in the system that can take young talent and consistently get them into the top five in the world.

Sebastian Coe

I'm not sure there are enough coaches in the system

Declining success

Despite these personal triumphs and successes nothing can hide the statistics that show this was the worst World Championship for Great Britain on record. A general slide in the performance of British athletes over the years combined with the results in Helsinki prompted former Olympic medallists such as Dave Bedford and Sebastian Coe to comment on this disappointing championship. They have drawn attention to the definite lack of talent coming through in a generation where there is less emphasis and curriculum time on physical education in schools and fewer young adults continue to take part in sport after leaving school. Insufficient funding for coaches in this country is also evident – good coaches are tempted to work abroad and the outstanding athletes use their own coaches outside the official set-up. Steve Cram has suggested that the money available needs to be very specifically targeted to benefit those athletes who have the potential to produce world-class performances.

DES LYNAM MEETS

Tanni Grey-Thompson

Tanni Grey-Thompson tells Des Lynam how husband, Ian, gives her motivation and a competitive edge:

A big part of it is that Ian still trains and competes, and I want to beat him. On road races we'll be alongside each other. Technically we're not competing against one another, but in my own mind I compete against him, so I want to be faster and better and stronger than him. And when we train together there's a real competitive edge between us on the road all the time. He can still beat me and that makes me mad, and makes me train really hard.

There was a road race about ten years ago, Portsmouth half marathon, and about half a mile away from the finish, I was in with a pack of guys and I was killing myself just to try to make the world's best time, and I wasn't really aware of what he was doing. He got a pack of guys to sit around me and block me into the kerb, and he went and sprinted, and by the time I got out of being blocked and got around, he crossed the finish line in front of me. And the chief timekeeper was there saying, 'Congratulations, you broke the women's world best time,' and I just thought, I don't care, I want to protest, give me a protest form. 'Who do you want to process? Him! But it's your husband.' I said 'I don't care, I want to process him,' and I remember taking off my crash helmet and throwing it at him, throwing my gloves at him, but no one's ever done that to me again. And all Ian said was, 'You should have known better, you should have known I would have done everything I could to beat you, don't let that happen again.' And the worse thing was having to admit to him that he was right!

Above: *Wheelchair racer Tanni Grey-Thompson stormed home to take Britain's first gold in the T53 400 metres event at the inaugural Visa Paralympic World Cup held in Manchester in May. In this year's London Marathon she was delighted with her third place.*

LONDON MARATHON

I didn't have a clue how far ahead I was

Paula Radcliffe's victory in this year's 25th London Marathon has demonstrated her talent to the world. Finishing in two hours, seventeen minutes and 42 seconds she produced the third fastest time on record. Despite the much-publicized toilet stop that Radcliffe apologized for later, she took control of the race after the seven-mile marker and never looked back. Covering the first mile in just over five minutes she was initially chased by the Kenyan duo Margaret Okayo and Susan Chepkemei. They were unable to keep with the gruelling pace set by Radcliffe and Okayo, the 2004 champion eventually finished fourth. Romania's Constantina Dita moved into second place halfway through the race and was eventually placed second, five minutes behind Radcliffe. Ireland's Sonia O'Sullivan and Britain's Mara Yamauchi also had excellent races coming in eighth and tenth respectively.

Lel's London Marathon surprise

It took Kenya's Martin Lel just two hours seven minutes and 26 seconds to win the Marathon beating Jaouard Gharib of Morocco by a mere 23 seconds. The race began with fellow Kenyan Paul Tergat as the clear favourite and although he and last year's winner Evans Rutto were part of the large leading group Lel picked them off one by one. Tergat eventually finished eighth while Rutto, also from Kenya, was a disappointing tenth. Britain's Jon Brown produced an excellent performance achieving a personal best, coming in six seconds behind Italian Olympic champion Stefano Baldini. The pace of the field enabled Brown to pass runners in the latter stages as his careful tactical running paid off.

Below: Paula Radcliffe crosses Tower Bridge on her way to victory in the third fastest time on record.

I didn't have a clue how far ahead I was so I was really panicking at having stopped, and annoyed with myself because I knew the time wasn't that bad and I wanted to try to run a good time as well. Because of my stomach cramps, I didn't get the chance to run as hard as I was capable of doing. The crowd was great. In London 2012, if we get a crowd like that out there, no city is going to be better than London.

Paula Radcliffe

BADMINTON

It's got to be my best win yet

England's fortunes in the World Championships did not start well when Olympic silver medallist Nathan Robertson was forced to withdraw when he tore ligaments in his right ankle during a practice session the day before the tournament began. He and his partner Gail Emms were top seeds in the mixed doubles and tipped to win gold. However, Emms and Donna Kellogg successfully reached the quarter-finals of the women's doubles. Tracey Hallam who was seventh seed in the tournament also reached the quarter-finals before losing to China's Xie Xingfang, who later went on to win the women's title.

In the men's singles Aamir Ghaffar achieved England's best result by reaching the third round, before bowing out to Denmark's second seed, Kenneth Jonassen. In the previous round he had shocked Olympic silver medallist Shon Seung by defeating him 15–1 15–7.

Meanwhile the Americans claimed their first medal at a world championship when men's double partners Tony Gunawan and Howard Bach, who were 13th seeds, defeated Indonesia's Candra Wijaya and Sigit Budiarto much to the delight of the home fans.

Opposite: England's Tracey Hallam returns a shot during the 2005 Sudirman Cup World Mixed Team Badminton Championships against Tine Rasmussen of Denmark at the Capital Gymnasium in May.

Below: *Aamir Ghaffar in action for England.*

BBC RADIO FIVE LIVE

It's got to be my best win yet.

Aamir Ghaffar
England number one

I aimed to make the quarter-finals and I've done that, despite coming here with a few niggles.

Tracey Hallam
England number one

World Championships

English successes

Women's doubles
Donna Kellogg and Gail Emms reached quarter-finals

Women's singles
Tracey Hallam reached quarter-finals

Men's singles
Aamir Ghaffar reached third round

BOXING

'Hitman' Topples Tszyu

On 4 June 2005 Ricky 'The Hitman' Hatton became king of the ten-stone division
by defeating Kostya Tszyu, light-welterweight champion for a decade and the man regarded as among
the best pound-for-pound fighters on the planet.
Unbeaten in 38 fights, Hatton had held the lightly-regarded WBU title since 2001.
At 26, he had an 11-year age advantage over a man undoubtedly in the twilight of his career.
And the man from Hyde knew that his army of fans would be willing him on to
topple the champion on their home MEN Arena turf.

Champion since '95

Even so, a cursory glance at Tszyu's cv showed that it was a daunting proposition. Born in Siberia, Tszyu won his first Soviet title at the age of 16. He took gold at the 1991 world amateur championship in Sydney, relocating to Australia and turning pro shortly afterwards. Tszyu lifted his first world title in 1995, unifying the three major championship belts in 2001. The one blot on his pro copybook came in 1997, when he lost to Vince Phillips. Hatton saw off Phillips in 2003, though as the latter was then pushing 40, it would have been dangerously unwise to read too much into that when he and Tszyu met for the IBF light-welterweight crown in Manchester.

Gruelling battle

The champion was installed as 1–2 favourite, but this was to be Hatton's finest hour. It was a gruelling battle which looked to be going all the way. At the end of the 11th, with Hatton ahead on all three scorecards, his trainer, Billy 'The Preacher' Graham exhorted his man to make one last big effort. Hatton, pugnacious as ever, was more than ready to deliver, but in the event he wasn't required to join battle for those final three minutes. Tszyu's trainer Johnny Lewis called a halt to proceedings, and within a week was looking for a new job.

Hatton said the fight went exactly as planned. He sapped the champion's strength by taking the fight to him in the early rounds. He knew that Tszyu was at his most dangerous at the outer limit of his punching range, so came in close to mix it. He fully expected to take a few shots and be behind in the early stages, then come through to win after Tszyu's strength and sting were drawn. It worked like a dream, Hatton saying he knew he had victory within his grasp by Round Nine.

Unifying the division

Although he had beaten the main man, Hatton was not about to rest on his laurels or hand-pick fall-guy opponents for easy pay-days. He immediately targeted the other belt holders, aiming to unify a division brimming with stellar talent over the next three years before calling it a day. First on the Hitman's hit-list was the new WBA title holder Carlos Maussa – surprise seven-round winner over Vivian Harris in June – the fight scheduled to take place in Sheffield in November 2005.

Opposite: Ricky Hatton (l) in action against Kostya Tszyu during the IBF light-welterweight title fight at the MEN Arena.
Right: Hatton with the belt after the fight.

Khan avenges Athens defeat

Before bowing out of the amateur ranks in 2005, Amir Khan had some unfinished business. The 18-year-old boxing sensation was still smarting from the defeat by Cuba's Mario Kindelan in the previous year's Olympic final. Khan had gone to Athens as Great Britain's sole boxing representative, and the nation's youngest Olympian in the ring since Colin Jones competed in Montreal in 1976. After disposing of four opponents, the 17-year-old student was guaranteed the honour of returning to Bolton as Britain's youngest ever boxing medallist. The colour he eventually brought home was silver, defending champion Kindelan winning the 60kg division final by a 30–22 margin. It meant that Khan didn't quite manage to outshine the achievement of his hero Muhammad Ali, who swept the board in the light-heavyweight division in Rome in 1960 at the age of 18.

Boxing's hottest property

Nine months later, in May 2005, the Athens finalists met again at the Reebok Stadium. Khan was now ready for the veteran Cuban, winning the fight 19–13. Some had hoped he would remain in the amateur ranks through to Beijing 2008, but Khan was the hottest property in boxing and the pressure to turn pro was enormous. He was keen to follow in the footsteps of Robin Reid, Richie Woodhall and Alan Minter, the only Britons to have won an Olympic boxing medal and gone on to become world champions. His promoter Frank Warren has little doubt that Khan will emulate their achievements; he regards Khan as the best of the many Olympians to join the professional ranks since the great Sugar Ray Leonard.

Gunning for Naz's record

Khan's first two professional bouts didn't prove too onerous. David Bailey was dispatched by TKO, while he was a comfortable points winner over Baz Carey. Khan's avowed intention is to become world champion and a boxing legend, then retire in his mid-twenties. His first objective will be to lift the world crown before the age of 21. If he manages that feat, he would take over from Naseem Hamed as Britain's youngest ever world champion.

Joe Calzaghe wins one-handed

After a unanimous decision in his favour Joe Calzaghe retained his WBO super middleweight title for the 17th time with a victory over Kenyan Evans Ashira. It was a far from average win with the 33-year-old Welshman quickly taking control before injuring his left hand in the third round, which forced him to continue the match using only his right. The fight finally went to 12 rounds and a medical examination showed he had broken a metacarpal. Calzaghe first won the WBO title after a fight against Chris Eubank in 1997. Since then opponents have included Omar Sheika and Mario Veit and to date he has remained unbeaten after 40 fights that have included 31 knockouts. In 1991 he was voted BBC Wales Sports Personality of the Year. He was due to fight IBF title holder Jeff Lacy in November but Calzaghe's promoter Frank Warren has now confirmed that the match is off due to the injury sustained and admits that it could be difficult to reschedule.

Opposite: Amir Khan in action against Baz Carey during their lightweight clash at the Cardiff International Arena.

Right: Joe Calzaghe is unable to take his glove off after damaging his left hand in the fight against Evans Ashira during the WBO super middleweight title fight at the Cardiff International Arena.

BBC RADIO FIVE LIVE

I think I did good work and definitely one day I'm going to be in America, beating Don's boxers. It was a brilliant workout thanks to all the coaching I've been getting.

Amir Khan
after his fight against Baz Carey

Cricket

THE NPOWER ASHES SERIES

Ashes return after 16 years

Even before England and Australia joined battle at the Oval in the winner-take-all Fifth Test, the 2005 Ashes had been hailed as the greatest series in the history of the game. The build-up to the clash between the two top-ranked sides in the world had been febrile. Could England, the young pretenders who had risen from bottom of the Test heap in 1999, wrest the famous urn from Australia's vice-like grasp for the first time since the winter of 1986-87?

Michael Vaughan's men had won their last five series, and beaten every Test side save Australia. They had also won seven out of seven on home soil in 2004. It was a team brimming with confidence and, crucially, one largely untainted by past maulings at the hands of their Antipodean rivals. That was one of the reasons why the selectors opted for the brash Kevin Pietersen over Graham Thorpe. Even Andrew Flintoff was entering uncharted waters, injury and poor form having kept him out of the previous three Ashes encounters.

None of that held much sway with Glenn McGrath. As it was a five-Test series, the result would be 5–0. Simple.

As the drama unfolded, the nation went cricket mad. The tentacles of the 2005 Ashes series stretched far beyond the game's aficionados. Millions for whom the lbw law and reverse swing were as abstruse as particle physics were drawn to a gladiatorial contest played in a spirit of humility and mutual respect; it was sporting theatre at its finest.

Opposite: England's captain Michael Vaughan kisses the replica Ashes trophy after defeating Australia.

Below: England players celebrate in Trafalgar Square following their Ashes series victory.

FIRST TEST: LORD'S

First blood to Australia

England needed to get off to a good start, and to do that they were up against history as well as Ricky Ponting's acclaimed world-beaters, for Australia had not lost at headquarters since 1934. That record still stood when the match ended on the fourth day, and although there had been encouraging signs in England's performance – notably Kevin Pietersen's batting and a four-man pace attack that could bowl the Australians out – a ninth Ashes defeat seemed on the cards.

Ponting won the toss and elected to bat, more than happy to let his fine collection of run machines get to work. Two hours later the innings was hanging by a thread, England having sent five back to the pavilion even before the scoreboard reached three figures.

Brute from Harmison

Matthew Hoggard had the honour of taking the first wicket of the series, bowling Hayden for 12. Harmison softened Ponting up with a brute which struck him on the visor, drawing blood from the skipper's cheek. He soon departed to a Strauss slip catch off the same bowler.

Flintoff, into the attack at first change, began his Ashes career with a wicket maiden, a short-pitched delivery hurrying Langer into skying the ball to Harmison. Simon Jones entered the fray in a double change, and Australia, so used to bossing any bowling a Test side could throw at them, soon found that this England attack was going to ask some seriously probing questions. Jones forced an edge from Damien Martyn, who edged to the bowler's

namesake behind the stumps. Michael Clarke was then trapped lbw off Jones, with the score on 87. That was the superstitious score for Aussie batsmen – 13 away from a century – though they were less used to it representing the total with five men down.

Prize scalp

Katich and Gilchrist made it through to lunch, Aussie fans knowing that an explosive hour or two from the wicket-keeper would get the innings back on track. Gilchrist's Test average was over 55, and even better than that against England, while his mean score for his previous four Test innings in 2005 was 152. No wonder, then, that England considered the No. 7 a prize scalp, and it was taken soon after lunch, Flintoff having him caught behind for a rapid-fire 26.

Warne and Katich steadied the ship before falling in quick succession, the last four wickets falling for the addition of just 15 runs. Harmison took them all to finish with 5 for 43.

Skittled in 40 overs

To skittle the world's premier side for 190 in just 40.2 overs was an outstanding effort. But wounded Australians were also going to pose a danger, and with McGrath and Warne in the side – on the verge of claiming 1,100 Test victims between them – no total was undefendable.

Below: Simon Katich sees his shot stopped by Ian Bell during day one of the First Ashes Test match.

Opposite: England captain Michael Vaughan tosses the coin as Australia's Ricky Ponting watches at the start of the First Test.

We've always had a good feeling about this place. It's a great ground to play on, we've had a great deal of success here and a lot of the guys on this team have been here and done it all before. So we had a great feeling coming here and that's reflected in the way we've played.

Ricky Ponting
on Lord's

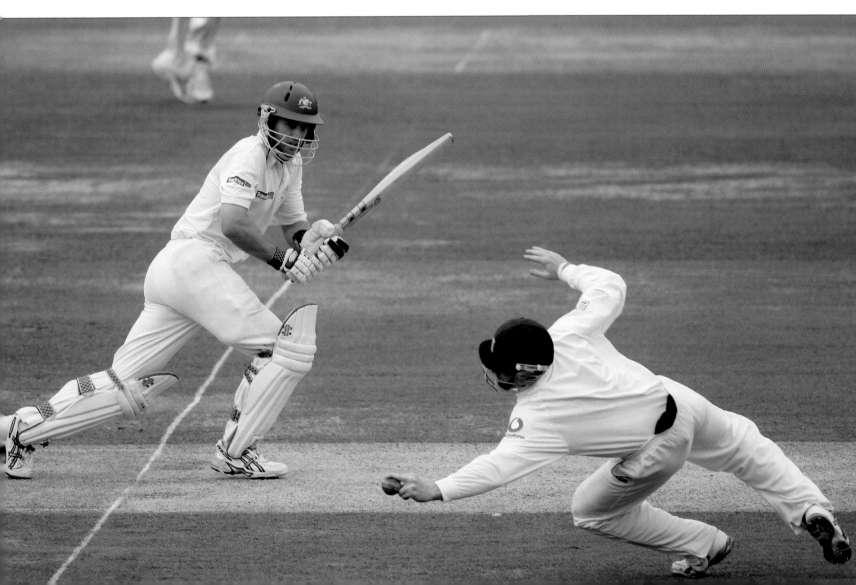

Opposite: Kevin Pietersen hits out on his way to a half-century during day four of the First Ashes Test match.

Below: Glenn McGrath celebrates the wicket of Ashley Giles with Simon Katich during day four of the First Test.

And so it proved. After tea the Australians hit back, courtesy of a blistering McGrath spell. He reduced England from 10 for 0 to 21 for 5, the first of those, Marcus Trescothick becoming his 500th Test scalp. McGrath had identified the Somerset man as one of his targets for the series, a ploy he'd used successfully over the years.

When Flintoff was bowled for a duck, McGrath's figures were 8.2–4–5–7, his 27th five-wicket haul. By now Australia's modest total had taken on a very different hue.

The belligerent Kevin Pietersen, England's 626th Test player, stopped the rot. After a brief partnership with the team's other debutant, Ian Bell, the Hampshire man put on 58 with Geraint Jones. England closed on 92–7, with Pietersen still there on 28 but with only tail-enders for support.

Maiden half-century for Pietersen

After Hoggard's early departure Pietersen opened his shoulders, clubbing McGrath for 14 off three balls to bring up his 50, including a towering six. He also put Warne into the stand, before another attempt at a monster was brilliantly caught just inside the rope by Damien Martyn. It had been a superb debut, 57 off 89 balls, 44 of them accumulated without the need to run. In the context of the match it was priceless, as was the contribution of Harmison and Jones, who put on a valuable 33, the second best partnership of a disappointing reply.

As the England selectors watched the collapse, news came through that Graham Thorpe had announced his retirement from international cricket, closing the door on that option, even if the batting continued to be brittle and changes needed to be considered.

If England want to become the best side in the world, it's not about one series, it's about a period of time, and I think that's why Australia have been so good for ten years at least, maybe longer. We've beaten everybody home and away. We want to keep that record going over here ... But England are a very good side. They have worked hard to get to number two in the world, and if they keep playing the way they are now, continue to play like this for the next two, three, four years, and keep beating everyone home and away, they can be the best side in the world.

Shane Warne

BBC RADIO FIVE LIVE

The bowling of Shane Warne in the second innings seemed like a genius at work, after the genius had done the work for you in the first innings.
Ricky Ponting

Opposite: Glenn McGrath acknowledges the crowd after taking four wickets during day four.

Below: Brett Lee of Australia takes the wicket of Andrew Strauss of England during day three.

Expensive drop

20 wickets had fallen inside 90 overs, and an hour into the second day Australia embarked on their second innings with a lead of 35. Pietersen's impressive debut continued as he brilliantly threw down the stumps to remove Langer for 6. But the next five batters all made a healthy contribution, Michael Clarke bagging 91 to reinforce his credentials as the rising young star of the team. He was dropped on 21, though, an expensive error by Pietersen which took the sheen off his personal contribution.

The tail-enders hung around as foil to Katich, who was last man out after the total had reached a formidable 384.

England needed a record 420 to win. Trescothick and Strauss provided a solid platform, putting on 80, but there followed a regular clatter of wickets. Pietersen once again was the man left to carry the fight. There was one mighty six off Lee, though he was somewhat lucky to survive a full toss lbw appeal off the same bowler.

England mopped up in 61 balls

England closed on 156–5, bad light ending the third day's proceedings prematurely. England's best chance lay in a rain-affected draw, but that proved a vain hope as the skies cleared on the afternoon of the fourth day. Australia needed only an hour and 61 balls to take the last five wickets for the addition of just 22 to the total, completing a comprehensive 239-run victory. Pietersen ran out of partners on 64, becoming only the eighth player to score two half-centuries on his England debut.

McGrath's 9 wickets earn him man of the match

McGrath and Warne had taken 15 wickets between them, a curt response to those who said that the two veterans – with an aggregate 70 years – were past their best. McGrath's 9 for 82 earned him the man of the match award, and he was quick to extrapolate from one result the pattern for the rest of the summer: 'If we bat and bowl as well as we can, I don't think England are going to get near us.' His captain endorsed that view, remarking that the difference between the sides was vast.

Michael Vaughan was naturally disappointed at the way his team had batted – Pietersen apart – and was also left ruing six dropped catches which, if taken, might have given the team a reachable fourth innings target.

BBC RADIO FIVE LIVE

...that's what Test cricket is all about, repeating high quality day in and day out. I think if you look at the play throughout this game it has been exceptional, absolutely outstanding.

Ricky Ponting

First Test 21 July 2005 at Lord's
Australia won the toss and decided to bat
Australia beat England by 239 runs

Australia 1st Innings

J L Langer	c S J Harmison	b A Flintoff	40
M L Hayden		b M J Hoggard	12
R T Ponting	c A J Strauss	b S J Harmison	9
D R Martyn	c G O Jones	b S P Jones	2
M J Clarke	lbw	b S P Jones	11
S M Katich	c G O Jones	b S J Harmison	27
A C Gilchrist	c G O Jones	b A Flintoff	26
S K Warne		b S J Harmison	28
B Lee		b S J Harmison	3
J N Gillespie	lbw	b S J Harmison	1
G D McGrath	not out		10
Extras	11nb 1w 5b 4lb		21
Total	all out	(40.2 overs)	190

Bowler	O	M	R	W
S J Harmison	11.2	0	43	5
M J Hoggard	8.0	0	40	1
A Flintoff	11.0	2	50	2
S P Jones	10.0	0	48	2

England 1st Innings

M E Trescothick	c J L Langer	b G D McGrath	4
A J Strauss	c S K Warne	b G D McGrath	2
M P Vaughan		b G D McGrath	3
I R Bell		b G D McGrath	6
K P Pietersen	c D R Martyn	b S K Warne	57
A Flintoff		b G D McGrath	0
G O Jones	c A C Gilchrist	b B Lee	30
A F Giles	c A C Gilchrist	b B Lee	11
M J Hoggard	c M L Hayden	b S K Warne	0
S J Harmison	c D R Martyn	b B Lee	11
S P Jones	not out		20
Extras	5nb 1b 5lb		11
Total	all out	(48.1 overs)	155

Bowler	O	M	R	W
G D McGrath	18.0	5	53	5
B Lee	15.1	5	47	3
J N Gillespie	8.0	1	30	0
S K Warne	7.0	2	19	2

Umpires: Aleem Dar, R E Koertzen

Australia 2nd Innings

J L Langer	run out		6
M L Hayden		b A Flintoff	34
R T Ponting	c sub	b M J Hoggard	42
D R Martyn	lbw	b S J Harmison	65
M J Clarke		b M J Hoggard	91
S M Katich	c S P Jones	b S J Harmison	67
A C Gilchrist		b A Flintoff	10
S K Warne	c A F Giles	b S J Harmison	2
B Lee	run out		8
J N Gillespie		b S P Jones	13
G D McGrath	not out		20
Extras	8nb 10b 8lb		26
Total	all out	(100.4 overs)	384

Bowler	O	M	R	W
S J Harmison	27.4	6	54	3
M J Hoggard	16.0	1	56	2
A Flintoff	27.0	4	123	2
S P Jones	18.0	1	69	1
A F Giles	11.0	1	56	0
I R Bell	1.0	0	8	0

England 2nd Innings

M E Trescothick	c M L Hayden	b S K Warne	44
A J Strauss	c and b	B Lee	37
M P Vaughan		b B Lee	4
I R Bell	lbw	b S K Warne	8
K P Pietersen	not out		64
A Flintoff	c A C Gilchrist	b S K Warne	3
G O Jones	c J N Gillespie	b G D McGrath	6
A F Giles	c M L Hayden	b G D McGrath	0
M J Hoggard	lbw	b G D McGrath	0
S J Harmison	lbw	b S K Warne	0
S P Jones	c S K Warne	b G D McGrath	0
Extras	3nb 6b 5lb		14
Total	all out	(58.1 overs)	180

Bowler	O	M	R	W
G D McGrath	17.1	2	29	4
B Lee	15.0	3	58	2
J N Gillespie	6.0	0	18	0
S K Warne	20.0	2	64	4

 RADIO FIVE LIVE

This bloke is going to leave a huge hole in the game of cricket when he disappears. When he comes on it's exciting – you just don't know what's going to happen. Everybody is watching; every ball is a major event – and long may it continue because every sport needs superstars, every sport needs people like Shane Warne. The longer he plays, the better … He's tough. He's competitive. He dares to do what other people don't do. He's brave and although you do want England to win the last Test match, if it's going to be his last game in England, you'd like to see him do something special as well.

Angus Fraser on Shane Warne

Right: *Warne (2nd from r) appeals in vain for lbw against Andrew Strauss during day three.*

SECOND TEST: EDGBASTON

Narrowest win in Ashes history

The Second Test at Edgbaston witnessed the closest ever finish to an Ashes encounter, and one of the most extraordinary matches in the annals of the international game. As a pulsating drama headed towards its denouement on the fourth morning all three results were still possible until Geraint Jones held on to a ball gloved by Kasprowicz off Harmison to clinch victory and level the series.

The drama began even before a ball was bowled, a freak accident during the warm-up costing McGrath a place in the starting line-up. It was a major blow to Australia: in the 13 matches the premier paceman had missed in the previous four years, the opposition had scored an average 120 runs more per innings. As just two runs would separate the teams after ten remarkable sessions, Ricky Ponting would have cause to rue the stray ball which found its way beneath McGrath's feet on the Edgbaston outfield.

Freak accident paves way for Kasprowicz

McGrath's departure for hospital treatment on damaged ankle ligaments meant Michael Kasprowicz entered the fray. The England selectors resisted the calls for change following the Lord's defeat, fielding the same XI.

Ponting's decision to put England in backfired as Strauss and Trescothick piled on 112 for first wicket on a pitch offering no help to the bowlers. After a top-notch 90 from the Somerset man, the Aussies found Flintoff and Pietersen in belligerent mood in the afternoon session, their century partnership coming at better than a run a ball. It was here that Flintoff, on whose broad shoulders had been heaped so much expectation, stepped up to the plate. Having scored 0 and 3 at Lord's, and taken four wickets for 173, Australia's fans must have wondered what all the fuss was

about. At Edgbaston, and the last three Tests, they would find out. Freddie eventually fell for 68 to Gillespie, 'Dizzy's' 250th Test victim. Freddie's was the fifth wicket to fall, for 290 – rather healthier than the 21–5 to which England had crumbled on the first day at Lord's.

Pietersen made it three consecutive 50s, before falling in the deep off Lee for 71, plundered off just 76 balls. The tail wagged on a placid strip to get England up to 407. What could have been a ticklish few overs for the Australian openers was prevented by rain.

To beat Australia you need to have a good team performance and you need individual brilliance as well. Freddie Flintoff, this week, was outstanding for us.

Michael Vaughan

Below: English bowler Simon Jones (c) is congratulated by teammates after dismissing Justin Langer for 82 runs on the second day of the Second Test.

Opposite: Flintoff comforts Brett Lee at the end of the Second Test.

Vaughan sets his trap

There had been no deviation off the pitch or in the air for the Australian attack, but in the very first over of the second day Harmison got the ball to swing. And in the first delivery of the second over Hayden's poor run of form continued as Hoggard had him caught on the drive for a golden duck, the first of his Test career. It was an excellent piece of captaincy, Vaughan setting three men in position for one of Hayden's favourite shots, Strauss being the one to swallow the catch.

Ponting led the fightback, no doubt aware of his need to take charge after taking the wrong option the previous morning. He hit a sparkling 61 – his 28th Test half-century – before his mistimed paddle sweep off Giles top-edged to Vaughan, with the score on 88. The England off spinner enjoyed the moment; he was stung by criticism aimed at the team in general, and him in particular, following the Lord's defeat. A brilliant piece of fielding by Vaughan just before lunch removed Damien Martyn, the captain swooping from mid-on and throwing down the stumps with the batsman a fraction short of his ground.

BBC RADIO FIVE LIVE

It's important that you take your opportunities in the field, especially against good teams like Australia. It's a huge positive factor that we actually created opportunities. I'd be a lot more worried if we weren't creating opportunities and they were getting 550 or 600. The start on day one was pretty good, the best start of an Ashes by an England side for a long time.

Michael Vaughan

Opposite: *Michael Vaughan (l) and Ian Bell congratulate Andrew Flintoff after he took the wicket of Ricky Ponting during day three.*

Right: *England off spinner Ashley Giles appeals to the umpire for the wicket of Australia's Justin Langer on the second day.*

Jones answers critics

Another man who had come in for criticism for his performance at Lord's was Geraint Jones. He, too, began repaying the selectors' faith by taking the catches which dismissed Clarke and Katich, the former off Giles, the latter from the bowling of Flintoff. Suddenly, Australia were 208–5 as the dangerous Gilchrist arrived at the crease for his 100th Test innings. He would see a succession of partners come and go. Anchorman Langer, who had taken a couple of meaty blows off Harmison, fell to a fast, full late-swinging delivery from Jones; and Warne's premeditated foray down the pitch against Giles produced the death rattle rather than a boundary.

Reverse swing

Simon Jones, who had been working hard on his reverse swing over the previous 12 months, put that effort to good use against Lee, and the irrepressible Flintoff mopped up Gillespie and Kasprowicz in successive balls. Gilchrist was left stranded one short of another Test 50.

Facing a 99-run first-innings deficit, Australia hit back in the 35 minutes remaining at the end of the second day. Warne bowled Strauss with an absolute jaffa, reminiscent of the delivery which removed Gatting on the leg spinner's Test debut in 1993. Hawkeye showed that the ball deviated three feet between pitching and hitting the stumps. Close of play: 25–1.

On Saturday morning nightwatchman Matthew Hoggard saw two senior partners depart in quick succession. Trescothick swished at a wide one from Lee, while Vaughan had his timbers clattered for the third time in the series and a worrying aggregate 32 runs in four innings. Master technician Geoff Boycott was quick to point out a flaw in the England captain's defence, the bat coming through at an angle from first slip to mid on, and only straightening after the ball had passed.

Slog sweep

When Hoggard's resistance was ended, England were suddenly wobbling at 31–4, Lee having taken three wickets for four runs in 11 balls. Pietersen provided cheer for the home fans, planting Warne into the stand with two terrific slog sweeps, but the bowler had his revenge with the score on 72. Pietersen was clearly unhappy at being given out caught behind, the ball ricocheting off thigh, chest and elbow. But having appeared to glove one earlier, perhaps justice was served.

Warne picked up Bell again, though the Warwickshire man may have been unlucky this time: the Snickometer suggested that he had struck pad with bat while playing his forward defensive.

With Flintoff and Jones, England's last recognized pair, at the crease and a lead of just 174, the game seemed to be swinging Australia's way. That looked even more the case when Flintoff pulled up sharply holding his shoulder after stroking a Warne delivery into the off side. Freddie not only made it through to lunch for remedial work, but came out afterwards with all guns blazing.

Opposite: Umpire Billy Bowden signals six runs for Andrew Flintoff during day three.

Right: Andrew Flintoff hits out during day three of the Second Test.

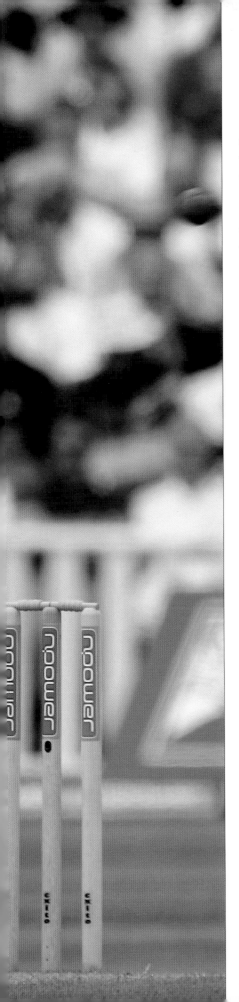

Record nine 6s for Freddie

Geraint Jones fell to a brute of a ball from Lee, the latter's fourth victim giving him his best ever return against England. And when Warne picked up Giles and Harmison in successive deliveries to record yet another 5-for, England were 131 with one wicket to fall. That partnership put on 50 in 40 balls, Flintoff setting a new Ashes record in plundering nine sixes in his 73 off 86 balls. At one point there was the extraordinary sight of every Australian fielder bar the bowler and Gilchrist guarding the boundary, but that mattered little as Freddie was at his brutal best. He was eventually bowled by Warne, the latter's 599th Test victim giving him figures of 6 for 46.

182 all out set Australia a target of 282. No one disputed that if they set a new Edgbaston record and mounted a successful chase to take a 2–0 lead in the series, the Ashes were highly unlikely to be changing hands this time round.

Langer and Hayden put on 47 for the first wicket before Flintoff continued his destructive form, this time with the ball. He bowled Langer, then, with just one more run on the board, had Ponting caught behind. A brilliant slip catch by Trescothick accounted for Hayden, and with the score on 107, Hoggard came on and Martyn immediately holed out to Bell at mid-wicket.

Trescothick gathered at the second attempt Katich's snick off Giles, and England smelled blood. Having claimed the extra half-hour, Vaughan reaped dividends when Harmison bowled Clarke with a superb slower ball for 30. The loss of the last recognized batsman in the final delivery of the day surely meant the final nail in Australia's coffin.

BBC RADIO FIVE LIVE

It's been an epic game and full credit to the way Australia came out this morning. I really thought that 100 runs on the last morning was going to be too much, but Shane Warne had an outstanding game and so did Brett Lee. But the way my team just came out and showed a bit of character at the end there! I think most of our guys thought it had gone but we fought hard. Throughout the whole Test match we fought very, very well and played a really good game under a lot of pressure. 1–0 down against a good team like Australia – you can't afford to go 2–0 down. We've won and it's really set us up for the rest of the series now.

Michael Vaughan

England clinch the Test by 2 runs

Last two wickets chase 107

Warne and Lee emerged on day four at 175–8. Lee had two Test 50s to his name, while the leg spinner's batting credits included a 99; even so, it needed a record-breaking effort for the last two Australian wickets to put on 107 and snatch victory. With a combination of some terrific proper cricket shots and some slices of fortune, the score moved on to 220 at an alarming rate from the England fans' point of view. Flintoff again made the breakthrough. His full-length delivery appeared to have cleaned up Warne's leg stump, the batsman having shuffled across to expose it on a number of occasions. Replays showed that the ball missed the woodwork; the batsman slipped and his back foot did the damage.

Home supporters' fears were eased as Kasprowicz, a more typical No. 11 'rabbit', came to the crease. However, he gave sterling support to Lee and the two edged ever nearer the target. But after putting on 59 in 77 balls – just three runs short of victory – Kasprowicz gloved Harmison to Jones. At least,

umpire Bowden raised his famous crooked finger; replays subsequently showed that Kasprowicz's hand had not been in contact with the bat when the ball struck him.

Perhaps the enduring image of the summer was Flintoff's gesture of consolation towards the unbeaten Lee; magnanimity in victory, after a fiercely contested four-day battle, was sport at its best.

First 'live' series win since '97

It was the narrowest win in the 308-match, 128-year history of Ashes cricket, one run closer than Australia's win at Old Trafford in 1902, and England's victory in Melbourne 80 years later.

Perhaps more significantly, it was England's first victory in an Ashes series that was still 'live' since 1997.

Shane Warne's ten-wicket haul and defiant 42 in the run chase would, ordinarily, have assured him of the man-of-the-match award. But in this extraordinary game, the leg spinner's terrific performance was eclipsed by the man Ponting had identified as the sole Englishman who would get into the Australian XI. Flintoff, with a brutal 68 and 73, plus aggregate bowling figures of 7–131 and a couple of catches for good measure, was the man who had done most to inflict defeat on Australia, level the series and give England momentum going into round three, Old Trafford, just four days later.

Opposite: Stephen Harmison claims the wicket of Michael Kasprowicz caught by Geraint Jones to give England a two-run win during day four.

Left: Geraint Jones celebrates after taking the winning catch off the bowling of Steve Harmison.

BBC RADIO FIVE LIVE

It was a finish and a match that brought immense credit to both sides. Australia, for the way they batted this morning, for their positive attitude and physical bravery. England, for sticking to the task and keeping their nerve.

Julian Worricker

Second Test 4 August 2005 at Edgbaston
Australia won the toss and decided to field
England beat Australia by 2 runs

England 1st Innings

Batsman			Runs
M E Trescothick	c A C Gilchrist	b M S Kasprowicz	90
A J Strauss		b S K Warne	48
M P Vaughan	c B Lee	b J N Gillespie	24
I R Bell	c A C Gilchrist	b M S Kasprowic	6
K P Pietersen	c S M Katich	b B Lee	71
A Flintoff	c A C Gilchrist	b J N Gillespie	68
G O Jones	c A C Gilchrist	b M S Kasprowicz	1
A F Giles	lbw	b S K Warne	23
M J Hoggard	lbw	b S K Warne	16
S J Harmison		b S K Warne	17
S P Jones	not out		19
Extras	14nb 1w 9lb		24
Total	all out	(79.2 overs)	407

Bowler	O	M	R	W
B Lee	17.0	1	111	1
J N Gillespie	22.0	3	91	2
M S Kasprowicz	15.0	3	80	3
S K Warne	25.2	4	116	4

England 2nd Innings

Batsman			Runs
M E Trescothick	c A C Gilchrist	b B Lee	21
A J Strauss		b S K Warne	6
M J Hoggard	c M L Hayden	b B Lee	1
M P Vaughan		b B Lee	1
I R Bell	c A C Gilchrist	b S K Warne	21
K P Pietersen	c A C Gilchrist	b S K Warne	20
A Flintoff		b S K Warne	73
G O Jones	c R T Ponting	b B Lee	9
A F Giles	c M L Hayden	b S K Warne	8
S J Harmison	c R T Ponting	b S K Warne	0
S P Jones	not out		12
Extras	9nb 1lb		10
Total	all out	(52.1 overs)	182

Bowler	O	M	R	W
B Lee	18.0	1	82	4
J N Gillespie	8.0	0	24	0
M S Kasprowicz	3.0	0	29	0
S K Warne	23.1	7	46	6

Australia 1st Innings

Batsman			Runs
J L Langer	lbw	b S P Jones	82
M L Hayden	c A J Strauss	b M J Hoggard	0
R T Ponting	c M P Vaughan	b A F Giles	61
D R Martyn		run out	20
M J Clarke	c G O Jones	b A F Giles	40
S M Katich	c G O Jones	b A Flintoff	4
A C Gilchrist	not out		49
S K Warne		b A F Giles	8
B Lee	c A Flintoff	b S P Jones	6
J N Gillespie	lbw	b A Flintoff	7
M S Kasprowicz	lbw	b A Flintoff	0
Extras	10nb 1w 13b 7lb		31
Total	all out	(76.0 overs)	308

Bowler	O	M	R	W
S J Harmison	11.0	1	48	0
M J Hoggard	8.0	0	41	1
S P Jones	16.0	2	69	2
A Flintoff	15.0	1	52	3
A F Giles	26.0	2	78	3

Australia 2nd Innings

Batsman			Runs
J L Langer		b A Flintoff	28
M L Hayden	c M E Trescothick	b S P Jones	31
R T Ponting	c G O Jones	b A Flintoff	0
D R Martyn	c I R Bell	b M J Hoggard	28
M J Clarke		b S J Harmison	30
S M Katich	c M E Trescothick	b A F Giles	16
A C Gilchrist	c A Flintoff	b A F Giles	1
J N Gillespie	lbw	b A Flintoff	0
S K Warne	hit wicket	b A Flintoff	42
B Lee	not out		43
M S Kasprowicz	c G O Jones	b S J Harmison	20
Extras	18nb 1w 13b 8lb		40
Total	all out	(64.3 overs)	279

Bowler	O	M	R	W
S J Harmison	17.3	3	62	2
M J Hoggard	5.0	0	26	1
A F Giles	15.0	3	68	2
A Flintoff	22.0	3	79	4
S P Jones	5.0	1	23	1

Umpires: B F Bowden, R E Koertzen

BBC RADIO FIVE LIVE

An amazing finish! Billy Bowden waited for a moment and the England players are surrounding themselves and slapping each other on the back. Flintoff came over and shook Brett Lee's hand. Both the Australian batsmen just stood there — dumbfounded for a moment or two — that the game could have ended like that. They got so close. It would have been a miraculous win, and at the death Harmison has produced a lifting ball down the leg-side that brushed Kasprowicz's glove. Jones has taken the catch. England has levelled the series in the most dramatic fashion here. They have won the Test match by just two runs!

Right: *The England team huddles together before the start of play on day four of the Second npower Ashes Test.*

THIRD TEST: OLD TRAFFORD

Australia escape with a draw

The 1,761st match in the annals of Test cricket more than matched the proceedings at Edgbaston for pure theatre, and ensured that legions of converts would be glued to their televisions and radios for the final two battles of the series. The Old Trafford game had everything, not least the fact that the result was in doubt until the very last ball, Brett Lee surviving Steve Harmison's assault on his stumps to earn his side a draw which, in the context of both the match and the series, was greeted by the holders as a triumph.

Following the Edgbaston defeat, the Australians were rocked by the news that Lee had developed a knee infection requiring hospital treatment. But just five days later he was passed fit to play, and the team was further buoyed by Glenn McGrath's miraculous recovery, just a week after sustaining ankle ligament damage. If there was any doubt about the fitness of either, it would soon be exposed, for Vaughan won his first toss and had no hesitation in electing to bat. The strip looked full of runs, while denying the opposition's two front-line pacemen the luxury of an extra day's rest was an added bonus.

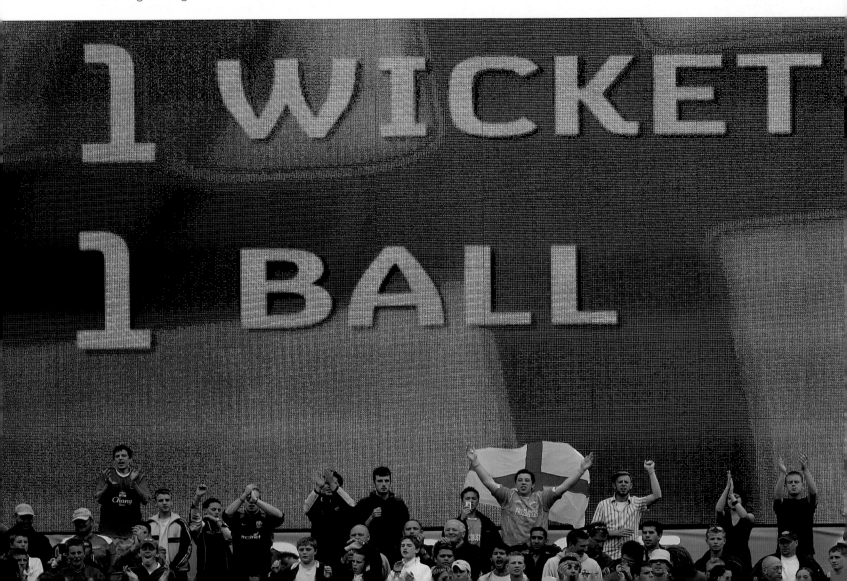

600th Test victim for Warne

Lee showed no after-effects of his injury. He softened Strauss up with some 90-plus mph short-pitched stuff, including a brute which struck the batsman in the neck. He then removed Strauss's off stump with a superb slower delivery, Lee celebrating the departure of his 150th Test victim.

Shane Warne had taken 449 more scalps than Lee, and this would be the day when Test cricket would acclaim the first bowler to reach the 600 mark. Marcus Trescothick played the supporting role in that statistic, though not before he and Vaughan had put on 137 for the second wicket. Then, 13 years and 126 matches on from making his Test debut, the greatest spinner in the game's history set a new high watermark, making a mockery of those who had suggested that he was a spent force. There may have been less variety these days, but even with a reduced menu of ripping leg-breaks, interspersed with the quicker, straight-on 'slider' and top-spinner, Warne was still the greatest exponent of his art.

BBC RADIO FIVE LIVE

It's hard to look back on these sort of achievements when you're still playing because I'm so wrapped up in the game and trying to do my best to win the Test match and tie up and do all those type of things. I feel very proud of that achievement at the moment. It was a pretty emotional time then but I knew I had a job to do, to try to tie up and get some wickets. Unfortunately there weren't too many going but I thought I bowled really well without much luck.

Shane Warne
talking about his 600th Test wicket

Opposite: *The screen shows the situation with one ball left and England chasing one final wicket, during day five of the Third Test.*

Left: *Shane Warne of Australia celebrates his 600th Test wicket, that of Marcus Trescothick during day one of the Third Test.*

Vaughan becomes first centurion

Vaughan, who had been in poor form with the bat, finally found his touch and became the series' first centurion. His average was already over 54 against Australia, and that went up as he hit a magnificent 166. He did ride his luck, though: he offered a difficult chance to Gilchrist, and was also cleaned up by McGrath off a no-ball. Gilchrist also missed a much easier chance early in Trescothick's innings, making it two expensive mistakes for the Australians.

Two late wickets – Pietersen and nightwatchman Hoggard – made the scoreboard slightly happier reading for Ricky Ponting as England ended the day on 341–5.

Bell went without adding to his overnight score of 59, edging a mistimed hook off a sharply rising Lee delivery to Gilchrist. Flintoff and Geraint Jones then put on 87 before Freddie was caught in the deep. That made it 433–7, and with just one run added to the total, Gillespie, who had been going for six an over, removed Jones' off stump for his first wicket of the match. The last three wickets added only another ten, and though England no doubt would have settled for a total of 444 at start of play, at one stage the platform looked to have been set for 500.

BBC RADIO FIVE LIVE

Cricket fever. Yes, I've got it. It's rampant. It's raging. I just can't get rid of it. I'm loving every moment of it this summer so far as the cricket is concerned. When you've got someone like Richie Benaud, great commentator that he's been for so long, saying that this is the best series he's seen in his history of sports broadcasting (which is 40-odd years), then I think that tells you all that you need to hear.

John Rawling

Opposite: *Australian batsman Justin Langer (l) watches as England's Ian Bell takes the catch which dismissed him on the second day. Another wicket to Giles.*

Right: *England captain Michael Vaughan celebrates his century against Australia on the first day of the Third Ashes Test.*

Aussie batting misfires

When Australia were reduced to 217–7 at stumps on the second day, England were in the box seat. The much-vaunted batting line-up again misfired, several batsmen getting a start but failing to build. Current form was certainly out of kilter with the world rankings, which had three men – Ponting, Martyn and Gilchrist – in the top ten, while only Trescothick featured for England.

Gilchrist was given a couple of lifelines in reaching 30, though his knock did take him past Alec Stewart's record aggregate for a wicket-keeper. Warne ended the day on 45 n.o., with Australia in danger of falling short of the follow-on target, the first time England had found themselves in that position since 1988.

Warne misses out on maiden ton

A rain-truncated Saturday saw just 14 overs bowled, which Australia survived without loss. They eventually climbed to a total of 302, thanks mainly to Warne, who fell ten runs short of a first Test century. Simon Jones, with 6 for 53 off 17.5 overs, was England's hero with the ball.

With a 142-run lead, England's first objective was to take the game away from Australia, preferably with some rapid scoring to leave plenty of time to bowl the opposition out. For once the men most likely to do that – Pietersen and Flintoff – missed out, though a fine century from Strauss laid the foundations for Vaughan to be able to declare on 280–6. McGrath, having somewhat unluckily, and highly unusually, gone through an entire innings without taking a wicket, was back in more customary five-for mode.

Australia reached 24 without loss at close of play, leaving a simple equation for the final day: England needing ten wickets, Ponting's men a record 399 runs – or failing that, survival to force a draw.

I thought it was another fantastic team performance here. The captain led from the front in the first innings. We bowled well and Straussy played unbelievably well. Then the bowlers came out today and I thought we bowled well. We stuck at our task, and we kept getting back into the game. With six or seven overs left and one wicket, we were trying everything, but they just kept us out ... I think every one of us can walk off that pitch proud of what we have done.

Andrew Flintoff

Ponting's heroic 156

Captain's innings

England got a dream start, Matthew Hoggard finding the edge of Justin Langer's bat with his first ball. Enter Ricky Ponting, who played a true captain's innings in returning his best score against England. 156 off 275 balls was superb stuff given the circumstances; but more crucial was the fact that he occupied the crease for six hours.

The first partner Ponting lost was Hayden, who exposed his leg stump and had it gleefully knocked over by Flintoff with the score on 96. At lunch Australia were 121–2. Eight runs later it looked to be England's day as they enjoyed a large slice of good fortune, Damien Martyn given out lbw off Harmison despite getting an inside edge onto his pad. Umpire Steve Bucknor only heard one noise, however, and Martyn had to walk.

Clarke bats through pain barrier

Flintoff picked up Katich and Gilchrist, who both fell cheaply. That brought Michael Clarke belatedly to the crease, a back injury again forcing him down the order. He made a doughty 39 before being bowled by Jones. The resilient Gillespie came in ahead of Warne, leaving no one in any doubt as to Australia's priority. It didn't work, however, as Hoggard had him leg-before for a duck.

With the score on 313 and the last hour approaching, Warne was dropped by Pietersen at mid-wicket, a sharp chance but one where the fielder did get both hands to the ball as he dived low to his right. It was his fifth fumble of the series, with zero in the successes column.

Warne finally departed for 34 in dramatic fashion: his edge off Flintoff flew to Strauss in the slips. He failed to take the catch, but the beleaguered Geraint Jones reacted brilliantly to grasp the ball inches above the deck.

McGrath and Lee see Aussies home

At 340–8 Australia's slim hopes of victory had disappeared. The question now was whether Lee and McGrath could support their skipper and save the game. England tried to target Lee, but it was Ponting who perished next, Harmison catching a sliver of glove and Jones taking comfortably down the leg side. It was a very faint contact and an excellent decision by Billy Bowden.

McGrath arrived at the crease with 24 balls remaining. Lee was now the senior batsman, but he could only spectate as McGrath took guard against Harmison in the final over. The No. 11 nicked a single off the third ball, and Lee survived the final three deliveries. As Australia celebrated, England were left ruing the loss of Simon Jones with cramp. Had he remained on the pitch his reverse swing may well have unlocked the rugged defence of the Australian tail.

The first drawn Ashes match since the encounter at the Gabba in November 1998 must have felt like a glorious victory to the Aussies, both in terms of the match, in which they were always playing catch-up, but more importantly in terms of a series which the holders had only to finish on level terms in order to retain the trophy.

BBC RADIO **FIVE LIVE**

I always look back on the positives and there are a hell of a lot of positives to come out of that game. The character a lot of the players showed from Edgbaston to Old Trafford, and their individual performances, was outstanding.

Michael Vaughan

Opposite: Ricky Ponting in action during day five of the Third Test.

Left: Brett Lee (l) and Glenn McGrath of Australia celebrate after holding on to draw the match on the last day of the Third Test.

Third Test 11 August 2005 at Old Trafford
England won the toss and decided to bat
Match Drawn

England 1st Innings

M E Trescothick	c A C Gilchrist	b S K Warne	63
A J Strauss		b B Lee	6
M P Vaughan	c G D McGrath	b S M Katich	166
I R Bell	c A C Gilchrist	b B Lee	59
K P Pietersen	c sub	b B Lee	21
M J Hoggard		b B Lee	4
A Flintoff	c J L Langer	b S K Warne	46
G O Jones		b J N Gillespie	42
A F Giles	c M L Hayden	b S K Warne	0
S J Harmison	not out		10
S P Jones		b S K Warne	0
Extras	15nb 3w 4b 5lb		27
Total	all out	(113.2 overs)	444

Bowler	O	M	R	W
G D McGrath	25.0	6	86	0
B Lee	27.0	6	100	4
J N Gillespie	19.0	2	114	1
S K Warne	33.2	5	99	4
S M Katich	9.0	1	36	1

Australia 1st Innings

J L Langer	c I R Bell	b A F Giles	31
M L Hayden	lbw	b A F Giles	34
R T Ponting	c I R Bell	b S P Jones	7
D R Martyn		b A F Giles	20
S M Katich		b A Flintoff	17
A C Gilchrist	c G O Jones	b S P Jones	30
S K Warne	c A F Giles	b S P Jones	90
M J Clarke	c A Flintoff	b S P Jones	7
J N Gillespie	lbw	b S P Jones	26
B Lee	c M E Trescothick	b S P Jones	1
G D McGrath	not out		1
Extras	15nb 8w 8b 7lb		38
Total	all out	(84.5 overs)	302

Bowler	O	M	R	W
S J Harmison	10.0	0	47	0
M J Hoggard	6.0	2	22	0
A Flintoff	20.0	1	65	1
S P Jones	17.5	6	53	6
A F Giles	31.0	4	100	3

England 2nd Innings

M E Trescothick		b G D McGrath	41
A J Strauss	c D R Martyn	b G D McGrath	106
M P Vaughan	c sub	b B Lee	14
I R Bell	c S M Katich	b G D McGrath	65
K P Pietersen	lbw	b G D McGrath	0
A Flintoff		b G D McGrath	4
G O Jones	not out		27
A F Giles	not out		0
Extras	14nb 1w 5b 3lb		23
Total	for 6 dec.	(61.5 overs)	280

Bowler	O	M	R	W
G D McGrath	20.5	1	115	5
B Lee	12.0	0	60	1
S K Warne	25.0	3	74	0
J N Gillespie	4.0	0	23	0

Australia 2nd Innings

J L Langer	c G O Jones	b M J Hoggard	14
M L Hayden		b A Flintoff	36
R T Ponting	c G O Jones	b S J Harmison	156
D R Martyn	lbw	b S J Harmison	19
S M Katich	c A F Giles	b A Flintoff	12
A C Gilchrist	c I R Bell	b A Flintoff	4
M J Clarke		b S P Jones	39
J N Gillespie	lbw	b M J Hoggard	0
S K Warne	c G O Jones	b A Flintoff	34
B Lee	not out		18
G D McGrath	not out		5
Extras	19nb 2w 5b 8lb		34
Total	for 9	(108.0 overs)	371

Bowler	O	M	R	W
S J Harmison	22.0	4	67	2
M J Hoggard	13.0	0	49	2
A F Giles	26.0	4	93	0
M P Vaughan	5.0	0	21	0
A Flintoff	25.0	6	71	4
S P Jones	17.0	3	57	1

Umpires: B F Bowden, S A Bucknor

 BBC RADIO FIVE LIVE

The '81 series was a fairytale. It had always been the benchmark for a commentator – but not now! This series just shades it. I've never been so excited about a series in all my life from the commentating point of view, and I think there are millions around the country who feel exactly the same. Perfectly logical people who might write a cheque in the morning for their business, might sack a few people, take a few people on and make big decisions, have been walking out of rooms not wanting to watch the screen, walking out the room and standing by the door with their backs to the TV screen listening to the commentary ... It was so exciting.

Richie Benaud

Right: *Brett Lee and Glenn McGrath of Australia celebrate at the end of the match which ended in a draw during day five of the Third Ashes Test.*

FOURTH TEST: TRENT BRIDGE

Vaughan's men squeeze home

He's the greatest I've ever seen. He is an out and out champion.

Richie Benaud
on Shane Warne

Jason Gillespie's poor form – three wickets at 100 apiece – finally cost him his place in the side. Australia drafted in 22-year-old Shaun Tait, the 392nd man to wear the baggy green. A speed merchant prone to waywardness, Tait had had a disastrous stint with Durham in 2004, but his form over the previous Australian summer had impressed the selectors. The pressure was certainly on the young firebrand, as McGrath picked up an elbow injury and failed a late fitness test. Kasprowicz was therefore back in the starting XI. If the attack wasn't Ponting's first choice unit, at least he had a fully fit Michael Clarke in the ranks.

England had the luxury of being able to field an unchanged team yet again, and under bright skies Michael Vaughan won an important toss and elected to get runs on the board. Confidence was high, every England batsman having posted a half-century, and on a placid pitch there was every expectation of another sizeable total.

Bowled off a no-ball

At lunch England were 129–1. None of the pacemen could make an impact, although Lee did bowl Trescothick off a no-ball – one of 18 in the first session. It was the third time in the series that the Aussies thought they'd struck, only to find the bowler had overstepped the mark.

It was left to Warne, introduced as early as the 18th over, to give Australia a breakthrough. Strauss had made 35 when his mistimed paddle sweep struck his boot and looped into Hayden's grateful hands.

In a rain-affected day in which 30 overs were lost, the Australians hit back well in the final session to make honours just about even at stumps. A superb late inswinger gave Tait his first Test wicket, Trescothick the batsman. It was the Somerset man's third fifty of the series and 27th in total, and in helping England reach 137–2 he had again provided the side with a decent platform on which the middle order could build.

However, with just nine runs added, Ian Bell edged Tait to Gilchrist. It was the latter's 300th Test dismissal, Gilchrist becoming only the fourth glove-man in history to reach that mark.

Opposite: The England team win the Fourth Ashes Test.

Left: Shane Warne successfully appeals for the wicket of Andrew Strauss on the first day. Strauss, who made 35, was caught in the slips off an inside edge onto his boot. The third umpire gave the decision.

Vaughan and Pietersen ride their luck

England rode their luck. Pietersen offered a caught and bowled chance to Kasprowicz which the latter refused; Hayden put down Vaughan at backward point; and a mix-up between the batsmen could easily have resulted in a run-out, Hayden again the fielder involved.

Ponting, with just four Test wickets to his name, had brought himself on in what seemed a desperate move, and yet it paid dividends. Vaughan had just reached his 28th Test 50, and statistics showed that once he reached that mark his conversion rate to centuries was better than even money. Yet just before the close he feathered a Ponting delivery to Gilchrist. Rain brought an early close, England ending the day 229–4, with Pietersen on 33 and Flintoff 8.

Flintoff's ton

The second day was all England's. Pietersen went early, caught behind, an excellent decision by Aleem Dar as bat hit ground just as the ball passed the blade. But then Flintoff and Geraint Jones put on 177, the highest partnership of the series, as England moved on to 477. That total looked even more impressive as the Aussies were reduced to 99–5 at stumps.

Flintoff's fifth Test century – his first against Australia – came off 121 balls, including three memorable boundaries in one Tait over.

Giles, Hoggard and Jones all weighed in with useful runs. Brett Lee, who would finish with unflattering figures of 1–131, raised a wry smile as a ball got through Simon Jones' defence and rattled the stumps, but failed to disturb the bails.

Hoggard immediately settled into a spell of penetrating swing bowling. He trapped Hayden plum in front of his stumps, and Langer bat-pad; only Martyn, who got some wood on the ball, could feel aggrieved about the lbw decision which sent him back to the pavilion. Ricky Ponting got a tough one too, another lbw off an inside edge. When the luck is going with you, you have to take advantage, and in the final ball of the day Harmison nipped one back to Clarke and Steve Bucknor rewarded him with the fourth leg-before of the innings.

BBC RADIO FIVE LIVE

He's now the complete cricketer. Up until his 100 the other day against Australia he was an international class player. Now he's scored 100 to go with his fantastic bowling against the number one side in the world – he is world class. Along with Jacques Kallis, they are the two best all-rounders in the world at present.

Alec Stewart
on Andrew Flintoff

Catch of the series

If it was the catch of the decade, I think it was certainly the catch of the century! It was a great catch – personally I think the low catches are probably more difficult at slip than the ones you have to come forward to. I think he was trying to try to catch it with two hands and realized he couldn't. He got it in the one hand, he was horizontal and was going to drop it on the floor. He had to break his fall somehow and it was terrific the way he put his hand out.

Rodney Marsh
talking about
Andrew Strauss' catch

On the third morning Katich and Gilchrist came out all guns blazing, seemingly having decided attack was the best form of defence. They plundered 41 in three overs before Jones came on to break the partnership, Katich caught by Strauss at gully. Warne went first ball, a leading edge gobbled up by Bell at cover. Lee made sure there were no hat-trick celebrations for Jones, but just three overs later England struck again, Strauss taking a spectacular diving catch to remove Gilchrist off Flintoff. In a summer of sensational catches, this was the best.

The outswinger from Jones that beat Kasprowicz would have troubled far better batsmen. The last wicket eked out 43 dogged runs, Lee again proving himself no mean batsman. Even his valiant efforts weren't enough to rescue Australia from the follow-on, the first time for 18 years that an Aussie team had been invited to have another bat.

Right: Australia's Brett Lee (l) celebrates after dismissing England's Andrew Flintoff on the fourth day of the Fourth Test.

Opposite: Andrew Strauss dives to catch Adam Gilchrist of Australia during day three of the Fourth Test.

Sub fielder row

Ponting's men were much more resilient second time round. The 150 came up for the loss of Hayden and Langer. The captain then fell for 48, run out by substitute fielder Gary Pratt as he tried to nick a quick single. Ponting later fulminated at England's use of sub fielders, which he felt was against the spirit of the game. In fact, in this instance Pratt was on for Simon Jones, who, far from taking an extra rest, was being treated for the ankle injury that would keep him out of the Fifth Test.

Australia began the fourth day on 224–4. Clarke and Katich took them past England's total – just – before Clarke went, caught behind chasing a wide one from Hoggard. The Aussies were effectively 2–5 and looking down the barrel.

Wagging tail sets England ticklish target

The last four wickets had been averaging a commendable 92 in the series thus far, and once again they contributed enough to at least set England a target to bowl at. Katich played the anchor role. He took 160 balls to reach his eighth Test 50 before being given out lbw to a ball which pitched outside leg and was also dubious regarding height. Warne's 45, on the other hand, came at better than a run a ball. He was stumped taking a wild swing at Giles, whom he had just planted for six.

Harmison splattered Tait's timbers to leave England needing 129 for victory. It shouldn't have presented a problem, though thoughts inevitably drifted towards the 130 Australia had chased at Headingley '81.

King of Spain hits winning runs

Vaughan's men did squeeze home to take a 2–1 series lead, but it was a jittery affair. England slumped from 32 without loss to 57–4. Pietersen and Flintoff put on 46 for the fifth wicket, but both fell in quick succession to an inspired Lee. Warne, who would end with 4–31, was at his mesmerizing best. Geraint Jones was one player Warne had never claimed as a victim; he put that right in England's nervy second innings, Jones trying to hit his way out of trouble and taken by Kasprowicz three-quarters of the way to the long-off boundary.

England, still 13 short, now had Hoggard and Giles at the crease. Hoggard capitalized on some wayward Lee deliveries to reach 8, including a fine punch through the covers for four. But it was the King of Spain who had the honour of clipping Warne through mid-wicket for the two runs which gave England their first Trent Bridge victory over Australia since 1977. It meant that a draw would now be enough for England at the Oval. 'We realize we're on the brink of something special,' said Michael Vaughan after the game. For Australia, nothing less than a Fifth-Test win would do.

Right: Ashley Giles is jubilant after scoring the winning runs on day four of the Fourth Test.

We were a little bit nervous, of course, when we needed 14 – it seemed more like 140 – but Hoggie played Brett Lee magnificently. The ball was tailing in at a high pace and I just tried to survive against Warnie. He's not a bad bowler actually – I've just worked that out!

Ashley Giles

I think I chewed the bat handle waiting to go in to bat. It's been a big change round and I've been working hard at my batting and thankfully it came to fruition today.

Matthew Hoggard

Fourth Test 25 August 2005 at Trent Bridge
England won the toss and decided to bat
England beat Australia by 3 wickets

England 1st Innings

M E Trescothick		b S W Tait	65
A J Strauss	c M L Hayden	b S K Warne	35
M P Vaughan	c A C Gilchrist	b R T Ponting	58
I R Bell	c A C Gilchrist	b S W Tait	3
K P Pietersen	c A C Gilchrist	b B Lee	45
A Flintoff	lbw	b S W Tait	102
G O Jones	c and b	M S Kasprowicz	85
A F Giles	lbw	b S K Warne	15
M J Hoggard	c A C Gilchrist	b S K Warne	10
S J Harmison	st A C Gilchrist	b S K Warne	2
S P Jones	not out		15
Extras	25nb 1w 1b 15lb		42
Total	all out	(123.1 overs)	477

Bowler	O	M	R	W
B Lee	32.0	2	131	1
M S Kasprowicz	32.0	3	122	1
S W Tait	24.0	4	97	3
S K Warne	29.1	4	102	4
R T Ponting	6.0	2	9	1

Australia 1st Innings

J L Langer	c I R Bell	b M J Hoggar	27
M L Hayden	lbw	b M J Hoggard	7
R T Ponting	lbw	b S P Jones	1
D R Martyn	lbw	b M J Hoggard	1
M J Clarke	lbw	b S J Harmison	36
S M Katich	c A J Strauss	b S P Jones	45
A C Gilchrist	c A J Strauss	b A Flintoff	27
S K Warne	c I R Bell	b S P Jones	0
B Lee	c I R Bell	b S P Jones	47
M S Kasprowicz		b S P Jones	5
S W Tait	not out		3
Extras	16nb 1w 2lb		19
Total	all out	(49.1 overs)	218

Bowler	O	M	R	W
S J Harmison	9.0	1	48	1
M J Hoggard	15.0	3	70	3
S P Jones	14.1	4	44	5
A Flintoff	11.0	1	54	1

Australia 2nd Innings (follow on)

J L Langer	c I R Bell	b A F Giles	61
M L Hayden	c A F Giles	b A Flintoff	26
R T Ponting	run out		48
D R Martyn	c G O Jones	b A Flintoff	13
M J Clarke	c G O Jones	b M J Hoggard	56
S M Katich	lbw	b S J Harmison	59
A C Gilchrist	lbw	b M J Hoggard	11
S K Warne	st G O Jones	b A F Giles	45
B Lee	not out		26
M S Kasprowicz	c G O Jones	b S J Harmison	19
S W Tait		b S J Harmison	4
Extras	14nb 1b 4lb		19
Total	all out	(124.0 overs)	387

Bowler	O	M	R	W
M J Hoggard	27.0	7	72	2
S P Jones	4.0	0	15	0
S J Harmison	30.0	5	93	3
A Flintoff	29.0	4	83	2
A F Giles	28.0	3	107	2
I R Bell	6.0	2	12	0

England 2nd Innings

M E Trescothick	c R T Ponting	b S K Warne	27
A J Strauss	c M J Clarke	b S K Warne	23
M P Vaughan	c M L Hayden	b S K Warne	0
I R Bell	c M S Kasprowicz	b B Lee	3
K P Pietersen	c A C Gilchrist	b B Lee	23
A Flintoff		b B Lee	26
G O Jones	c M S Kasprowicz	b S K Warne	3
A F Giles	not out		7
M J Hoggard	not out		8
Extras	5nb 4lb		9
Total	for 7	(31.5 overs)	129

Bowler	O	M	R	W
B Lee	12.0	0	51	3
M S Kasprowicz	2.0	0	19	0
S K Warne	13.5	2	31	4
S W Tait	4.0	0	24	0

Umpires: Aleem Dar, S A Bucknor

FIFTH TEST: THE OVAL

The bails are off.
England have won the Ashes

And so to the Oval, the ground which staged the first England-Australia encounter in 1880, and where the Ashes legend was born two years later. The history books showed that this was England's happiest hunting ground by far against the Australians, 15 wins in 33 Tests. If Vaughan's side was to make it 16, or even manufacture the required draw, it would have to do so without the man who topped the England bowling averages with 18 wickets at a miserly 21 runs apiece and a strike rate of 34. Simon Jones failed to recover from the ankle injury which kept him off the pitch in the latter stages at Trent Bridge, preventing the selectors from setting a record for the modern era by naming the same XI for the entire series.

Collingwood gets the nod

Hampshire's Chris Tremlett, having made every squad thus far, missed out as Paul Collingwood and James Anderson were drafted into the squad. The Durham all-rounder, with six centuries to his name already during the season, would strengthen the batting in a game where England only needed to avoid defeat, while Lancashire's Anderson was the better wicket-taking option. The decision went in favour of Collingwood, the man with 80 one-day internationals behind him but just two previous Test appearances. Most pundits saw his inclusion as the safer bet, allowing Geraint Jones to come in at eight, though the selectors fervently tried to portray their decision as a positive move, not one born of caution.

Left: England's Kevin Pietersen shakes hands with Shane Warne as he leaves the field after being bowled out for 158 against Australia during the last day of the Fifth Test match.

Opposite: Michael Vaughan joins his teammates in song as they celebrate with a replica Ashes urn.

I think we're doing a good job of it at the moment and let's just pray for five days of rain.

Kevin Pietersen
after the Fourth Test

The astonishing thing is that the Australians have been outplayed in the three Test matches – Edgbaston, Old Trafford and then Trent Bridge. Ponting has said after each game that we were outplayed but we've hung in there and we're now in the situation where there is only a whisker separating the teams and yet England have clearly been the better side since Lord's.

Richie Benaud

Vaughan opts to bat

Vaughan wins third toss

Vaughan won his third successive toss and had no hesitation in electing to bat on a glorious morning, especially as the forecast was for unsettled weather. The tactics were clear: get runs on the board – 450 looked a par score – and avoid having to face Warne on a wearing 4th-innings pitch.

The big plus for the Aussies was the return of McGrath. Ponting had lost both matches when he didn't have his No. 1 pace bowler at his disposal, and McGrath's personal tally against the old enemy was an impressive 73 wins out of 111 contests. The other crumb of comfort for the Aussie skipper was the scheduling: 8 September was the latest start ever to a Test match, and there would be undoubtedly be some early help for the bowlers.

The first hour of the first session was more crucial than ever, and at the end of it England were in a very healthy position, 70–0 off just 14 overs. Trescothick, averaging 85 in Oval tests, looked set for another big score in 2005.

BBC RADIO FIVE LIVE

We can't afford to give a good side like England a head start.

Ricky Ponting

Warne strikes early

But the second half of the morning went to the visitors. Yet again Ponting turned to Warne early in the innings, and yet again the world's top wicket-taker came up trumps. A terrific delivery, matched by an outstanding ankle-high catch by Matthew Hayden, dismissed Trescothick for 43. It was a quicker leg break with top spin, taking less than 0.4 seconds to travel from bat to Hayden's lightning-quick hands. Michael Vaughan then chipped to Clarke at mid-wicket, and Bell went without scoring, trapped leg-before to a straight one. At lunch, with England reduced to 115–3, Warne's figures were 7–1–3–27.

In the afternoon session Strauss went past 50 before Warne struck again, winning the battle of the Hampshire teammates as he bowled Pietersen through the gate, the batsman ill-advisedly trying to clip the ball into the on side against the spin.

It will be the biggest week of our lives, this last Test match. Going in 2–1 is a great feeling, but we know that we have got to finish the job off, and we want to make sure that we clinch the series. Team England – that's exactly what we are. We've been a team now for the last 18 months and we've had very few changes. It shows in the way that we unite and bond together.

Geraint Jones

Opposite: England captain Michael Vaughan and Australia captain Ricky Ponting look on ahead of day one of the Fifth npower Ashes Test.

Left: Shane Warne (l) celebrates the wicket of Marcus Trescothick of England with teammates during day one of the Fifth Test.

Seventh ton for Strauss

England stood firm till tea, Strauss and Flintoff putting on 82 in 90 minutes to take England past the 200 mark. Freddie reached his 50 with three successive fours off Warne, and in the next over Strauss celebrated his seventh Test hundred, and second of the summer. It put him fourth in the all-time list for the number of centuries made from a player's first 19 Tests, no less a figure than the Don himself standing at the top of that particular tree.

Australia claimed three further wickets to make it a decent day's return for a fielding side on a flat track. Warne, never out of the game, took Flintoff at slip off McGrath. A rapid Tait inswinging yorker struck Collingwood's boot for an lbw dismissal which made the decision to play an extra batsman look in danger of backfiring. Strauss also went late in the day for 129, which he described as his best effort in an England shirt. That wicket gave Warne yet another five-for, and as England closed on 319–7, most felt honours were about even. If the last three wickets could get England's total past 400, then the decision to bat would be vindicated; if they fell cheaply, Ponting would feel he and his men had wrested the initiative after losing the toss.

On day two, with a ball just four overs old, Lee made the breakthrough in the second over. Having seen his first delivery to Jones dispatched to the boundary, Lee clattered the England wicket keeper's off stump with a very swift delivery, Jones playing inside the line.

Snicko proves McGrath unlucky

At 343–8 there was high drama as McGrath – who had just induced an edge from Giles, only to see Ponting put it down – was left with head in hands as another wicket-taking opportunity slipped by. This time the ball safely found its way from Giles' bat into Gilchrist's gloves. Rudi Koertzen dampened the celebrations by indicating he hadn't heard a noise. The Snickometer confirmed that the Aussies had been hard done by, and McGrath made his feelings known by asking Clarke to retrieve his cap from the umpire at the end of the over.

Leg spin masterclass

McGrath finally had some luck with a beautiful slower ball which deceived Hoggard, who was through his shot far too early, resulting in a tame chip to mid-on.

England were finally all out for 373, after Warne picked up Giles for the fifth time in the series, though Hawkeye's view of the lbw decision suggested that this time fortune had favoured the bowling side. That couldn't detract from the maestro's performance; Warne had given a leg spin masterclass to finish with 6–122.

32 from Giles, plus 20 plundered by Harmison from as many balls, gave England a late flourish. Having lost Jones so early, Vaughan would have been satisfied with the efforts of the tail, not for the first time in the series, though most felt that England had fallen some way short on such a benign pitch.

First century stand for Aussie openers

Going into the match, former Australian captain Steve Waugh's advice to the team was delivered in three simple words: Patience, Pressure, Partnerships.

Langer and Hayden showed great diligence in building their first century stand of the series, comfortably eclipsing their previous best of 58, made at Old Trafford. Hayden finally delivered, though he was very much the junior partner in the early stages. Having failed to get past 36 in four Tests, he was understandably cautious in trying to build an innings to answer those who felt he should have been dropped.

At 76–0 Collingwood, working up a great head of steam, hurried Langer into a false stroke, but Trescothick couldn't hold on to a difficult chance. Langer then survived an lbw appeal off Giles, Hawkeye suggesting that he was struck in line and that the ball would have hit.

Australia haven't had a great tour by their standards. Before they left, they built up what they were going to do over here. So it's been nice to be able to put them under some pressure and because of that I think we've earned their respect, which as a side probably hasn't been done for a while. It's been a great feeling.

Geraint Jones

Those long nights in front of the radio or television following losing causes – watching baggy green giants crushing England for years on end. These are very special moments for these fans who have invested so much in the England cricket team down the years.

Arlo White

Opposite: Andrew Strauss of England in action during day one of the Fifth npower Ashes Test match.

Left: Australia's Glenn McGrath shows his frustration after his appeal for the wicket of England's Ashley Giles is turned down by umpire Koertzen.

Langer justifies bad light decision

Just after tea, with the total on 112, the batsmen were offered the light and opted to troop off. Rain later set in and they didn't return. Langer defended the decision, saying that they didn't want to risk losing wickets in adverse batting conditions, and that the aggressive cricket played over the summer meant games were tending to be four-day affairs, so the loss of time was unlikely to be crucial. Even so, the England players could barely hide their astonishment – and glee – at having the day's proceedings truncated.

England look to make it Ashes double

England's women's cricket team, which had just regained the Ashes after an even longer time in the wilderness – 42 years – paraded around the Oval in what home fans were hoping would be the first leg of a famous double. If that were to be achieved, England needed to make inroads into Australia's batting line-up. Hayden reached his first 50, though the fact that he had taken 137 balls and more than 3 hours to reach it showed how out of touch one of the most brutal hitters in the game had been during the Test series.

Australia reached 185 before Langer played on to Harmison, having just notched his 22nd century, and also passed the 7,000-run mark, putting him ahead of Bradman in the all-time list. He must have been aggrieved that he couldn't have survived the delivery, for another rain break intervened even before Ponting could reach the middle.

After almost five hours at the crease, Hayden also reached his ton, a fine effort considering the fact that he hadn't passed 70 in his previous 31 innings. He also reached 6,000 Test runs at an average of over 50, proving the old adage that form is temporary, class permanent.

Flintoff matches Botham feat

A brilliant low catch by Strauss from a sharp lifter from Flintoff accounted for Ponting, Freddie following Botham into the record books by taking 20 wickets and scoring 300 runs in an Ashes series.

At 277–2 the batsmen again departed in poor light, though with just five overs remaining this was a much less controversial decision than that of the previous day. There was little to gain, especially with the new ball due within the next two overs, and much to lose.

Aussies lose eight wickets for 90

The pundits were pontificating as to whether the Australians should declare early and get England in or bat on and establish a sizeable lead. In fact, the most unlikely scenario of all happened: Australia batted through the card, yet fell short of England's total by six runs.

Hayden finally fell for 138, only 42 runs short of his aggregate for the previous eight innings. On the day Australia lost eight wickets for the addition of just 90 runs. Flintoff, who finished with 5–78, and Hoggard, 4–97, did the damage.

When the weather closed in yet again, England had reached 34 for the loss of Strauss, who perished bat-pad to Warne. Effectively, Vaughan's men were 40–1 going into the final day.

It was a much brighter picture as the gladiators entered the arena with the strains of *Jerusalem* still ringing in their ears. With a possible 98 overs to be bowled, the equation was simple: for Australia to have any chance they needed to roll England over in 60 overs at most, then mount a quick-fire run chase. England, meanwhile, would be intent on batting the opposition out of the game.

I think England have had a magnificent summer. They have shown to everyone that they have the potential to become the best side in the world. If they are outplayed over the next five days I think they still leave this summer with having achieved a huge amount, and with everybody feeling good about English cricket's future. If Australia lose the Ashes you wouldn't want to be a member of that side. They are the ones that have got to go back down under. They are the ones that are going to face the recriminations – they are the players.

Angus Fraser

Opposite: *Justin Langer (l) and Matthew Hayden of Australia leave the field together at lunch during day two of the Fifth Ashes Test.*

Left: *Andrew Flintoff of England appeals unsuccessfully for lbw against Matthew Hayden of Australia as Hayden (l) and teammate Justin Langer take a leg bye during day two of the Fifth npower Ashes Test.*

Series result rests on the final day

McGrath close to second Test hat-trick

The key man was surely going to be Warne, on his final day in the Test arena in England. But it was the other legendary bowler bidding farewell to Ashes cricket in England who gave Australia early hope. McGrath reduced England from 67–1 to 67–3 in the 23rd over. Vaughan's edge brought a stunning catch from Gilchrist, diving to his right. Then Bell went first ball to another edge, this time snaffled by Warne in the slips. McGrath invited Billy Bowden to award him his second Test hat-trick as Pietersen reared back to fend off a steepling delivery. Bowden, completely unfazed, correctly judged that the ball had missed the batsman's glove by a whisker and flicked the shoulder.

In the next over Pietersen edged Warne, but the ball deflected off Gilchrist's glove and not even Hayden at slip was able to react quickly enough. On 75–3 Warne produced a delivery reminiscent of the famous Gatting ball: it pitched a yard outside Trescothick's off stump, then jagged back and, had it not hit the pad, was heading in the direction of leg stump. It deviated so much – 31 inches to the batsmen, almost four feet had it reached the timbers – that it actually bamboozled Hawkeye technology for a time. The fact that it hit Trescothick outside the line saved him, but the prodigious amount of turn augured well from the Australian perspective.

Warne shells regulation catch

Nerves were jangling as Pietersen, attempting a quick single off Warne, got home by a whisker as Clarke threw down the stumps. Then, with the total on 93 and Pietersen having accumulated a scratchy 15, came the turning point. Warne, an ultra-reliable slip-catcher, shelled a regulation take to throw yet another lifeline to Pietersen, Brett Lee the unlucky bowler.

Pietersen immediately began taking advantage of his good fortune, hoisting his teammate into the stand for two big sixes, taking England past the three-figure mark.

Another huge ripper from Warne saw Trescothick depart with the score on 109. Hawkeye again showed that it would have clipped leg stump, the difference this time was that it hit the batsman in line.

The team have played to a consistent standard, as they have done for the last few years. The selectors deserve a lot of credit over the last couple of years because they have been consistent in their selection. They have backed players and continued to give them a run of games. It really helps with the management of the team when you're working with a regular set of players on a regular basis.

Michael Vaughan

This is a momentous moment for English cricket. It's not just winning one match, or drawing one match. It's the ultimate test – winning the five-match series.

Graham Gooch

Opposite: Supporters look on as rain comes down during day two of the Fifth npower Ashes Test.

Left: Australian bowler Glenn McGrath appeals after bowling to England's Kevin Pietersen on the fifth day of the Fifth Test.

Match swings Australia's way

Just before lunch the match turned in Australia's favour as Warne picked up the prize wicket of Flintoff, taking a smart low catch as Freddie attempted to punch the ball straight down the ground. Suddenly, the decision to book Trafalgar Square for a victory parade began to look premature.

With Pietersen beginning to open up, crease occupation at the other end was vital. Collingwood and Giles performed heroics in that respect, batting for over 24 overs between them. Collingwood made only 10 but hung around for 51 balls, over an hour in tandem with the destructive Pietersen. Giles, the hero of Trent Bridge, playing in his 50th Test, did even better, hitting a career-best 59 off 97 deliveries.

Maiden ton for Pietersen

But it was Pietersen's maiden Test century that settled the issue of where the Ashes urn would rest for the next two years. His 158 off 187 balls included a ton in boundaries, an innings of so many majestic shots all around the ground that even Flintoff was left purring when interviewed after the game. He was finally cleaned up by McGrath, the latter's 19th victim of the series giving him a career total of 518, equalling Courtenay Walsh's record for a pace bowler.

Opposite: Kevin Pietersen hits out as Matthew Hayden and Adam Gilchrist of Australia watch on during day five of the Fifth Test.

Below: England's Marcus Trescothick walks back to the Pavilion after losing his wicket to Australia's Shane Warne for 33 runs on the fifth day of the Fifth and final Ashes Test.

Pietersen's century wins the match

Warne mopped up the last two wickets to take him to 40 wickets at 19.92, easily the best return from a bowler on either side, and his best Ashes performance in four trips to England.

Warne had signed off by taking a remarkable 12 wickets, yet there was only one candidate for man of the match. Since top scoring at Lord's, Pietersen had had a quiet couple of matches; his bludgeoning performance which steered England over the line meant he was the only batsman to end the series with an average of over 50.

Langer and Hayden took to the field for a token four Harmison deliveries before coming off for bad light. The draw was already sealed, the non-Antipodean Oval crowd already in party mood. Yet when umpire Bowden removed the bails to officially bring the 2005 Ashes series to a close, the euphoria reached a new intensity. Australia remained the No.1 side in the ICC rankings, but that mattered little to the home fans. After a summer in which cricket fever swept the nation, the longest period of Ashes domination since the 19th century had come to an end.

Just listen to the roar! Pietersen is turning round. His helmet's off. His bat's in the air. What a hero he has been today for England. As soon as the ball struck the stumps, people stood up to applaud Kevin Pietersen – one of the greatest Ashes knocks of all time by an England player. What a time to do it!

*The bails
are off.
The game is
drawn.
England
have won
The Ashes!*

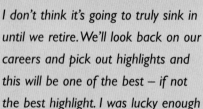

*I don't think it's going to truly sink in
until we retire. We'll look back on our
careers and pick out highlights and
this will be one of the best – if not
the best highlight. I was lucky enough
to be there at the end and it was
just a fantastic moment in the Ashes.*

Matthew Hoggard

Man of the Series
The best all-round cricketer in the world

BBC RADIO FIVE LIVE

Flintoff is a genuinely nice man, he's a shy fellow, he doesn't seek the spotlight. He's just a regulation guy — well rounded. That's why people are drawn to Flintoff. Everyone knows that he can hit a ball out the ground and bowl at 90 miles per hour, but his real special extra charm is that he's just so normal, so approachable. He's the best all-round cricketer in the world, no question about it. Flintoff is absolutely fundamental to England's success. He's a character, he's a talisman in the dressing room. The players follow him — he's the guy who cranks up the ghetto blaster with Rod Stewart and Elton John — Rocket Man and Maggie May. His importance to England can't be overstated. His whole demeanour is of a guy at the top of his game.

John Ethridge

Fifth Test 8 Sept 2005 at the Brit Oval
England won the toss and decided to bat
England drew with Australia

Opposite and below: Andrew Flintoff, who scored 402 runs and took 24 wickets at 27.29, was named man of the series. He was also given the freedom of his home town, Preston, for the part he played in England's first Ashes victory since the winter of 1986–87.

England 1st Innings

M E Trescothick	c M L Hayden	b S K Warne	43
A J Strauss	c S M Katich	b S K Warne	129
M P Vaughan	c M J Clarke	b S K Warne	11
I R Bell	lbw	b S K Warne	0
K P Pietersen		b S K Warne	14
A Flintoff	c S K Warne	b G D McGrath	72
P D Collingwood	lbw	b S W Tait	7
G O Jones		b B Lee	25
A F Giles	lbw	b S K Warne	32
M J Hoggard	c D R Martyn	b G D McGrath	2
S J Harmison	not out		20
Extras	7nb 1w 4b 6lb		18
Total	all out	(105.3 overs)	373

Bowler	O	M	R	W
G D McGrath	27.0	5	72	2
B Lee	23.0	3	94	1
S W Tait	15.0	1	61	1
S K Warne	37.3	5	122	6
S M Katich	3.0	0	14	0

Australia 1st Innings

J L Langer		b S J Harmison	105
M L Hayden	lbw	b A Flintoff	138
R T Ponting	c A J Strauss	b A Flintoff	35
D R Martyn	c P D Collingwood	b A Flintoff	10
M J Clarke	lbw	b M J Hoggard	25
S M Katich	lbw	b A Flintoff	1
A C Gilchrist	lbw	b M J Hoggard	23
S K Warne	c M P Vaughan	b A Flintoff	0
B Lee	c A F Giles	b M J Hoggard	6
G D McGrath	c A J Strauss	b M J Hoggard	0
S W Tait	not out		1
Extras	9nb 2w 4b 8lb		23
Total	all out	(107.1 overs)	367

Bowler	O	M	R	W
S J Harmison	22.0	2	87	1
M J Hoggard	24.1	2	97	4
A Flintoff	34.0	10	78	5
A F Giles	23.0	1	76	0
P D Collingwood	4.0	0	17	0

England 2nd Innings

M E Trescothick	lbw	b S K Warne	33
A J Strauss	c S M Katich	b S K Warne	1
M P Vaughan	c A C Gilchrist	b G D McGrath	45
I R Bell	c S K Warne	b G D McGrath	0
K P Pietersen		b G D McGrath	158
A Flintoff	c and b	S K Warne	8
P D Collingwood	c R T Ponting	b S K Warne	10
G O Jones		b S W Tait	1
A F Giles		b S K Warne	59
M J Hoggard	not out		4
S J Harmison	c M L Hayden	b S K Warne	0
Extras	5nb 7w 4b		16
Total	all out	(91.3 overs)	335

Bowler	O	M	R	W
G D McGrath	26.0	3	85	3
B Lee	20.0	4	88	0
S K Warne	38.3	3	124	6
M J Clarke	2.0	0	6	0
S W Tait	5.0	0	28	1

Australia 2nd Innings

J L Langer	not out		0
M L Hayden	not out		0
Extras		4lb	4
Total	for 0	(1 over)	4

Bowler	O	M	R	W
S J Harmison	0.4	0	0	0

Umpires: B F Bowden, R E Koertzen

BANGLADESH TESTS

Crushing victory

England warmed up for the Ashes series with two Tests against Bangladesh. These were routine victories over a side playing barely county standard, according to some commentators. Michael Vaughan wasn't interested in questions regarding Bangladesh's Test status; he took the view of all match-tough captains, that you could only beat the side that was put in front of you. And win they did. In the First Test at Lord's England rolled over the opposition by an innings and 261 runs in less than seven sessions. Trescothick fell six runs short of a double hundred, and Vaughan also made a ton.

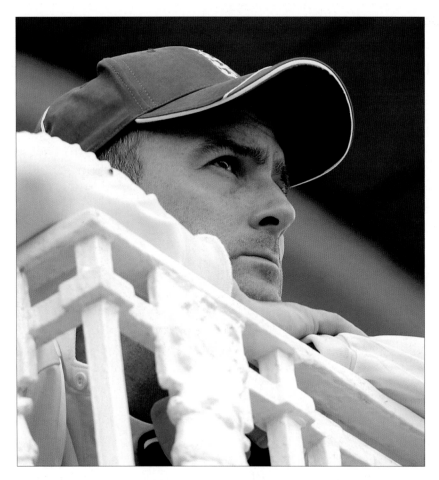

Above: Graham Thorpe of England looks on from the the balcony during day one of the First npower Test match between England and Bangladesh at Lord's.

Opposite: England players watch as their team bat during the NatWest International Twenty20 match between England and Australia at the Rose Bowl.

Dilemma over Thorpe

The decisions of the selectors were of more interest than the one-sided game. Graham Thorpe won his 99th cap, but then announced he wouldn't be available for the winter tour of India and Pakistan. It meant that if selected for the Ashes series, it would be the swansong for the classy 35-year-old who had been a mainstay of England's middle order for a decade.

Hampshire's Kevin Pietersen, who had set the one-day series in South Africa alight with some scintillating performances, was omitted from the squad to face Bangladesh, leaving many wondering whether he was seen as a limited-overs tub-thumper rather than a Test player. Rob Key, averaging 31 in his 15 tests to date, also missed out. Warwickshire's 23-year-old star Ian Bell was included – making an unbeaten 65 – a strong indication that the selectors had decided to go into the Ashes series with him at No. 3, despite the fact that his one Test to date had been a 'dead' match against West Indies in 2004.

Bangladesh routed again

The Second Test, at Chester-le-Street, again barely got into the third day. In another crushing England win, this time by an innings and 27 runs, Trescothick scored 151, Bell 162 in a total of 447–3. Bangladesh offered stiffer resistance in their second innings, opener Javed Omar making 71 for an aggregate 155 over the four innings. He was the visitors' man of the series, with Trescothick taking that honour for England for his 345 from just two knocks.

TWENTY20

First blood to Ashes underdogs

Next up was a one-off Twenty20 international between England and Australia, played at the Rose Bowl. The first match in this format between the two sides went well for England, the Ashes underdogs striking an early psychological blow with a 100-run victory and five overs to spare. Australia were out of it after losing seven wickets in 20 balls, though Ricky Ponting didn't appear unduly perturbed at being on the wrong end of a slogging match.

NATWEST SERIES

All square in the final

One of the all-time great one-day matches! Over the whole series it was probably a fair result. We had got off to a great start with the bat on a tough wicket. But Paul Collingwood and Geraint Jones produced a great stand to get England back in the game, so credit to them.

Ricky Ponting

'Best one-day innings ever'

A week later, Australia's captain was probably a little more concerned, his team having suffered three further reverses. They went down to Somerset in a one-dayer, and also suffered a three-wicket defeat to England at Bristol in the NatWest Series. The latter featured a blistering 91 off 65 balls by Pietersen, described by the England skipper as the best one-day innings he'd ever seen. At this point Pietersen's average from ten one-day internationals was 162.

If that defeat could be put down to early-tour rustiness against a strong limited overs side, tripping up against Bangladesh was completely unfathomable. Prior to inflicting a five-wicket defeat on Australia at Cardiff, Bangladesh had won only nine one-day internationals out of 107. The star of the show was Mohammad Ashraful. He had become the youngest player to hit a Test match hundred when he scored a ton against Sri Lanka on his debut, at the age of 16. Another century, this time against the best side in the world, was of a different order of magnitude.

Record for Collingwood

Another record fell in England's crushing tri-nations victory over Bangladesh at Trent Bridge. In the second of three straight victories over Bangladesh in the series, Durham all-rounder Paul Collingwood became the first man to take six wickets and score a century in a one-day international.

Australia recovered from the blip against Bangladesh to face England in the final. In overcast conditions both sides struggled as the new white ball moved around, both in the air and off the pitch. Australia, put in by Michael Vaughan, raced to 50 off the first seven overs, but wickets tumbled and the scoring rate dropped thereafter, notably after Harmison was brought into the attack. They eventually reached 196 in 48.5 overs, Mike Hussey top scoring with an unbeaten 62. Harmison (3–27) and Andrew Flintoff (3–23) were the pick of the England bowlers.

Match tied

England, now strong favourites to win, crashed to 33–5 as McGrath and Lee ripped through half the side within ten overs. Collingwood (53) and Geraint Jones (71) got the innings back on track with a sixth-wicket stand of 116. When both fell the initiative seemed to swing back to Australia, but Giles (18 n.o.) and Gough (12) took England to within a whisker of victory. Ten were needed off the final Glenn McGrath over; that became three off the last two balls. The equation remained the same one delivery later, McGrath running out Gough off his own bowling. Giles scrambled two leg-byes off the last ball, the match was drawn and the trophy shared. Geraint Jones won the man of the match award for his 71 and five catches; Andrew Symonds was named man of the series.

BBC RADIO FIVE LIVE

It was a pretty nerve-racking game to play in. We were outstanding in the field to restrict them to 196 and we were happy to be chasing 197 to win. But I think the tie was the right result.

Michael Vaughan

Opposite: Michael Vaughan, captain of England and Ricky Ponting, captain of Australia share the trophy after the game was tied.

Below: Geraint Jones of England hits out watched by Adam Gilchrist of Australia during the NatWest Series one-day final.

NATWEST CHALLENGE

It's been close for a while. I've been playing pretty well for most of the summer. I just need to hone my technique, and I've worked hard in practice over the past couple of weeks.

Marcus Trescothick

Decider at the Oval

Many commentators felt England's Ashes hopes had not been helped by the scheduling. Had the tests begun earlier, there was more chance of catching Australia cold, the argument ran. With the Natwest Challenge next in the order – three head-to-head one-dayers between the sides – there was yet more time for Ponting's men to shake off any ring-rustiness and be in prime form when the teams took the field at Lord's for the First npower Test.

England were out of the blocks first, cruising to a nine-wicket win at Headingley. Australia's total of 219–7 never looked enough, particularly as the clouds rolled away and Trescothick and Strauss were able to bat under blue skies. Strauss, caught attempting to reverse sweep Brad Hogg, was Australia's only success. Trescothick, with his tenth century in one-day internationals, and Vaughan saw England home with four overs in hand, inflicting Australia's worst defeat in two years.

Guard of honour for Shep

Aussies come from behind to win

The Aussies hit back in fine style to win the series, Ricky Ponting – who would be named man of the series – leading from the front. At Lord's England's top order collapsed yet again. At one stage 45–4, England recovered thanks to a fifth-wicket stand of 103 between Flintoff and Collingwood. Vaughan needed early wickets, used six bowlers in the first 12 overs in an effort to prise a breakthrough. Ponting scored his 18th one-day ton, equalling Mark Waugh's record, as Australia won by seven wickets to set up a decider at the Oval.

Shepherd's last stand

On 12 July the teams met for the final time before the Ashes series. There was a note of camaraderie and respect as the players formed a guard of honour to mark the retirement of David Shepherd, who had stood in 92 Tests and 172 one-day internationals. When the action began, England again struggled early on with the bat. Pietersen, at least, was in good touch, playing a succession of power strokes through his favoured leg side. His 74 came in 84 balls, and a half-century by Vikram Solanki, together with a fine cameo by Giles, got England up to 228-7 from their allotted overs.

The bowlers found Adam Gilchrist in ominously good form. He sped to 50 in 42 balls, and went on to complete his 11th one-day ton. His unbeaten 121 included 80 in boundaries. Hayden and Ponting were England's only successes by the time Martyn hit the winning runs with 15.1 overs to spare.

We batted in overcast conditions for our entire 50 overs and then, when it was their turn to bat, the sun came out and dried everything out! If the weather had stayed the way it was when we batted I think there would still have been enough in the wicket. It was probably the toughest conditions I've ever been confronted with in a one-day international.

Ricky Ponting

Opposite: The Australian cricket team celebrate victory.

Above: David Shepherd, best known for his antics on nelson or multiples thereof, performs his superstitious ritual as Australia reach 222 in the final.

Below: The England and Australian teams stand for a minute's silence in front of the Pavilion for the London bombings.

C&G TROPHY

Ervine victorious in battle of the centurions

The Cheltenham & Gloucester Trophy final was lit up by two sparkling centuries, Warwickshire captain Nick Knight anchoring his team's reply after Sean Ervine's brilliant 104 off 93 balls had formed the backbone of Hampshire's impressive 290 from their allotted 50 overs. When the Bears reached 200 for the loss of just three wickets, it seemed as if Knight's decision to put the opposition in had been vindicated. But the last six Warwickshire wickets fell for just 57 runs and Shaun Udal became the first Hampshire skipper since 1992 to hold a major trophy aloft.

Knight elects to chase

Knight, in his final campaign as Warwickshire captain, could hardly be criticized for electing to bat second; in six of the previous eight finals the winners had mounted a successful chase. John Crawley and Nic Pothas put on 57 inside 14 before Crawley was caught behind. That brought 22-year-old left handed Zimbabwean Sean Ervine to the crease. He and the South African wicket-keeper batsman added 134 in just 20 overs for the second wicket. When the total passed the 100 mark at five an over, Bears fans must have been drooling as a mix-up left both batsmen stranded and the ball in the hands of ace fielder Trevor Penney. But he threw to the wrong end – not very accurately – and Hampshire survived. All the bowlers were taking stick, with the exception of Makhaya Ntini, who got early movement off the pitch and whose first six overs went for just 12 runs.

We deserve it; we've played some magnificent cricket all the way through the competition. We were behind the eight ball after 15 overs but we clawed it back – this side's got some serious spirit. We've come so far in two years, Shane Warne is astonishing with his never-say-die spirit; this is for him as much as anybody. Sean Ervine scored a wonderful 100 in the semi-final and 100 in the final, it doesn't get any better than that. We were a little concerned that we didn't get 310–315 but we knew that as the ball got softer it would be harder to score and we just kept hanging on in there.

Shaun Udal

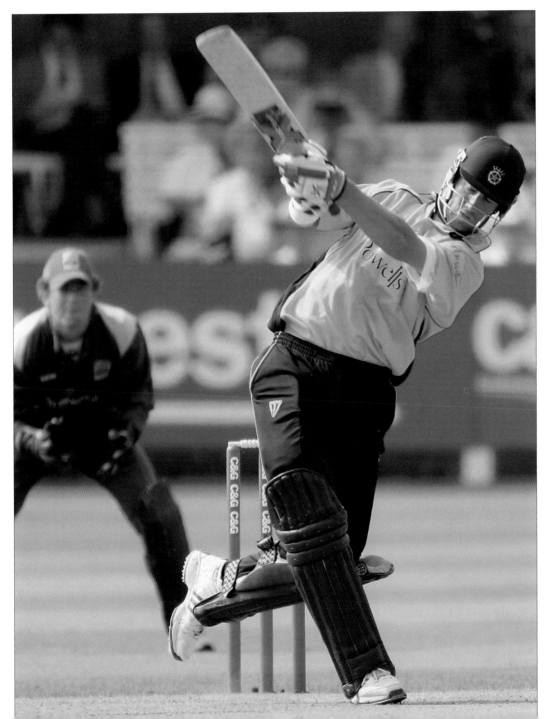

Opposite: The Hampshire team celebrate with the trophy after beating Warwickshire in the C&G final at Lord's.

Left: Sean Ervine of Hampshire hits a boundary during his knock of 104.

Giles wins battle of the England stars

Opposite: Andrew Bichel of Hampshire celebrates the wicket of Nick Knight of Warwickshire during the C&G Trophy final.

Below: Ashley Giles of Warwickshire is congratulated after catching Kevin Pietersen off the bowling of Ian Trott during the C&G Trophy final.

Pothas eventually fell for 68, caught behind in attempting to hook Neil Carter, a carbon copy of Crawley's dismissal. That seemed to offer little respite as it brought Kevin Pietersen to the crease, ahead of Shane Watson. He had predicted that he would mete out some severe treatment to his England colleague Ashley Giles. But when Pietersen had made just five, the 'King of Spain' snaffled a glorious low catch in the deep off Jonathan Trott.

From that moment on, Warwickshire applied the brakes with a regular clatter of wickets, although they couldn't prevent Ervine from reaching his ton, a repeat performance of his superb innings in the semi-final victory over Yorkshire.

Greg Lamb, the seventh man to perish, was comfortably short of his ground when Ntini threw down the stumps. But the Zimbabwean bowler's outstretched arm made contact with Lamb, and Andy Bichel, at the non-business end, made it clear that he felt there had been blatant obstruction. The third umpire saw no misdemeanour.

Carter's 5–66 restricts Hampshire total

The score was then 282–7, and both Udal and Bichel went before the Hampshire tail added eight more runs. Neil Carter finished with 5 for 66, while his captain would undoubtedly have been pleased that his men had reined in the opposition, Hampshire at one stage looking certain to exceed 300.

After his fine spell with the ball, Carter took on the pinch-hitting role, plundering 32 of the 44 runs scored for the first wicket before being run out by Ervine from mid-on. Knight and Ian Bell then set up what appeared to be a solid platform for victory with a second-wicket partnership of 122.

Bell goes down with cramp

The turning point came when the England man suffered cramp and needed a runner. He was out almost immediately for 54, his discomfort plain for all to see. At 166–2 Warwickshire were still well in the game, but two Andy Bichel overs, which accounted for Troughton and Penney for the addition of just six runs, was a blow from which the Bears never recovered. Only Dougie Brown managed to get into double figures thereafter, and when Knight perished at deep square leg, with his team still needing 40 off 2.5 overs, the game was up.

I thought at one point we were going really well. We just couldn't get a partnership together, the new guys coming in found it hard and the rate kept going up. We weren't at our sharpest in the field – we let a few runs through our legs and there were a lot of extras.

Nick Knight

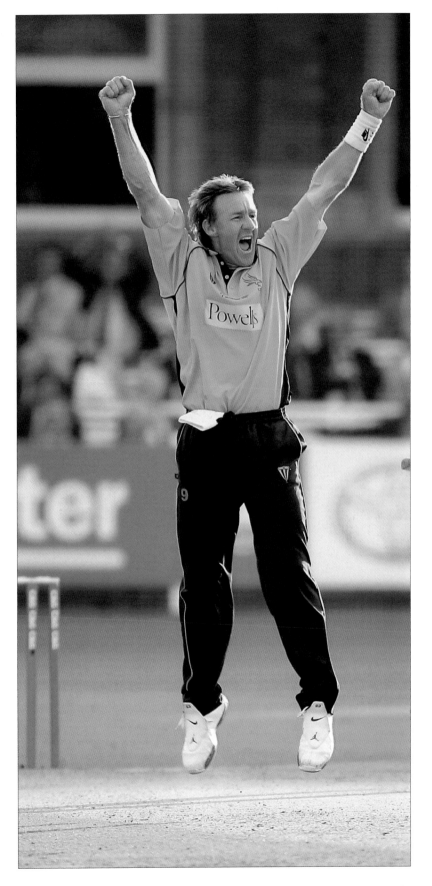

TWENTY20 CUP

Sabres rattle Freddie and co.

The popularity of Twenty20 cricket continued apace in 2005, the third year since the introduction of the competition. A rain-interrupted finals day at the Brit Oval boasted a strong cast: holders Leicestershire Foxes were there again, as were Surrey Lions, inaugural winners and runners-up in 2004. Lancashire Lightning's prodigious batting prowess made them the bookies' favourite, with Somerset Sabres completing the semi-final line-up.

Lions edge Bears in quarter-final bowl-out

Surrey and Lancashire contested the first semi. Lions fans might have thought it was their year again, following an extraordinary match against Warwickshire in the previous round. The Bears, needing three off the last ball to reach a Duckworth-Lewis revised total, could only tie the scores. Surrey trooped off, believing they'd won, only for the teams to re-emerge after the umpires had scratched their heads and consulted the rule-book. Surrey did squeeze through in a nervy bowl-out in one of the more bizarre endings to a first-class cricket match.

Flintoff bludgeons 49 off 28 balls

Surrey failed to make it a hat-trick of final appearances, though. Lancashire scored 217, the seventh highest total in the competition's history. Andrew Symonds hit 52, with Flintoff, Loye and Law all making over 30. Freddie's 49 came off just 28 balls. Alistair Brown led the charge for Surrey, and after six overs they had matched Lancashire's score of 63. But despite a 76-run partnership between Ramprakash and Mahmood, Lions' fans hopes of repeating their narrow 2004 semi-final win over the same opposition faded as they came up 22 runs short.

Woeful batting costs holders

In the other semi, Somerset Sabres won the toss and elected to bat. Some top-notch fielding from the Foxes, along with Dinesh Mongia's 3-30 from his four overs, restricted the West Country side to 157–9, Matthew Wood top scoring with 38. Leicester looked in control when Darren Maddy reached his 50 off just 27 deliveries. The wheels then came off for Leicester as Ian Blackwell took three scalps, and Richard Johnson dismissed Gibson and Henderson with successive balls. The Foxes finished on 153–8, leaving captain Hylton Ackerman bemoaning an abject batting display.

I had a really good feeling – I thought we were going to win it – but I don't think it's a case of choking.

Mark Chilton
Lancashire captain

Opposite: Captain Graeme Smith and his Somerset teammates celebrate victory in the Twenty20 Cup final.

Below left: Richard Johnson of Somerset celebrates bowling Claude Henderson of Leicestershire Foxes during the Twenty20 Cup semi-final.

Below right: Mark Ramprakash of Surrey Lions is clean bowled by Andrew Flintoff during the semi-final.

TWENTY20 CUP

Semi-finals

Lancashire Lightning 217-4 (20 overs)
Surrey Lions 195-7 (20 overs)

Somerset Sabres 157-9 (20 overs)
Leicestershire Foxes 153-8 (20 overs)

Final Scorecard

Lancashire Lightning

M B Loye	c Johnson	b Caddick	2
S G Law	run out		59
A Flintoff	c Blackwell	b Caddick	2
A Symonds	run out		12
D G Cork	c Trescothick	b Johnson	1
G Chapple		b Johnson	0
M J Chilton		b Blackwell	9
A R Crook	c Gazzard	b Johnson	15
W K Hegg	not out		6
Extras			5
Total	(8 wkts, 16 overs)		114

Somerset Sabres

G C Smith	not out		64
M E Trescothick	c Hegg	b Flintoff	10
M J Wood		b Flintoff	22
I D Blackwell	c Law	b Keedy	3
J C Hildreth	not out		16
Extras			3
Total	(3 wkts, 14.1 overs)		118

Somerset won by 7 wickets

Lightning batters fail to spark

A rain-affected final saw the match reduced to 16 overs per side. Lancashire won the toss and elected to bat, no doubt hoping to post another daunting total, particularly as the ball was swinging considerably as the evening wore on at the floodlit Brit Oval. For once, however, the much vaunted top order failed to spark, Stuart Law apart. He made a fine 59 off 45 balls as Lancashire reached 114, a total they must have been more than happy with having stood at a parlous 41–5 in the sixth over. Andy Caddick and Richard Johnson, with two early wickets apiece, were the men chiefly responsible for reining in the favourites.

Smith unbeaten

Lancashire needed wickets; what they got was a classy display from opener Graeme Smith, playing his last game for Somerset before returning to South Africa. He hit an unbeaten 64 off 47 balls and Somerset were always in the driving seat. Flintoff captured the wickets of England teammate Marcus Trescothick and Matthew Wood, but with Smith still there Lancashire were always up against it. Needing just 15 off the last three overs, Smith bludgeoned Freddie for 14. England prospect James Hildreth hit the winning boundary, giving Somerset a seven-wicket victory with 11 balls to spare.

Right: Mark Chilton is clean bowled by Ian Blackwell.

TOTESPORT LEAGUE

Essex Eagles take Totesport crown

Essex Eagles romped to the Totesport League Division One title, suffering just one defeat and two no-results in their 16 matches. The Eagles finished 14 points clear of second-placed Middlesex. The Second Division race was much closer. A run of five straight victories brought Sussex Sharks the championship. Sussex's eight-wicket victory over Yorkshire Phoenix on the final day was enough to pip Durham by two points.

Below: Simon Katich of Hampshire in action during the Totesport Sunday League match between the Hampshire Hawks and the Essex Eagles at the Rose Bowl.

National Cricket League Division One	P	W	L	T	N/R	R/R	Pts
Essex	16	13	1	0	2	7.28	56.0
Middlesex	16	10	5	0	1	5.54	42.0
Northamptonshire	16	7	7	0	2	-0.13	32.0
Glamorgan	16	6	6	0	4	-0.24	32.0
Nottinghamshire	16	6	7	0	3	5.83	30.0
Lancashire	16	6	9	0	1	-0.69	26.0
Gloucestershire	16	6	9	0	1	-8.39	26.0
Worcestershire	16	5	10	0	1	-2.53	22.0
Hampshire	16	5	10	0	1	-6.23	22.0

COUNTY CHAMPIONSHIP

Nottinghamshire win county title

Victory over Kent brought Notts their first Championship since 1987 and their first major trophy in 14 years. Notts are the first side since the Championship was split in 2001 to win the title after being promoted from Division Two the previous year.

Victorious Notts captain Stephen Fleming paid tribute to Kent's David Fulton for agreeing a declaration to keep Kent's own title ambitions alive: 'Dave Fulton is a guy who loves to win, and that is the sort of captain I think needs to be promoted in county cricket. There were some boos and jeers about what we did. That is where county cricket has to go – with guys who want to win games rather than getting caught up too much in bonus points.'

Opposite and below: Nottinghamshire celebrate winning the Frizzell County Championship following their victory over Kent at Kent county cricket ground.

County Championship – Division One Table

		P	W	D	L	Batting	Bowling	Pts
1	Nottinghamshire	16	9	4	3	50	44	236.0
2	Hampshire	16	9	4	3	46	46	233.5
3	Sussex	16	7	6	3	57	45	224.0
4	Warwickshire	16	8	3	5	42	44	209.5
5	Kent	16	6	7	3	57	42	202.5
6	Middlesex	16	4	7	4	56	42	181.5
7	Surrey	16	4	9	3	53	44	180.5
8	Gloucestershire	16	1	5	10	26	46	104.0
9	Glamorgan	16	1	1	14	33	38	88.5

County Championship – Division Two Table

		P	W	D	L	Batting	Bowling	Pts
1	Lancashire	16	7	6	3	43	47	212.0
2	Durham	16	6	8	2	45	44	205.0
3	Yorkshire	16	5	10	1	49	42	200.5
4	Northamptonshire	16	5	8	3	45	46	193.0
5	Essex	16	5	7	4	51	36	185.0
6	Worcestershire	16	5	4	7	53	46	179.5
7	Leicestershire	16	3	7	6	45	45	159.5
8	Somerset	16	4	5	7	42	37	155.0
9	Derbyshire	16	1	7	8	31	43	116.0

It's the sort of thing that you dream about, it's been a long time coming. We haven't done a great deal for seven years. But the last two or three years we've been steadily getting better and this is the pinnacle of that.

Chris Read

We have got an ageing side but with that comes experience and it's been very valuable throughout the year.

Stephen Fleming

It's been a good two years, a good two seasons. Winning the second division last year was fantastic and then to come into the first division and actually win it was outstanding considering we were just looking to consolidate – to make sure we stayed up this year. But to actually win it was really good …The team is very well experienced, it's quite an old side. But the side is performing well. Our bowlers this year have certainly stood up to the play and bowled sides out.

Jason Gallian

CYCLING: TOUR DE FRANCE

Seven times champion retires

Lance Armstrong competed in his first Tour de France in 1993. Twelve years and a record six victories later, the 33-year-old Texan announced that the 2005 race would be his last. In 1996 Armstrong was diagnosed with testicular cancer, which then spread to his brain. Mere survival was extraordinary enough; but to go on to triumph in the gruelling 2,241-mile marathon on seven occasions made him, arguably, the most driven athlete in sport.

Armstrong announced his intentions early on in his swansong race. In the very first stage, a 19km time-trial, he finished second to fellow-countryman David Zabriskie. Yet the significant moment came 4km from the finish, when Armstrong flashed past his great rival Jan Ullrich, who had started a full minute ahead of him. For almost a decade Armstrong had been the German rider's nemesis. 31-year-old Ullrich, the 1997 champion, had finished runner-up to Armstrong on five occasions, and the American's early form suggested that this year he would once again be the rider to beat. And by Stage 4, the team time-trial, Armstrong was in his familiar yellow jersey as his Discovery team led the way home.

Armstrong didn't have things all his own way. After Stage 9 he lay third overall, trailing Jens Voigt and Christophe Moreau. But everyone knew these weren't his main challengers; all the chief pretenders to the throne – Ivan Basso, Alexandre Vinokourov, Floyd Landis – and Ullrich – were behind him. Spain's rising star Alejandro Valverde pipped Armstrong to win Stage 10, the climb to Courchevel, but the latter regained the overall lead and put even greater distance between himself and his main rivals. Valverde would drop out through injury on Stage 13, though he confirmed his potential as Spain's heir to the legendary Miguel Indurain, while Armstrong dubbed him 'the future of cycling'.

Opposite: *Lance Armstrong puts on the yellow jersey as overall leader on the podium after the 20th stage of the 92nd Tour de France, an individual time-trial in Saint-Etienne.*

Left: *The cyclists make their way up to the Col D'Aubisque during Stage 16 between Mourenx and Pau.*

Right: *Jan Ullrich of T-Mobile Team in action during the finish of the Stage 20 time-trial.*

Armstrong's lieutenant wins stage

France was able to acclaim a stage winner on Bastille Day, David Moncoutier leading the rest into Digne-les-Bains. However, Armstrong was able to ride conservatively, ever mindful of the time advantage he held at the top of the leader board.

Stage 15, Lezat-sur-Leze to Saint-Lary-Soulan, had special significance for the race leader. It was during this stage in 1995 that his teammate Fabio Casartelli crashed and sustained fatal head injuries. Armstrong wore an armband inscribed with the word 'Fabio' during the stage, which passed by the sundial memorial to the man who won Olympic gold in 1992. He and Basso came in together, sixth and seventh, behind Armstrong's Discovery teammate George Hincapie, who won his first stage after a decade of competing in the Tour.

By now Armstrong was 2 minutes 46 seconds ahead of Basso, with Michael Rasmussen a further 23 seconds adrift and Ullrich over five minutes behind the leader. Few now doubted the outcome; the question was whether Armstrong could add to the 19 stage wins amassed in his previous six Tour victories.

Going into the penultimate stage, a 55.5km individual time-trial around St Etienne, it looked as if Armstrong might repeat his 2003 victory, when he became only the third man to win the Tour without a single road stage victory to his name. But, fittingly, the Texan notched his twentieth stage win in this, his final opportunity. It put him 4 minutes 40 seconds clear of Basso, and barring disaster his seventh coronation was assured. Basso's runner-up spot was also looking impregnable, but the big loser was Michael Rasmussen. He had a disastrous day – two crashes and four bike changes – allowing Ullrich, who finished the stage in second place, to nudge him out of the top three in the overall standings. Rasmussen's consolation was the confirmation of his victory in the King of the Mountains classification.

Vinokourov won the sprint for the line up the Champs-Elysees on the final day, but Paris on 24 July was all about hailing a remarkable seventh Tour victory for an extraordinary athlete, the man who said of his annual encounter with one of the greatest sporting challenges: 'I don't do this for pleasure; I do it for pain.'

It's nice to win. It's nice to finish your career on a high note – not just the stage but the race overall. For me, there was no pressure for this victory – it's just something I had within myself and as a sportsman I wanted to go out on top. It's part and parcel of being a person who has overcome and survived a life-threatening illness and come back and participated in a very famous event. I just try to be an example of the person that was lucky and believed he would get better and believed he would ultimately make it back to life.

Lance Armstrong
following his seventh Tour de France victory.

Final Classification Tour de France 2005

Yellow Jersey (General Cassification):	Lance Armstrong
(+ 4 min, 40 sec.) Second:	Ivan Basso
(+6min. 21 sec.) Third:	Jan Ullrich
Polka Dot Jersey (King of the Mountains):	Michael Rasmussen
Green Jersey (Winner of the Points):	Thor Hushovd
White Jersey (Best Young Rider):	Jaroslav Popovych
Team (General Cassification):	Discovery Channel

Left: George Hincapie of the Discovery Channel Team celebrates after winning Stage 15 between Lezat-sur-Leze and Saint-Lary-Soulan.

Right: Lance Armstrong (yellow jersey) rides with teammates from the Discovery Channel team during Stage 21 on the Champs-Elysees in Paris.

DARTS

Van Barneveld's fourth world crown

By common consent, the world's best darts player is Phil 'The Power' Taylor, but he's contracted – to the rival darts organization the Professional Darts Corporation, whose own world championship was taking place at the same time in January. While the British Darts Organization maintains that theirs remains the premier event, Raymond Van Barneveld was picking up his fourth title and cheque for £50,000 following his defeat of England's Martin Adams at the Lakeside Club.

'Dazzler' and 'Wolfie' make semis

English players Daryl 'The Dazzler' Fitton and Martin 'Wolfie' Adams put up strong opposition during the final weekend of the tournament. In a closely fought semi-final Fitton played Raymond Van Barneveld from the Netherlands and proved to be a tough opponent for the Dutchman 'Barney'. Van Barneveld hit doubles in the first five sets which took him 4–1 ahead of Fitton. However, Fitton soon fought back to bring the score round to 4–3 before Van Barneveld took the

lead to win the match 5–3. In the other semi-final Martin 'Wolfie' Adams was placed against Australian Simon Whitlock. Adams controlled the match throughout winning a convincing 5–0, which took him into the final.

In the final contest between Van Barneveld and Adams it was Adams who took the first set before Van Barneveld began to hit doubles and regain control of the match. Adams continued to fight back but it was Van Barneveld who was to win the match 6–2, giving him his fourth World Championship.

England's Martin Adams (above) and Raymond Van Barneveld (top and left) of Holland during the final of the BDO World Professional Darts Championships at the Lakeside Club, Frimley Green, in January.

Opposite: *Martin Adams at the oche in the final.*

BDO World Professional Darts Championships

Semi-final	Raymond Van Barneveld NED	31.79
	Daryl Fitton ENG	31.30
Semi-final	Martin Adams ENG	32.61
	Simon Whitlock AUS	28.74
Final	Raymond Van Barneveld	32.26
	Martin Adams	30.45

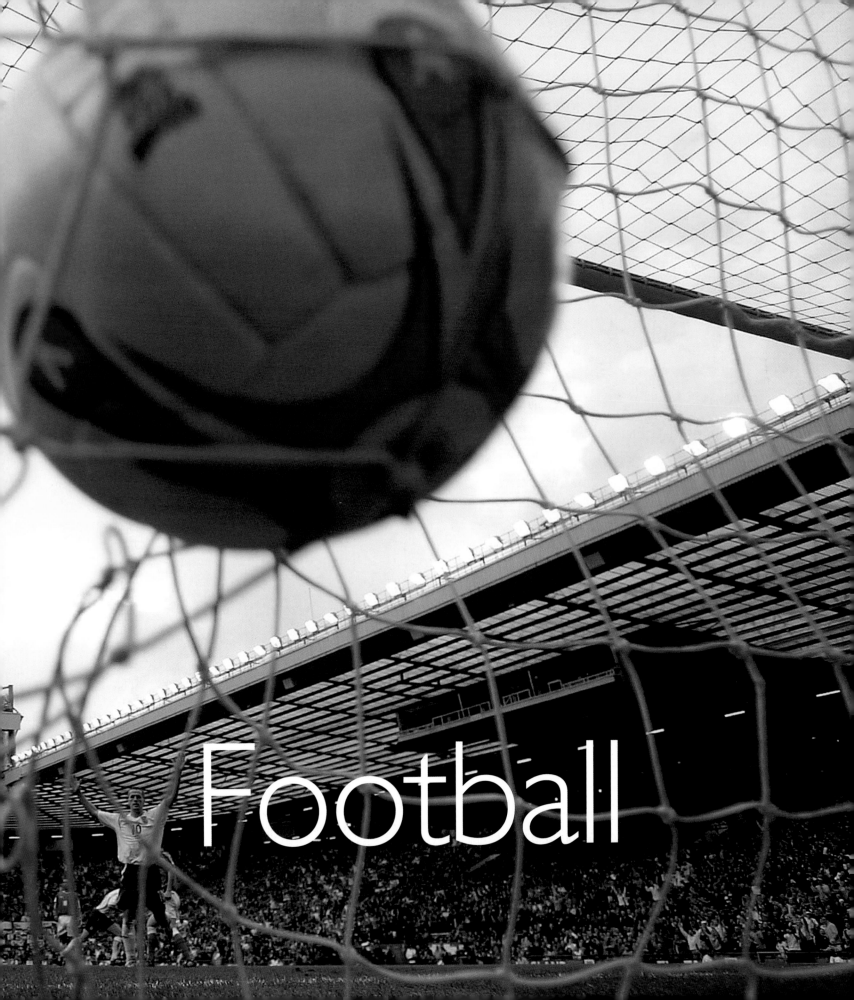

Football

THE PREMIERSHIP

Chelsea's first in 50 years

In the 12 seasons prior to the 2004–05 campaign, only Blackburn Rovers had managed to prevent the Premiership becoming a perennial two-horse race. And that proved to be a temporary blip; Jack Walker's millions could not prevent Rovers being relegated a
mere four years after the club's 1995 championship success, while United and Arsenal continued to vie for domestic supremacy.

City spoil Chelsea party

Roman Abramovich's arrival at Stamford Bridge in the summer of 2003 gave manager Claudio Ranieri a near-bottomless pit of resources with which to mastermind the dismantling of the duopoly. He came up just short; runners-up in the Premiership and semi-finalists in the Champions League wasn't enough to secure another season at the helm; enter Jose Mourinho, the man who had steered Porto to UEFA Cup and Champions League victory in successive seasons.

Defeat at Manchester City was the sole blot on Chelsea's 2004–05 copybook as far as the league was concerned. That meant the team didn't quite match the achievement of Arsène Wenger's side the season before, but it was still a mightily impressive, record-breaking campaign. Chelsea won 29 of their 38 games

– 15 of those on the road – in amassing a 95-point haul which saw them finish 12 points clear of the reigning champions from Highbury. Both statistics set a new Premiership benchmark.

In 57 hours of league football Chelsea shipped just 15 goals, two fewer than Arsenal in 1998–99. Die-hard Liverpool fans would no doubt point out that their team conceded only 16 goals in 1978–79, in the days of a 42-match programme, but few would dispute the quality of Chelsea's niggardly defence, which was superbly marshalled by the team's own Captain Marvel, John Terry. He would be named PFA Player of the Year, the first defender to receive the award since Paul McGrath in 1993.

For me this Premiership was the most difficult one. I've won the UEFA Cup, I've won the Champions League – but this was the most difficult for me. I have to say I didn't enjoy the game today because there was no pressure. It was a game for nothing. It was a game just to wait for the cup – not a game to achieve the cup. As a football game – I didn't like it.
I did enough to be regarded as a great manager. To win the Premiership with Chelsea after 50 years – I was voted by the fans last week as manager of the century!

Jose Mourinho

Opposite: *Chelsea players Petr Cech (l) John Terry (r) and Frank Lampard (c) look at the league trophy with their manager Jose Mourinho (2nd r) after winning 29 of their 38 league games.*

Left: *Damien Duff of Chelsea beats Sylvain Distin of Manchester City during the Barclays Premiership match between the teams at the City of Manchester Stadium.*

Cech breaks Schmeichel shut-out record

Former Rennes 'keeper Petr Cech exuded the same kind of aura of unflappable authority as Peter Schmeichel during United's most dominant period. The Czech Republic international played for 1,025 minutes without having to pick the ball out of the net, breaking Schmeichel's record for shut-outs. How Wenger and Ferguson must have wished for a 'keeper as imposing and consistent as the Chelsea man; they were left ringing the changes between Lehmann and Almunia on the one hand, and Howard and Carroll on the other, none of whom inspired total confidence. Ferguson would finally address the issue by signing Edwin van der Saar from Fulham at the end of the season. For many fans the arrival of Holland's most capped 'keeper was six months overdue, his name having been linked with a move to Old Trafford in the January 2005 window.

Chelsea were also devastatingly potent going forward. Only Arsenal topped Chelsea's 72-goal haul from their 38-match league programme, and even the Gunners couldn't match 37 goals away from home, a fraction under two per game.

Championship in centenary year

Chelsea sealed the championship at Bolton with three games to spare – exactly as Mourinho had predicted. Frank Lampard, runner-up to Terry in the PFA poll but winner of the Football Writers award, scored both goals in the 2–0 win at the Reebok, the result which confirmed that the class of 2005 had emulated the success of Ted Drake's side exactly 50 years earlier. The fact that it was the club's centenary neatly added to the symmetry of the achievement.

Above: Chelsea's goalkeeper Petr Cech misses a penalty kick from Bayern Munich's Michael Ballack during their first leg Champions League quarter-final at Stamford Bridge.

Left: Tal Ben Haim of Bolton Wanderers tackles Joe Cole of Chelsea during the Barclays Premiership match between Bolton Wanderers and Chelsea at the Reebok Stadium.

BBC RADIO FIVE LIVE

It's going to be a massive, massive task for someone to follow him [Alex Ferguson] – and sooner or later he's going to retire. He's done it all. He did it at Aberdeen before he went to Manchester United, and almost packed it in a few years back, but kept going. His record speaks for itself. I think he's a genius. He's in the same class as Sir Matt, and the amount of trophies he's won is amazing. How do you replace Fergie?

George Best

Fergie blames lack of firepower

In clinching the Premiership runners-up spot, Arsenal maintained their remarkable record in the Wenger era of never finishing outside the top two. Sir Alex Ferguson, meanwhile, blamed the lack of firepower for the fact that his team had to settle for third place for the third time in four years, the club's 'worst' run since the inception of the Premiership. United suffered from the loss of Ruud van Nistelrooy through injury for a large chunk of the season, and although £28 million signing Wayne Rooney regularly showed his credentials as the most exciting young talent in the land, United conjured just 58 goals from their 38 games. That was 16 fewer than

2002–03, the last time the Premiership title went to Old Trafford.

Towards the business end of the campaign the United management and playing staff had to contend with speculation over the ownership of the club as American entrepreneur Malcolm Glazer relentlessly bought up shares and got ever nearer the critical mass for complete control. 'United not for sale' was the passionate cry of many Red Devils fans; but they were to find that when it came to listed companies, the juggernaut of commercialism easily trampled over such dewy-eyed concepts as the soul and tradition of a football club.

 BBC RADIO FIVE LIVE

Wayne Rooney is fantastic, fantastic! One of the biggest talents you can have. He's a very good boy. He's very happy – especially when he can kick a football. Always a smile on his face. He doesn't talk very much and if he talks it's not that easy to understand him – for a Swede! A very good boy! Very easy to handle.

Sven-Goran Eriksson
talking to Des Lynam

Left: *Manchester United's Wayne Rooney scores the first goal during the Barclays Premiership match between Liverpool and Manchester United at Anfield.*

I arrive here with my ego big. Now it is even higher

Jose Mourinho

'I arrive here with my ego big. Now it is even higher.' Thus commented Jose Mourinho after guiding Chelsea to the 2004–05 Premiership title in his first season in English football. The self-appointed 'Special One' had ended a 50-year wait for the Stamford Bridge faithful, and also taken his personal tally to a remarkable seven trophies in three seasons, including victory in both European cup competitions.

From an early age Mourinho realized he lacked the talent to make the grade as a professional footballer, and saw coaching as his route to the top level. He was an astute student of the game, and his mentors included Bobby Robson, with whom he worked at Sporting Lisbon just after the latter had steered England to the semi-final at Italia '90. Mourinho was a polyglot and gifted communicator, skills which the former England boss valued so highly that he took his young protégé with him to Porto in 1993, and thence to Barcelona. Mourinho became increasingly involved in the coaching side, and when Robson left the Nou Camp, his successor Louis van Gaal retained the Portuguese as his number two.

The Catalan side won back-to-back La Liga titles in 1998 and 1999, and the following year Mourinho was given his first top job, at Benfica. Boardroom wrangling meant his tenure there was brief, but after working his magic at unheralded club Uniao Leiria, steering them to fifth in the league and a UEFA Cup spot, Mourinho was again in demand.

He returned to Porto, taking over as the club finished third in 2001–02, the first time in over a decade that the 1987 European Cup winners had finished outside the top two. Mourinho halted the slide in dramatic fashion.

Porto led the league from start to finish in 2002–03, ending the season 11 points clear of runners-up Benfica. The domestic double was completed with victory over his former club Uniao Leiria in the cup final. Porto then made it a glorious treble by beating Celtic 3–2 in the UEFA Cup final in Seville.

In 2003–04 Mourinho guided Porto to a successful defence of the Portuguese title, and brought the European Cup to the club's trophy room with a 3–0 demolition of Monaco in the showpiece final.

Those credentials were enough to persuade Roman Abramovich that Mourinho was the man to repay his huge investment at Chelsea with silverware. He arrived at Stamford Bridge in the summer of 2004 charged with eclipsing predecessor Claudio Ranieri's achievement of Premiership runners-up and Champions League semi-finalists. Victory over Liverpool in the Carling Cup final provided the first trophy of his Chelsea reign, and although the Reds got their revenge in the last four of the Champions League, Mourinho's men romped to the Premiership title. Chelsea finished 12 points clear of reigning champions Arsenal, with Manchester United a further six points adrift. In a single season Mourinho had broken the stranglehold Old Trafford and Highbury had exerted on English football for over a decade.

Opposite: Jose Mourinho during a Chelsea training session at Stamford Bridge.

Left: Mourinho gestures to a player during a Premiership match against Southampton at St Mary's.

Everton claim first European Cup place for 35 years

In contrast to Chelsea's runaway championship victory, the race for fourth place and the final Champions League spot went to the wire. Everton eventually edged their city rivals and Bolton Wanderers to claim their first Champions Cup adventure since winning the title in 1970, Howard Kendall's title-winning side of 1984–85 having been denied by the ban following the events at Heysel. It was an outstanding achievement, David Moyes' men having been widely tipped as relegation candidates at the start of the campaign following Wayne Rooney's departure to Old Trafford, and the further weakening of the side when influential midfielder Thomas Gravesen departed to Real Madrid in the January transfer window.

Everton faced a discomforting wait before having their Champions League qualification confirmed. Speculation grew that if Liverpool went all the way in the Champions League, the 2005–06 competition would surely have to accommodate the holders. For Everton supporters there was an uncomfortable precedent: in 2000 Real Madrid were crowned European champions but finished only fifth in La Liga. They were allowed to defend their title the following season at the expense of fourth-placed Real Zaragoza, whom the Spanish FA consigned to the UEFA Cup.

Reds' Istanbul win gives Goodison jitters

Liverpool's stunning victory over AC Milan in Istanbul left UEFA and the FA with exactly the same scenario, which was ultimately resolved when the Reds were granted a place in the qualifiers alongside some of European football's lesser lights. The final twist in the saga came as Liverpool comfortably made it through to the main draw of the 2005–06 competition, while Everton fell at the final qualifying hurdle, beaten 4–2 on aggregate by Villareal, and found themselves in the UEFA Cup anyway.

Fowler miss costs City UEFA place

With both FA Cup finalists and the Carling Cup winners already in the Champions League, the UEFA Cup places went to the sixth- and seventh-placed teams in the Premiership. Bolton finished sixth to secure a place in Europe for the first time in the club's history, while Middlesbrough pipped Manchester City for the final spot with a draw at the City of Manchester Stadium on the final day of the season. Had Mark Schwarzer not saved Robbie Fowler's stoppage-time spot-kick, it would have been Stuart Pearce's side planning a European adventure.

However, for sheer nailbiting tension the relegation dogfight was hard to beat. On the last day of the season it was a case of perm any three from four for the drop, the first time in Premiership history that the fate of at least one club hadn't been sealed going into the final round of matches. The protagonists were the previous year's promoted sides – Norwich, Crystal Palace and West Bromwich Albion – plus Harry Redknapp's Southampton, and they played out a 90-minute drama in several acts, all of which contained a twist.

Opposite: Everton celebrate after scoring against Newcastle at Goodison Park.

Above: *Mark Schwarzer the 'Boro goalkeeper gets down to save Robbie Fowler's penalty during the Premiership match between Manchester City and Middlesbrough, held at the City of Manchester Stadium.*

 BBC RADIO FIVE LIVE

It was never in doubt that fourth place would qualify. For a long time we've been focusing on the Champions League. Suddenly this situation has arisen and every man and his dog has got an opinion on it. The fact of the matter is when we set out at the start of the season everybody knew that the top four would probably qualify for the Champions League. Suddenly we're trying to find different rules.

David Moyes
talks about Everton qualifying for the Champions League

Win over Pompey keeps Baggies up

Norwich were in the survival spot at kick-off, the only team with its destiny in its own hands. During the afternoon all four occupied the vital 17th place at one time or another. But when the final whistle blew it was the Baggies who clinched another season at the top table. Bryan Robson's outfit was the only side to manufacture a win – a 2–0 victory over Portsmouth – although had Crystal Palace not conceded an equalizer eight minutes from time at Charlton, they would have pipped Albion by a point.

In surviving, West Brom made Premiership history. Statistics showed that the writing was invariably on the wall for the team propping up the table at Christmas. West Brom had not only anchored the Premiership at yuletide but had stood eight points adrift of the pack. As the Baggies fans celebrated their great escape, Southampton were left to contemplate life outside the top flight for the first time in 27 years.

BBC RADIO **FIVE LIVE**

Fabulous scenes at The Hawthorns. News has just come through and the place has gone absolutely barmy! The full-time whistle went here ahead of the whistle at The Valley. The West Brom players waited on the pitch until the final whistle there, but when it came – what celebrations! West Bromwich Albion have done it. Bryan Robson has led them to 'The Great Escape'. Albion – bottom at Christmas, eight points adrift of the rest, bottom of the table this morning. But it's West Bromwich Albion who have come out on top on 'Survival Sunday' in the Premiership!

Opposite: *West Bromwich Albion manager Bryan Robson celebrates after securing Premiership status at the end of the game against Portsmouth at The Hawthorns.*

Left: *Southampton fans show their disappointment at being relegated.*

Right: Bobby Zamora runs with Mark Noble on his back after scoring West Ham's winning goal during the Coca-Cola Championship Play-off against Preston North End.

Above: Gary Breen, the Sunderland captain, lifts the Championship trophy after his side's 1–0 victory in the match against Stoke City.

Opposite: Wigan celebrate going up to the Premiership after the Coca-Cola Championship match between Wigan Athletic and Reading at the JJB Stadium.

Wigan's fairytale rise

Mick McCarthy's Sunderland took top honours in the Championship, finishing seven points clear of the field. Wigan Athletic edged Ipswich for the other automatic promotion spot. Elected to the league as recently as the end of the 1977–78 season, Wigan had been bought in 1995 by Dave Whelan, 68-year-old founder of the JJB sportswear empire. His money, together with Paul Jewell's shrewd management, had produced a fairytale rise to the top of the English game. 'What we've done has given hope to every club in England that they can also achieve the impossible dream,' said a jubilant chairman as his team clinched promotion on the final day of the season.

Third-placed Ipswich finished nine points clear of Derby County, but it was the fifth- and sixth-placed teams, Preston and West Ham, who emerged to contest the play-off final. A Bobby Zamora goal earned the Hammers a return to the top flight, a vindication as well as a triumph for boss Alan Pardew, who had come in for considerable criticism from the Upton Park fans.

At the wrong end of the table Nottingham Forest, European champions in 1979 and 1980, were relegated to English football's third division for the first time since the early 1950s.

We've had some tricky days and nights at West Ham. This club is all about the fans – you've only got to look at the history of this club to know that sometimes we've had periods where we've played attractive football and not won anything.

But I want to win and we won something today – we've won a trophy. Let's not just settle for playing good football the West Ham way – let's win things as well.

Of course criticism hurts, but you have to use it in the right manner. If people throw bricks you have to build a wall with it and we've done that. We've built a wall of confidence around ourselves that we're good enough – and we've proved it today.

Alan Pardew

BBC RADIO **FIVE LIVE**

We've waited so long for our first big trophy together. We won the Carling Cup last year which was a great feeling for us – our first one together as a team. But now that we've had a taste of the Premiership – it's not just about winning one. If you look at the great players, they've all got five, six or seven trophies and medals. That's what I want to do. I want to retain the Premiership.

John Terry

I think Chelsea is the favourite to win the Premiership this season. But I think it will be more difficult because everyone wants to beat Chelsea today. Jose Mourinho is a character; he's a good organizer. You can see that when you watch Chelsea playing football and when Porto played football. I think he's a great motivator.

Sven-Goran Eriksson

Barclays Premiership 2004–2005

	Pld	W	D	L	F	A	GD	GFA	GAA	PpG	Pts
Chelsea	38	29	8	1	72	15	57	1.89	0.39	2.50	95
Arsenal	38	25	8	5	87	36	51	2.28	0.94	2.18	83
Manchester United	38	22	11	5	58	26	32	1.52	0.68	2.02	77
Everton	38	18	7	13	45	46	-1	1.18	1.21	1.60	61
Liverpool	38	17	7	14	52	41	11	1.36	1.07	1.52	58
Bolton Wanderers	38	16	10	12	49	44	5	1.28	1.15	1.52	58
Middlesbrough	38	14	13	11	53	46	7	1.39	1.21	1.44	55
Manchester City	38	13	13	12	47	39	8	1.23	1.02	1.36	52
Tottenham Hotspur	38	14	10	14	47	41	6	1.23	1.07	1.36	52
Aston Villa	38	12	11	15	45	52	-7	1.18	1.36	1.23	47
Charlton Athletic	38	12	10	16	42	58	-16	1.10	1.52	1.21	46
Birmingham City	38	11	12	15	40	46	-6	1.05	1.21	1.18	45
Fulham	38	12	8	18	52	60	-8	1.36	1.57	1.15	44
Newcastle United	38	10	14	14	47	57	-10	1.23	1.50	1.15	44
Blackburn Rovers	38	9	15	14	32	43	-11	0.84	1.13	1.10	42
Portsmouth	38	10	9	19	43	59	-16	1.13	1.55	1.02	39
West Brom Albion	38	6	16	16	36	61	-25	0.94	1.60	0.89	34
Crystal Palace	38	7	12	19	41	62	-21	1.07	1.63	0.86	33
Norwich City	38	7	12	19	42	77	-35	1.10	2.02	0.86	33
Southampton	38	6	14	18	45	66	-21	1.18	1.73	0.84	32

GD: Goal Difference   **GFA:** Goals For Average per match

GAA: Goals Against Average per match   **PpG:** Points per Game

Below: Chelsea line up prior to the UEFA Champions League match between Chelsea and RSC Anderlecht at Stamford Bridge.

PREMIERSHIP 2005–2006

The champions will come from a small group of one

Even before the clocks had gone back, it seemed that Peter Kenyon's prediction that the Premiership title would come 'from a small group of one' was well on the way to being realized.

Chelsea had spent £50 million acquiring the services of Michael Essien, Shaun Wright-Phillips and Asier del Horno, while the return of Hernan Crespo after a season-long loan at AC Milan effectively added a fourth world-class player to the champions' squad. Aston Villa's Luke Moore had the honour of becoming the first player to score against Chelsea – in their seventh league match – though David O' Leary's side still went down 2–1.

Meanwhile, the attempts of Chelsea's main rivals to kickstart their season were misfiring. Manchester United dropped seven points from their first six games, and when the team suffered a 2–1 home defeat against Blackburn, the fans vented their frustration on Sir Alex Ferguson, the man who had delivered eight Premiership titles and Champions League success. Arsenal, who had lost Henry to injury as well as Vieira to Juventus, fell eight points behind Chelsea in their first six matches. European champions Liverpool, spearheaded by their £7 million summer signing Peter Crouch, opened with four draws out of five, while their city rivals were in free fall. Fourth in 2004–05, Everton were propping up the table at the beginning of October, still looking for their first win.

Falling attendances

Off the pitch, the health of the game occupied acres of newsprint. Falling attendances brought on by a dearth of entertainment at exorbitant cost led some to conclude that the golden goose was unwell, perhaps terminally so. Altering the points system to reward goalscoring was discussed by the Premier League and rejected – for now. However, Premier League Chief Executive Richard Scudamore expressed concern over the inexorable rise in televised football, with the European Commission the villain of the piece: 'It wasn't us that wanted to go to 138 (live televised matches), that was the EC. Clearly, they see our competition as designed for the benefit of broadcasters, even though it was created in 1888 for people to watch as a spectator sport.'

Right: Michael Owen of Newcastle is congratulated by Alan Shearer on scoring the second goal during the Barclays Premiership match between Blackburn Rovers and Newcastle United.

CARLING CUP

Chelsea 3 Liverpool 2 (a.e.t.)

The Carling Cup provided Jose Mourinho with his first piece of silverware in English football. Chelsea's third success in the competition came with a victory over Liverpool in the final at the Millennium Stadium. Within seconds John Arne Riise put the Reds ahead, and they came within 15 minutes of extending their lead at the head of the all-time list of League Cup winners. But a Paulo Ferreira free-kick deflected off Steven Gerrard's head for the equalizer and the game went into extra-time. Drogba and Kezman put Chelsea 3–1 up, and although Liverpool pulled one back through an Antonio Nunez header, Chelsea took the first honours of the 2004–05 season.

Right: Joe Cole holds aloft the Carling Cup.

Opposite: Chelsea's Frank Lampard is tripped by Liverpool's Dietmar Hamann during the Carling Cup final.

It's a dream come true. It's been a long time coming and the fans deserve this today. It's been a great day – what a fantastic achievement for us!

John Terry
after Chelsea beat Liverpool to win the Carling Cup

A big win! The cup, the silverware is the first since the new Chelsea under Mr Abramovich. It's the first time for a lot of players. We are having a very, very good season. We don't receive the credit we should.

Jose Mourinho
after Chelsea beat Liverpool to win the Carling Cup

FA CUP

In 1872 there was a mere 15-strong entry for the inaugural FA Cup, Wanderers beating Royal Engineers 1–0 in the final. One hundred and thirty-two years later a record 661 teams entered the world's oldest knockout cup competition. After 781 matches the two most successful teams in FA Cup history, Arsenal and Manchester United, battled through to meet in the final, although both suffered major scares along the way.

FA Cup upsets

Exeter City became the pride of the West Country for their superb goalless draw at Old Trafford in the Third Round. United did a professional job with a 2–0 win at St James's Park in the replay, but the tie showed that the big boys focused on the Premiership and Champions League at their FA Cup peril. Rafael Benitez found that out the hard way, fielding an under-strength side at Burnley and 90 minutes later finding that Liverpool would not be adding to their six wins in the competition. Scunthorpe had the temerity to score at Stamford Bridge, something that Premiership sides would manage only six times in the course of the league programme, but Mourinho's table-toppers came through safely in the end 3–1.

Opposite: The Arsenal team celebrate after winning the penalty shoot-out during the FA Cup final against Manchester United at the Millennium Stadium.

Left: Alex Inglethorpe and Scott Hiley of Exeter City at the final whistle during the FA Cup tie between Manchester United and Exeter City at Old Trafford.

Above: The Burnley team celebrates the own goal scored by Djimi Traore of Liverpool, as Jerzy Dudek looks on during the FA Cup Third Round match between Burnley and Liverpool at Turf Moor.

 BBC RADIO FIVE LIVE

It is fantastic to be in another FA Cup final because when I was a young boy I used to dream of FA Cup finals – and now I'm involved in so many. It also shows the remarkable consistency of the club and that's where I feel the most difficult thing is in modern football at the top, top level – to be consistent.

Arsène Wenger
following the semi-final win against Blackburn to take Arsenal into the FA Cup final

Plaudits for plucky Yeading

The tie of the round as far as romance was concerned was Yeading v Newcastle. The game took place at Loftus Road, where the Ryman League minnows held the Magpies at bay for 50 minutes before eventually going down 2–0. Six divisions separated the two teams, thought to be the widest gap of any FA Cup tie, but Yeading bowed out with enormous credit.

In Round Four, a more illustrious giant-killing side, Yeovil, travelled to take on Alan Curbishley's Charlton. The team famous for beating Sunderland in 1949, when they were a Southern League outfit, again acquitted themselves well, though it was the Premiership side which edged the tie 3–2.

Oldham, conquerors of Manchester City in the Third Round, fell to Bolton in another local derby. There were four all-Premiership clashes: Spurs needed a replay to see off West Brom, while Manchester Utd and Chelsea enjoyed home advantage in beating Middlesbrough and Birmingham City respectively.

Harry's move adds spice to south coast battle

But the match which captured everyone's imagination was Southampton v Portsmouth. Harry Redknapp's arrival at St Mary's so soon after leaving Pompey added extra spice to the battle of the bitter south coast rivals. An extra-time penalty coolly converted by Peter Crouch gave Saints a 1–0 win and they went marching on. However, on the final day of the Premiership season many Pompey fans were jubilant as their side went down at West Brom and news came through that Southampton had been relegated.

Arsenal had two titanic matches with Sheffield Utd in the Fifth Round, the teams locked at 1–1 after 210 minutes of football. Arsène Wenger's men went through 4–2 on penalties, showing once again that a good cup run invariably requires a slice of good fortune – and Arsenal would enjoy the rub of the green on several more occasions before Patrick Vieira lifted the trophy at the Millennium Stadium.

Right above: Matthew Oakley of Southampton scores their first goal during the FA Cup Fourth Round match against Portsmouth at St Mary's.

Right below: Lee Bowyer of Newcastle after scoring a goal during the FA Cup Third Round match between Yeading and Newcastle United at Loftus Road.

BBC RADIO FIVE LIVE

I was always a manager that did practise penalties. I understand that you can't replicate the nerves, but we used to go right through the proper routine, get the players in the centre of the field, walk them up to the goal. We knew what order we would take them in. We knew who would take them and I believe it is well worth practising.

Graham Taylor
talking after Liverpool had qualified for the final of the Champions League

Left: *Referee Mark Halsey sends off Chelsea 'keeper Carlo Cudicini during the Fifth Round FA Cup match between Newcastle United and Chelsea at St James's Park.*

Above: *Leicester City 'keeper Ian Walker celebrates his team's win in the FA Cup Fifth Round against Charlton Athletic at The Valley.*

Kluivert ends Chelsea's clean-sweep dream

Chelsea, meanwhile, were still vying to win four trophies, their odds of doing so shortening all the time. That dream ended at St James's Park, although they were somewhat unfortunate. Patrick Kluivert had been a huge disappointment since his arrival from Barcelona, but the Toon Army went delirious as the Dutch striker headed Newcastle ahead after four minutes. Mourinho played all his cards at half-time, making three substitutions, but that backfired as Wayne Bridge was stretchered off and Damien Duff became a passenger, injured but unable to be replaced. A red card for Carlo Cudicini, given for a foul on Ameobi, completed a miserable day for Chelsea.

Three other Premiership sides bit the dust in Round Five. Fulham's 1–0 defeat at the Reebok and Everton's 2–0 loss at home to Manchester United hardly constituted shocks; but Leicester City caused an upset with a 2–1 victory at Charlton.

I always wanted to coach and when I got into coaching I didn't miss playing at all. It's a different sort of satisfaction. When you're playing you've only got yourself to think about; when I lost I was inconsolable – I always wanted to win games. But when you're a manager you take it harder because you're responsible for the whole picture. You probably felt ten times worse when you lost, but ten times better if you won because you've put your mark on it and you're running this group of players.

Terry Venables
talking to Des Lynam

Foxes reach last eight

In the last eight United steamrollered Southampton, but a single goal won the other three ties. Kluivert was again Newcastle's hero in the match against Tottenham. He slotted home from Shearer's assist, though Shay Given would be named Player of the Round for a string of fine saves which kept Spurs' strikers at bay. Leicester City, languishing in the lower reaches of the Championship, was the only team outside the top flight to reach the quarters, and the only club never to have won the trophy. After their tie against Blackburn the Foxes were left having to wait at least one more year, a late Paul Dickov penalty dumping his former team out of the competition. Blackburn were into the semis for the first time since 1960. A typical Freddie Ljungberg goal settled the Bolton–Arsenal tie just three minutes into the game. The Swede burst through to latch onto Pires' through-ball before slotting home past the advancing Jaaskelainen. Ljungberg was also the culprit in one of the misses of the season late in the game, though it didn't prove costly. Bolton were hampered by the first-half dismissal of the fiery El-Hadji Diouf, an elbow on Jens Lehmann being the latest in a long line of incidents in which the red mist descended on the Senegal striker. The Gunners were in the last four for a record 25th time, while in the Wenger era the team had reached the semis five years in a row, matching Manchester United's achievement of 1962–66.

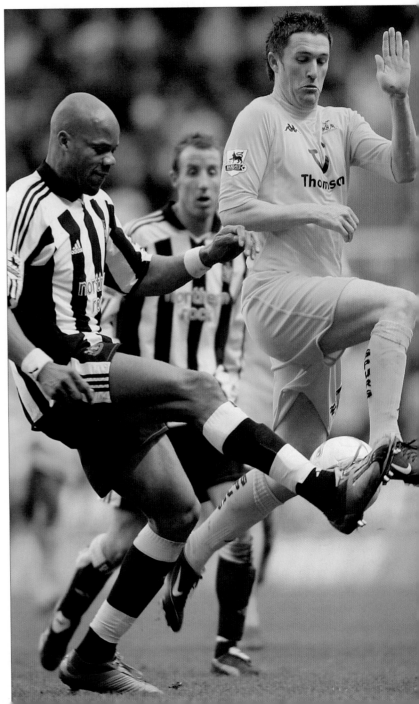

We're in the game to win trophies. It was nice to win a semi-final and we'll try to take care of the final when it comes. I think there's a lot of rivalry between ourselves and Arsenal (and the Chelseas, Liverpools, Leeds and Citys of this world) but we just look forward to the game and hopefully people can talk about the football.

Roy Keane
following the semi-final win against
Newcastle to take Manchester United into the FA Cup final

Seventeenth Cup Final for United and Arsenal

The semi-final draw kept Arsenal and Manchester United apart, and both won through to reach the final for the 17th time, putting them joint top in the all-time list. By now both were out of the Champions League, while hunting down Chelsea in the league seemed an unlikely prospect. The FA Cup thus represented both Wenger's and Ferguson's only realistic hope of silverware for the current campaign.

Blackburn stood joint fifth in the FA Cup record book with six wins, though the last of those had come in 1928. Current Cup pedigree comfortably won out in a disappointing match. Robert Pires put Arsenal ahead from close range just before the break, and Robin van Persie came off the bench to score twice in the second half. Arsenal thus booked their place in the final for the fourth time in five years.

Fifty-year Cup wait for Toon Army goes on

The pattern in the second semi was much the same. As with Blackburn, a long memory was needed to recall the last of Newcastle Utd's six FA Cup wins, 1955 in the Magpies' case. In contrast, Manchester Utd had won the trophy five times in the past 15 years. Newcastle needed to be at full strength and firing on all cylinders but in fact Graeme Souness was struggling with a spate of injuries. United cashed in, van Nistelrooy grabbing a brace and thus ending an eight-game drought – his worst run since arriving at Old Trafford. Paul Scholes came to the party with a header, and Ronaldo capped a bewitching performance with a goal, Newcastle fans having only an Ameobi strike with which to console themselves. This was Sir Alex Ferguson's seventh straight FA Cup semi-final victory, and certainly the most comfortable.

Opposite left: Nikos Dabizas of Leicester (r) in action with Paul Dickov of Blackburn during the FA Cup quarter-final between Blackburn Rovers and Leicester City at Ewood Park.

Opposite right: Newcastle's Jean Alain Boumsong (l) clears from Robbie Keane of Tottenham during the FA Cup quarter-final at St James's Park.

Below: Robert Pires of Arsenal scores the opening goal during the FA Cup semi-final against Blackburn Rovers at the Millennium Stadium.

United's match, Arsenal's cup

Arsenal 0 Manchester United 0 (a.e.t. Arsenal won 5–4 on penalties)

The Millennium Stadium, 21 May 2005, witnessed the 11th FA Cup meeting between United and Arsenal, though it was only the second occasion that they had locked horns in the final, the other being the memorable 1979 Wembley encounter, a game decided by the famous late Alan Sunderland strike.

The Cup holders had completed a double over the Gunners in the league, including a 4–2 win at Highbury, but couldn't make it a hat-trick in the Cardiff showpiece. United dominated the game, creating all the best chances, but failed to convert pressure and opportunity into goals. The much maligned Jens Lehmann was in top form, and on the one occasion when he was beaten, by Rio Ferdinand after 21 minutes, the referee's whistle came to the rescue. Rooney hit the woodwork, while Freddie Ljungberg did brilliantly to deflect a van Nistelrooy shot onto the bar and thence to safety.

Red card for Reyes

Jose Antonio Reyes was red-carded for a foul on Ronaldo, having already been yellow-carded, but with only seconds remaining in extra-time United were unable to capitalize on their man advantage and the FA Cup final went to penalties for the first time in history. Van Nistelrooy, Ronaldo and Keane all converted, but Lehmann's save from Scholes opened up a chink for the Gunners, who ended the shoot-out with a perfect record. Patrick Vieira put away the decisive spot-kick in what would prove to be

his final act in a competitive match for Arsenal before departing to Juventus in a £14 million deal.

'We really had to dig deep,' was Arsène Wenger's euphemistic assessment of a game in which his side was on the back foot for long periods. Inevitably, United's warrior-in-chief Roy Keane would rather have played indifferently and left Cardiff with the silverware. 'It's small consolation to say that we had all the chances,' said the defeated skipper. It meant that in 2004–05 Arsenal had added to their roll of honour, while United ended the campaign trophyless for only the fourth time in 16 years.

BBC RADIO FIVE LIVE

Patrick Vieira can win the FA Cup for his team here, captaining the side for the first time in the final. He has to beat Roy Carroll and send the Arsenal fans into ecstasy. One of Arsenal's great post-war players, Patrick Vieira steadies himself and ... wins the FA Cup for Arsenal. 100% they've been in the penalty shoot-out. In 90 minutes they were second best, Manchester United created the chances, they were the likeliest side, but Arsenal win the cup and Manchester United fail to retain it.

FA Cup Final match commentary

FA CUP RESULTS 2004-05

THIRD ROUND
Burnley 1-0 Liverpool
Notts County 1-2 Middlesbrough
Manchester United 0-0 Exeter City
Replay: Exeter City 0-2 Manchester United
Plymouth Argyle 1-3 Everton
Leicester City 2-2 Blackpool
Replay: Blackpool 0-1 Leicester City
Derby County 2-1 Wigan Athletic
Sunderland 2-1 Crystal Palace
Wolverhampton Wanderers 2-0 Millwall
Hull City 0-2 Colchester United
Tottenham Hotspur 2-1 Brighton & Hove Albion
Reading 1-1 Swansea City
Replay: Swansea City 0-1 Reading
Birmingham City 3-0 Leeds United
Hartlepool United 0-0 Boston United
Replay: Boston United 0-1 Hartlepool United
Milton Keynes Dons 0-2 Peterborough United
Oldham Athletic 1-0 Manchester City
Chelsea 3-1 Scunthorpe United
Cardiff City 1-1 Blackburn Rovers
Replay: Blackburn Rovers 3-2 Cardiff City
Charlton Athletic 4-1 Rochdale
West Ham United 1-0 Norwich City
Sheffield United 3-1 Aston Villa
Preston North End 0-2 West Bromwich Albion
Rotherham United 0-3 Yeovil Town
AFC Bournemouth 2-1 Chester City
Coventry City 3-0 Crewe Alexandra
Watford 1-1 Fulham
Replay: Fulham 2-0 Watford
Ipswich Town 1-3 Bolton Wanderers
Portsmouth 1-0 Gillingham
Northampton Town 1-3 Southampton
Queens Park Rangers 0-3 Nottingham Forest
Luton Town 0-2 Brentford
Arsenal 2-1 Stoke City
Yeading 0-2 Newcastle United
(at Queens Park Rangers FC)

FOURTH ROUND
Derby County 1-1 Fulham
Replay: Fulham 4-2 (a.e.t) Derby County
Manchester United 3-0 Middlesbrough
Blackburn Rovers 3-0 Colchester United
Chelsea 2-0 Birmingham City
West Ham United 1-1 Sheffield United
Replay: Sheffield United 1-1 (a.e.t) West Ham
(Sheffield United won 3-1 on penalties)
Oldham Athletic 0-1 Bolton Wanderers
Arsenal 2-0 Wolverhampton Wanderers
Everton 3-0 Sunderland
Nottingham Forest 1-0 Peterborough United
Brentford 0-0 Hartlepool United
Replay: Hartlepool United 0-1 Brentford
Reading 1-2 Leicester City
Burnley 2-0 AFC Bournemouth
Southampton 2-1 Portsmouth
West Bromwich Albion 1-1 Tottenham Hotspur
Replay: Tottenham Hotspur 3-1 WBA
Newcastle United 3-1 Coventry City
Charlton Athletic 3-2 Yeovil Town

FIFTH ROUND
Bolton Wanderers 1-0 Fulham
Tottenham Hotspur 1-1 Nottingham Forest
Replay: Nottingham Forest 0-3 Tottenham Hotspur
Everton 0-2 Manchester United
Charlton Athletic 1-2 Leicester City
Burnley 0-0 Blackburn Rovers
Replay: Blackburn Rovers 2-1 Burnley
Southampton 2-2 Brentford
Replay: Brentford 1-3 Southampton
Newcastle United 1-0 Chelsea
Arsenal 1-1 Sheffield United
Replay: Sheffield United 0-0 (a.e.t) Arsenal
(Arsenal won 4-2 on penalties)

SIXTH ROUND
Newcastle United 1-0 Tottenham Hotspur
Southampton 0-4 Manchester United
Bolton Wanderers 0-1 Arsenal
Blackburn Rovers 1-0 Leicester City

SEMI-FINALS
Arsenal 3-0 Blackburn Rovers
Newcastle United 1-4 Manchester United

FINAL
Arsenal 0-0 (a.e.t) Manchester United
Arsenal won 5-4 on penalties

It feels fantastic because it was a very difficult game. It was a fantastic achievement to win against Manchester United. For a long time I felt we had more chances to lose the game, but our mental strengths got us through. Manchester United defended very well. We didn't want to concede because in a Cup Final it is very important not to be too open, and in the end it worked.

Arsène Wenger
talking after Arsenal beat Manchester United in the FA Cup Final

Opposite: Manchester United's Wayne Rooney shoots from a free-kick during the FA Cup Final at the Millennium Stadium.

Above: Arsenal's Patrick Vieira lifts the FA Cup after Arsenal defeat Manchester United in a penalty shoot-out.

DES LYNAM MEETS

Alan Hansen

Paisley had never seen me play but signed me for 100 grand

Going back to those Liverpool days, you won eight championships, you won the European Cup three times. When you look back, can you put your finger on why Liverpool were able to maintain that consistency?

Obviously Shankley started the whole thing off, but when I was there, Bob Paisley was the manager. I went there and they won the championship, the European Cup '77, and got beaten in the FA Cup final. He picked me up at Lime Street Station, he'd never seen me play but signed me for 100 grand. His philosophy was unbelievably simple. Strength and weaknesses, you play to your strength and exploit their weaknesses, and then it doesn't matter how you win the game. Win it, then worry about it later. He had a great line about the long ball and the short ball, because there was a great debate in the early '80s about the long ball, and he comes in and he says, 'The long ball and the short ball, it's about neither; it's the right ball'. Simple but so effective.

Then Joe Fagan took over from the great man and then Kenny took over, and it just went from success to more success. But I was there and I'm thinking, Sooner or later this will end. And if you look at some of the signings after, that's the reason why they haven't won the big prizes for 14 years.

People say to me, 'I bet you wish you were playing now, and I bet you wish you were earning sixty grand a week', but you cannot take one minute of my time at Liverpool away from me. I had 14 of the best years of my life professionally at Liverpool, great players, great managers, great supporters, great times. It wasn't just the winning, it was the times you had winning, and I had such a great time there. So the guys that earn the money today, the best of luck to them.

In your prime at Liverpool, there were few foreign players. You're a Scot, you were a foreigner at Liverpool, now there's hardly a British player playing for Liverpool. What are your thoughts about the influx of all the foreign players? And has it benefited football in this country or is it detrimental to the national teams?

I think foreign players have brought a lot to the game. They've brought better technical ability. The first touch is king; you need two good feet. I think the players like Zola that came to Chelsea were great for the game. The influx of too many foreign players coming in and just taking the money and running, to me, has spoilt the game a bit.

The first year I was at Liverpool, we were playing the semi-final of the European Cup and we were on £200 to get to the final

It's put some of the clubs in terrible financial jeopardy.

But they've been badly run. You see, when I played, contracts were all in favour of the clubs, now they're all in favour of the players, so the clubs can't do anything about it. The other thing is, of course, when I played, you made up your money by winning. The first year I was at Liverpool, we were playing the semi-final of the European Cup and we were on £200 to get to the final, but were on six grand to win the final which, in 1978, was a fortune. So you win, and you get paid plenty, whereas now it doesn't matter what the bonuses are, because the basic salaries are so big. Another thing is, if you're not playing you don't need to fight your way back in the team: you just move on.

In your day Scotland had a pretty good team. What's happened?

Well, they haven't got any players. When I was growing up you played at school, after school you played, when you got home you kicked a ball against a wall. At the weekend you'd go into the local parks and play 54-a-side, so everybody played. I was going back to the same parks in 1982, which is a long time ago, and there was nobody playing. People had found other things to do. You mentioned foreign players: if you have an Old Firm game where there's Rangers against Celtic, there's one Scottish-born player playing in the match; that can't be good. I look at the Scotland line up and what they've got is 11 decent players — they haven't got any great players.

But you see it's not just the Old Firm, it's not just Rangers and Celtic, you look down the list of the other teams in Scotland, they're all bringing in foreign players, there's nowhere for the kids to come through.

It's Catch 22, they bring the foreigners in, paying them a lot of money, put the club in debt and there's no youth policy. I don't know how they're going to solve it, I really don't. I mean, if you think English clubs have got problems financially, you can multiply that by ten for the Scottish clubs. Again, you go back to the national team and it doesn't matter how good your coach is, and it doesn't matter what your preparation, or your team spirit is. At the end of the day, it's all about 11 players, and if you've only got five or six good players, then you've got a problem. That's why they really are struggling.

Can you see a time in British football where somebody is brave enough to play with just British players, perhaps an English team in the Premiership?

Not a chance, it's never ever going to happen. For the biggest clubs, if you're not in the Champions League, then you're history. Now everything is about money. Money rules English football. Is it getting better? No, it's not getting better, it's getting worse.

Who was the best player you ever played with in terms of sheer talent?

Dalglish. When you ask about the best player, Dalglish was unbelievable. When he was in his prime, you could play into him on either side; left or right foot, from four or five yards he would read it. Can you imagine how much confidence that gave the guy in possession? In the knowledge you could hit it five yards either side and he would get it. He was just a winner.

Above: The European Cup is raised in triumph by three Scotsmen: Graeme Souness, Kenny Dalglish and Alan Hansen. Liverpool won the trophy following their 1–0 victory over Real Madrid.

Below: Alan Hansen taking part in the 'Liverpool Legends Celebrity XI' Tsunami fundraiser match at Anfield.

UEFA CHAMPIONS LEAGUE

Liverpool kings of Europe once again

Liverpool had a curate's egg of a season in 2004–05. When they were poor – and they often were – they could look woefully inept; but the team also had the capacity to play champagne football. With such inconsistency the Reds always looked a better bet for a cup run than as a serious runner in the Premiership stakes, and a trip to Cardiff for the Carling Cup final seemed to bear that out. However, not even the most ardent Liverpool fan would have given much for the team's Champions League chances. How could a side which would eventually lose 14 Premiership matches, and in points terms finish nearer to bottom-placed Southampton than champions Chelsea, hope to overcome the cream of European football?

If there was an ace up the Anfield sleeve it was new manager Rafael Benitez; he may have struggled to adapt to the relentless demands of top-flight English league football in an injury-hit season; and he would be accused of misjudging the threat posed by Burnley, Liverpool's conquerors in the Third Round of the FA Cup; but the former Valencia boss was a battle-hardened European campaigner who certainly knew what it took to go the distance in the continent's premier competition.

Opposite: Liverpool's goalkeeper Jerzy Dudek surrounded by teammates at the end of the UEFA Champions League final against AC Milan at the Attaturk Stadium in Istanbul.

Left: Liverpool manager Rafael Benitez during the Champions League Group A match between Liverpool and Olympiakos at Anfield.

BBC RADIO **FIVE LIVE**

Benitez is a very good manager – he won two titles with Valencia, two championships, and also the UEFA Cup and now he's trying to do the same thing with Liverpool. Slowly he's understanding the League better, but in the Champions League he's very strong because the players are very focused. It's not the same in the Championship. It is a very big problem; he's had some injuries with Kewell and some strikers. It's not easy, but in my opinion Rafael Benitez has done a good job.

Claudio Ranieri

What a goal! What a fantastic goal by Steven Gerrard. Simply magnificent! It was a screaming half-volley left of Nikopolidis. Remarkably Liverpool, 1–0 down at half-time and heading out of the Champions League, are poised to go into the qualifying stages. Liverpool 3, Olympiakos 1 – would you believe it? The skipper delivers!

Match commentary on Gerrard's last minute goal to keep Liverpool in the Champions League

Three minutes from defeat against Olympiakos

Liverpool, having squeezed into the 2004–05 Champions League by finishing fourth in the Premiership, nearly came unstuck even before the main draw was made, only edging Grazer AK 2–1 on aggregate in the third qualifying round. Going into their final group match, Liverpool stood third, trailing Monaco by two points and Olympiakos by three. The French side ensured their safe passage by thrashing whipping boys Deportivo; who would join them in the last 16 hinged on the outcome of the Liverpool–Olympiakos clash. The Reds fell behind to a Rivaldo free-kick and came within three minutes of elimination, Steven Gerrard's stunning 87th-minute drive ensuring a win by the necessary margin to overturn their inferior goal difference.

Manchester United also went through as group runners-up. Sir Alex Ferguson's side took four points off both Lyon and Sparta Prague, but a 3–0 defeat at Fenerbahce in their final match meant that the winners of the French championship three years running topped the group.

Right: *Liverpool's Steven Gerrard (c), flanked by John Arne Riise (l) and Harry Kewell (r), celebrates scoring to make it 3–1 against Olympiakos.*

Below: *The teams of Manchester United and Sparta Prague line up at the start of the UEFA Champions League match at Old Trafford.*

Five-goal Gunners equal their record

Arsenal also made it to the last 16, by winning Group E, but it was a perilously close-run thing as just one point separated the Gunners, PSV and Panathinaikos in the final table. Arsenal were unbeaten in their six matches – only Juventus and Inter Milan managed to equal that – but four draws left Arsène Wenger's side needing to beat Rosenborg at Highbury to ensure qualification. With goals from Reyes, Henry, Fabregas and van Persie, plus a Pires spot-kick, Arsenal equalled the famous 5–1 win at Inter the season before, their best Champions League result.

Premiership runners-up Chelsea made it four out of four English clubs through to the knockout stage. Jose Mourinho's men were drawn with Porto, the team the 'Special One' had led to UEFA Cup and Champions League victory in successive seasons. They shared the honours with a win apiece, although Chelsea already had an unassailable lead at the head of the group when they went down 2–1 in Portugal in the final match. Duff put Chelsea in front at the Dragon Stadium, but Diego levelled and South African striker Benni McCarthy won the game with a late header. It was an academic result for Chelsea, their first defeat in the competition; not so for the reigning European champions, who thus edged CSKA Moscow for the group runners-up spot.

Above: *Arsenal's Robin van Persie (c) celebrates scoring against Rosenborg with teammates Mathieu Flamini (l), Fabregas (2nd r) and Jose Antonio Reyes.*

Left: *Damien Duff scores for Chelsea during the Champions League match against FC Porto at the Estadio Do Dragao.*

 BBC RADIO FIVE LIVE

We all try to be better tomorrow than we were yesterday and once you lose that you're ready to stop.

The challenge of a manager is to keep a club and team united.

Football is so attractive because there are people who have that talent to touch the ball and look around – and that demands a huge level of concentration that makes the sport specially difficult.

Arsène Wenger

talking to Nick Mullens reflecting on the milestone of 500 games in charge

Celtic miss out on UEFA Cup spot

In Group F Celtic found themselves up against two of the favourites, AC Milan and Barcelona, both of whom had secured their places in the last 16 before the fixtures were completed. Martin O'Neill's side beat Shakhtar Donetsk at Celtic Park and fought creditable draws at home to Milan and in the Nou Camp, but Shakhtar Donetsk's shock 2–0 home win over Barcelona in the final game meant that the Ukrainian side pipped them for third place and a UEFA Cup spot.

Valencia were reigning La Liga champions, having finished ahead of Barcelona in the 2003–04 title race. But while the Catalan giants, inspired by Ronaldinho, were looking ominously strong, Valencia limped home a distant third behind Inter and Werder Bremen in Group G. Perennial Champions League competitors Anderlecht were even worse, the only side in the group stage not to register a single point.

Leverkusen top Real's group

Bayer Leverkusen were the surprise winners of Group B, their progress based on a fortress-like home record. Real Madrid, Roma and Dynamo Kyiv all left Germany having shipped three goals. The Ukrainian side's defeat in the final match, combined with Real's 3–0 win at Roma, meant that Kyiv slipped from table toppers to a UEFA Cup place in 90 minutes.

Juventus cruised through Group C, their results including a double over Bayern Munich. The only blemish on the Italian giants' record was a draw away to Maccabi Tel Aviv. Bayern conjured four wins and a draw from their other four games to go through as runners-up.

Four years ago we actually had to qualify for the UEFA Cup by playing at Luxembourg, so tonight it's very disappointing to be out of European football. It probably won't really sink in until the draw is made sometime in February, but just about now might be time to take stock and see what we have to do.

Martin O'Neill
talking after Celtic's exit from the Champions League.

Below: AC Milan's Andrea Pirlo is congratulated by teammates after scoring against Celtic during their Champions League match at the Meazza Stadium in Milan.

Exit Arsenal and United

Arsenal and Manchester Utd both bowed out at the first knockout hurdle. United went to the San Siro needing to overturn a 1–0 deficit, Hernan Crespo having pounced on a Roy Carroll howler 11 minutes from time at Old Trafford. Ferguson brought in Tim Howard for the do-or-die trip to Italy, and gambled on throwing van Nistelrooy into the fray despite his recent long lay-off. But the only goal of the game was again scored by on-loan Chelsea striker Crespo, and United's hopes of emulating their 1999 glory year were over for another season.

Arsenal were woeful in their 3–1 defeat at Bayern Munich. Kolo Toure, who was at fault for the first two goals, both scored by Claudio Pizarro, made some kind of amends by scoring in the dying minutes to throw the Gunners a lifeline they barely deserved. A 2–0 win at Highbury would have been enough, and there was more than half an hour to go when Henry cracked a volley past Oliver Kahn – a goal which put him joint second with Cliff Bastin in the all-time Arsenal list, and just seven behind Ian Wright's record. But the Gunners couldn't find the net a second time, once again opening them up to the 'Champions League underachievers' tag.

Terry header dumps Barcelona out

Many thought Chelsea and Barcelona would have graced the final, but they came out of the hat together in the last 16. Barcelona came from behind to win 2–1 at the Nou Camp. Damien Duff's cross deflected off a defender to put Chelsea ahead after 32 minutes. Maxi Lopez equalized and Samuel Eto'o hit the winner. But the most controversial moment came after 55 minutes, when referee Anders Frisk showed Drogba the red card for a challenge on the 'keeper. The return leg at Stamford Bridge was extraordinary. Chelsea romped into a 3–0 lead, but a brace from Ronaldinho, the World Footballer of the Year, gave the initiative back to the visitors on away goals. John Terry headed the goal which gave Chelsea a 5–4 aggregate victory.

BBC RADIO FIVE LIVE

That's the way it is. Today we were one goal short once again. In the second half we showed the right Arsenal. I would like to say Phillipe Senderos played amazingly today and the likes of Edu and Gilberto Silva were massive. Obviously, with the standard that we set last year it is a disappointing season but there's still the FA Cup to go.

Thierry Henry

Left: A frustrated Thierry Henry during the UEFA Champions League, first knockout round, second leg match between Arsenal and Bayern Munich at Highbury.

Below: Oliver Kahn, the Bayern Munich 'keeper.

Liverpool hit Leverkusen for six

I think Liverpool have a better chance against AC Milan than they would have had against PSV. It will be a similar approach to the games against Juventus and Chelsea. I think they will be tight on people. No Chelsea player could get the ball without a Liverpool player being very close to him all of the time and I think they will do that to AC Milan as well. Liverpool have a very good chance of winning.

Graham Taylor
talking after Liverpool had qualified for the final of the Champions League

Liverpool's win over Bayer Leverkusen was barely less impressive, notably for the 3–1 win in Germany, a repeat of the Anfield scoreline. Luis Garcia scored twice, with Milan Baros adding a third before Leverkusen fired in a late consolation.

Juventus striker David Trezeguet wiped out Real Madrid's one-goal advantage gained at the Bernebeu, and Marcelo Zalayeta's extra-time goal won the tie for the Turin giants. Lyon confirmed their credentials as dark horses for

the title with a ten-goal mauling of Werder Bremen; Porto earned the dubious honour of being the first holders to fail to reach the quarter-finals when they went down 4–2 on aggregate to Inter. Brazilian striker Adriano did the damage with a second-leg hat-trick at the San Siro. PSV, who had won the old European Cup but never reached the knockout phase of the Champions League, enjoyed home and away wins over Monaco.

Right: Steven Gerrard climbs above Bernd Schneider during Liverpool's 3–1 victory over Bayer Leverkusen in Germany.

Milan derby abandoned

The battle of the Milan giants went the way of AC, in unsavoury circumstances. When Shevchenko scored on the half-hour of the second leg it put Milan 3–0 up on aggregate. It was a tempestuous affair, and the mood transferred to the supporters. With 15 minutes remaining Milan 'keeper Dida was struck by a flare and the players left the field. The referee tried to restart the match but objects continued to rain onto the pitch and the game was abandoned. Milan were through, Inter left to face the music before UEFA.

PSV and Lyon were locked at 2–2 after 210 minutes of football. Former Arsenal striker Sylvain Wiltord put Lyon, the competition's top-scoring side, in front in the second leg in Eindhoven. An Alex volley brought the home side level, and that's the way they stood at the end of extra-time. Two saves from PSV's Brazilian 'keeper Gomes – one of them from Michael Essien – settled the issue, PSV going through 4–2 in the shoot-out.

Right: AC Milan's Brazilian goalkeeper Nelson Dida is treated by doctors after he was injured by fireworks.

Below: A fireman collects fireworks as Inter Milan and AC Milan players wait for smoke to clear.

We play a lot of European teams at their own grounds. You have to tolerate a lot of histrionics from some teams in Europe – gamesmanship and playing for fouls and free-kicks. But AC Milan are perfectly professional. Even in the last minute they got a throw-in and Cafu took it quickly, took it immediately, not even thinking about running the clock down. Completely professional. It's that kind of professionalism and spirit they have that makes them a bit special and I think they can win the cup because of that.

Alex Ferguson

Wins over Bayern and Juve set up Premiership semi

Chelsea and Liverpool were both at home in their quarter-final first-leg matches, and both secured a win. Chelsea held a 4–1 lead over Bayern Munich in injury time when Ricardo Carvalho's challenge on Ballack in the box was deemed a foul. Ballack stepped up to beat Cech and breathe new life into the tie. A deflected shot from Lampard – who had scored twice at the Bridge – and a header from Drogba put Chelsea 2–1 up in Munich, and despite conceding two late goals and losing 3–2 on the night, Chelsea had done enough.

Sami Hyppia was Liverpool's unlikely hero against Juventus, giving his side the lead with a sweet left-foot volley. Luis Garcia doubled the advantage with a screamer into the top corner, but Juve clawed their way back with a priceless away goal. Fabio Cannovaro's header beat rookie teenage goalkeeper Scott Carson, and the odds swung in favour of Juve completing the job in Turin. When talisman and skipper Steven Gerrard was ruled out, Liverpool's task looked even more daunting. But a display of mature resilience and indomitable spirit earned Rafa Benitez's men a goalless draw and the prize of a semi-final clash with Premiership rivals Chelsea. It also meant that an English side would contest the final in Istanbul.

Below: Liverpool's Dudek clears from Marcelo Zalayeta (l) and Zlatan Ibrahimovic of Juventus during the UEFA Champions League quarter-final second leg at the Delle Alpi Stadium in Turin.

Biggest game in club football history

The Chelsea–Liverpool semi meant that the managers who had won the 2003–04 Champions League and UEFA Cup were going head to head. It was billed as the biggest game in the history of English club football, eclipsing Nottingham Forest and Liverpool, who met in the first round in 1978–79, and the Chelsea–Arsenal match of 2003–04, which had been at the quarter-final stage. Chelsea had won all three meetings between the sides during the current campaign, twice in the league and the Carling Cup final. But in the fifth encounter – the second leg at Anfield after a goalless game at Stamford Bridge – Liverpool finally scored the win which took them through. A controversial was-it-over-the-line goal from Luis Garcia saw the Reds reach their sixth Champions Cup final, 20 years on from the Heysel tragedy.

Below: Luis Garcia celebrates after scoring the controversial goal which decided the Liverpool–Chelsea Champions League semi-final.

Right: Jose Mourinho, Chelsea's manager, and Liverpool's manager Rafael Benitez, shouting instructions to their players.

We have good supporters, a good club, a good team and our team spirit is good – that's enough sometimes. Here, in England, it's more difficult for me – the language, the players, the style of football. Now we need to work hard for the future and think about the final because if you go to the final, it's to try and win and we will try and win.

Rafael Benitez
following Liverpool's defeat of
Chelsea in the Champions League
semi-final

Milan survive PSV scare

Liverpool's opponents in the final were AC Milan, though PSV gave the Italians a mighty scare. Guus Hiddink's side, which had just sewn up the domestic championship, trailed 2–0 from the first leg with goals from Shevchenko – his 34th in 65 Champions League matches – and Tomasson. Park Ji-Sung – who would depart to Old Trafford at the end of the season – reduced the arrears at the Philips Stadium inside ten minutes, and a Cocu header made the tie all square. PSV had troubled Milan in Italy, despite losing, and a 2–0 lead in the home leg certainly didn't flatter them. A 90th-minute Massimo Ambrosini header got Milan out of jail, for though Cocu volleyed his second of the match seconds later, it wasn't enough to prevent the Italian side going through on away goals.

It was Milan's tenth Champions Cup final and they were most pundits' favourites to record their seventh win. Liverpool, with four wins from their previous five appearances, also had a strong European Cup pedigree, and they needed to show it when they fell behind in the first minute, Maldini connecting on the half-volley from a Pirlo free-kick. A double from Crespo before the break seemed to have put the game out of Liverpool's reach. His first was a close range-effort from Shevchenko's cross, the second a delightful chip over the advancing Dudek following Kaka's pinpoint through-ball.

Below: Jerzy Dudek's save from Shevchenko makes Liverpool European Champions for the fifth time.

The game has completely turned on its head. They bolted the door after the horse has gone – but the horse has gone back in!

John Toshack

Gerrard inspires comeback

Benitez had already lost Kewell early on, replaced by Smicer. At half-time he threw on Hamann for Finnan, the German international bringing control and authority to the midfield. It also allowed Gerrard a freer rein, and it was the skipper who galvanized the team and led the fight-back. He powered home a header from Riise's cross on 53 mins. Then, after Smicer's drive from the edge of the area beat Dida, Gerrard's burst into the box was halted unfairly by Gattuso. Dida saved Xabi Alonso's spot-kick, but the latter reacted quickly and netted from the follow-up.

Milan then reasserted themselves, particularly in extra-time. Dudek made a wonder double save from Shevchenko and the game went to a shoot-out.

Hero Dudek does the Grobbelaar wobble

Dudek, said to be on borrowed time as No. 1 'keeper at Anfield, was the Reds' hero, emulating Bruce Grobbelaar's famous wobbly legs show, which successfully put off Graziani and Conti in the 1984 final shoot-out. Their 2005 counterparts were Serginho, who blazed over, and Pirlo, whose shot Dudek saved. Then, after Riise failed with his attempt, Dudek won the trophy for Liverpool by keeping Shevchenko out.

It was the greatest comeback in the history of European football; the Reds were being quoted at 300–1 at half-time, and many fans thought even those were generous odds against Milan's much vaunted defence. The icing on the cake was Steven Gerrard's post-match comment in which he committed his future to the club. The England midfielder had been the subject of fevered speculation over a move to Stamford Bridge, but amid the euphoric celebrations said that he couldn't entertain the thought of leaving his beloved club after such a dramatic victory. Liverpool would keep the trophy as well as their captain, the Reds' fifth win in the competition meaning that the cup would stay at Anfield.

I am delighted and very happy for the players, really happy for the supporters and for the club

 BBC RADIO FIVE LIVE

I thought it was going to be tears and disappointment and frustration at the end, but we kept going. We scored an early goal, which gave the team a bit of belief, and we kept fighting till the end. We've beaten some magnificent sides in this competition and no one can argue that we deserve to be Champions League winners. I just hope that the people above us let us defend it. It's called the Champions League, so the Champions should defend it.

Steven Gerrard

I am delighted and very happy for the players, really happy for the supporters and for the club.

Rafael Benitez

UEFA CUP

CSKA Moscow 3 Sporting Lisbon 1

England's UEFA Cup representatives, Middlesbrough and Newcastle, both fell to the same Portuguese opposition. Boro went down to Sporting Lisbon in the last 16, losing 3–2 at the Riverside and 1–0 at the Estadio Jose Alvalade. In the quarter-final Newcastle went to Lisbon in a strong position, leading from an Alan Shearer header at St James's Park. When Kieron Dyer put the Magpies two up after 20 minutes with a priceless away goal, the Toon Army might have been forgiven for believing this was finally their year for silverware. But Sporting levelled before the break, and Newcastle conceded three goals in the last 20 minutes for yet another bitterly disappointing cup exit.

Sporting went on to beat Dutch side AZ Alkmaar in the semis, though they had a Miguel Garcia header late in the second leg to thank: that meant a 3–2 defeat on the night but 4–4 on aggregate and progress to the final on away goals.

Sporting's opponents were CSKA Moscow, who had entered the UEFA Cup fray after finishing third behind Chelsea and Porto in their Champions League group. The other Roman Abramovich-backed team enjoyed a 3–0 aggregate win over Parma in the semis, then faced the daunting prospect of having to face Sporting on their own ground, the Jose Alvalade Stadium having been chosen to stage the final. It began well for the home side, Rogerio firing in from outside the box on the half-hour mark. But CSKA hit back with three second-half goals, playmaker Daniel Carvalho having a hand in all of them. CSKA's epic European adventure, which had begun with the Champions League qualifiers, ended 19 matches later with an entry into the record books as they became the first Russian club side to win a European final.

BBC RADIO FIVE LIVE

Tough times! Confidence isn't high, but I believe we're not far away. When we can get our first choice 11 out onto the pitch then we're a match for anyone. But once we get injuries we're a bit thin on the ground; we let seven or eight players go in the summer and didn't really have a big enough squad last year – that's what caught us out. In the UEFA Cup run, we were caught short with players. We need some players now and we haven't got long.

Alan Shearer

Opposite: *CSKA Moscow players display the trophy.*

Right: *Alexey Berezutskiy of CSKA Moscow celebrates scoring his team's first goal.*

UEFA SUPER CUP

CSKA Moscow 1 Liverpool 3

Reds' Super Cup

Liverpool began the 2005–06 season battling on six competitive fronts. The first piece of silverware was in the Anfield trophy room before August was out, the Reds coming from behind to beat CSKA Moscow in the European Super Cup, staged in Monaco. Liverpool trailed the Roman Abramovich-backed UEFA Cup holders 1–0 at the break, Carvalho capitalizing on a defensive lapse. Luis Garcia – who had missed several decent chances – finally put one away to take the game into extra-time, and a brace from Djibril Cisse saw Liverpool add to their Super Cup victories of 1977 and 2001.

Opposite: *Liverpool's Florent Sinama Pongolle battles for the ball with Elvir Rahimic of CSKA Moscow during the UEFA Super Cup match between Liverpool and CSKA Moscow at the Stade Louis II in Monte Carlo, Monaco.*

Right: *Liverpool celebrate their third victory in the Super Cup.*

Above: *A jubilant Djibril Cisse after scoring during extra-time.*

UEFA Champions League 2004-05

Quarter-finals

	1st leg	2nd leg	Agg.
Chelsea v Bayern Munich	4-2	2-3	6-5
AC Milan v Inter Milan	2-0	1-0	5-0
		2nd leg match abandoned. Milan awarded 3-0	
Liverpool v Juventus	2-1	0-0	2-1
Lyon v PSV Eindhoven	1-1	1-1	2-2
		PSV win on penalties	

Semi-finals

	1st leg	2nd leg	Agg.
Chelsea v Liverpool	0-0	0-1	0-1
Milan v PSV Eindhoven	2-0	1-3	3-3
		Milan win on away goals	

Final

Istanbul, Turkey

Milan v Liverpool	3-3
	(aet., Liverpool win 3-2 on penalties)

UEFA Cup 2004-05

Quarter-finals

	1st leg	2nd leg	Agg.
CSKA Moskva v Auxerre	4-0	0-2	4-2
Newcastle v Sporting Lisbon	1-0	1-4	2-4
Austria v Parma	1-1	0-0	1-1
Villarreal v Alkmaar	1-2	1-1	2-3

Semi-finals

	1st leg	2nd leg	Agg.
Parma v CSKA Moskva	0-0	0-3	0-3
Sporting Lisbon v Alkmaar	2-1	2-3	4-4
		Sporting Lisbon win on away goals	

Final

Lisbon, Portugal

Sporting Lisbon v CSKA Moskva	1-3

BBC RADIO FIVE LIVE

All the team knew it was important to work hard and then the game was almost ready for Cisse in the second half. We needed fresh legs and I always say the same in that we have good players and we need to use them. We always controlled the game. When we scored we had more space. We made one mistake and conceded a goal but I thought if we keep working the same we can score.

Rafael Benitez

COMMUNITY SHIELD

Drogba's double strike wins Shield

Didier Drogba openly admitted that despite Chelsea's Premiership and Carling Cup victories, he underperformed in his first season in English football. The former Monaco star began the 2005–06 campaign in fine style, scoring both goals in Chelsea's 2–1 win over Arsenal in the Community Shield curtain raiser.

Opposite: Chelsea are jubilant after beating Arsenal in the FA Community Shield at the Millennium Stadium in Cardiff.

Right: Chelsea's Didier Drogba celebrates his second goal.

If Didier Drogba feels under pressure from the return of Hernan Crespo to Chelsea, then he's responding in spectacular fashion. His two goals – one in each half – were beautifully taken and enough to give Chelsea the first available silverware of the season. Not everyone has been convinced by Drogba's value, but eight minutes in he breasted down a clipped pass for impressive new signing Asier del Horno and hit home a sweet left-footer. Drogba's second was a triumph for perseverance as he spread-eagled Senderos, Lehmann and Lauren to spin and score. Immediately he was replaced by Crespo – one of 11 substitutions on a steamy day. Arsenal replied through Fabregas, but despite plenty of ball and desire they fell short against The Champions.

Match report on the FA Community Shield

BBC RADIO FIVE LIVE

DES LYNAM MEETS

Arsène Wenger

England was ten years behind every other country

Arsène, critics of your team say that you haven't got the depth in your squad that, say, United or Chelsea have at this moment.

It is true, but we've gone for a policy of young players. I'm now in a situation where this season I've introduced many young players brought in from all over Europe, so to buy experienced players just to put in front of them would kill the policy we have established. That's why Fabregas, Clichy, Van Persie, Flamini and now Quincy have all come in. I don't know if I want to put somebody in front of them now, because it would destroy what we have built.

Where are the up-and-coming English players in your squad?

That's a very good question that I get asked many times. We have some very good young players including Justin Hoyte and Ryan Smith. We have been unlucky because both have suffered from injuries so we have to be a little bit patient. English teams attract the best players in the world but it is unfortunate for the English players that they have to compete with the best players in the world. We therefore invest a lot of money into our academy and spend between three and four million pounds per year to develop the young players. We do a good job because, if you look, our young players play at many other clubs and do very well.

But why are the young continental lads coming into your team now? They seem to be more talented than the young English players – why do you think that is?

Because England was ten years behind every other country in the development of the youth academies. They responded well four years ago, but the response time takes five or six years. Now for the first time you can see the under-16 and under-17 national teams beating big countries like France, Spain and Portugal, who were miles ahead. England has begun to claw back, but you will have to wait a little bit longer. The English football system always relied on schools, but schools can no longer cater for what is requested at the top level in the game so, unless the English Football Federation takes control of its own development, you will have no chance anymore – that is what happened in France.

So from what you are saying, can you foresee a time, say ten or fifteen years down the line, when you might not be involved with Arsenal, but that the Arsenal team might have more English players?

Yes, of course, I'm convinced of that because since I came here I have seen a huge improvement in the youth teams.

You go to bed early, you don't drink and you don't go out

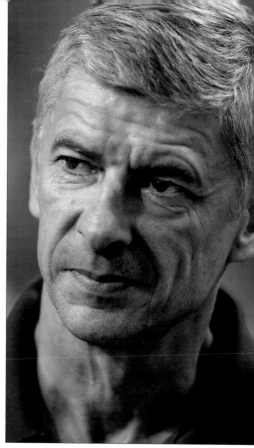

Going back to Europe, the Champions League is the gap in your Arsenal CV, isn't it?

We are a big club and I would be very proud to achieve that, and I will not give up, but you also have to consider some of the clubs who are in – Real Madrid, Juventus, Barcelona, Inter Milan, Manchester United and Chelsea. If I ask you now if Barcelona is a big club you would certainly say yes. They have 100, 000 people to every game but they have only won the Champions Cup once, so it shows you that, even for these clubs, it is not guaranteed that you win it.

You can't possibly have time off in the season. Do you ever get to the stage some days in your life when you think, I'm fed up with this, I'm low?

No, I sometimes get to the stage where I feel tired and when I get like that I think what would I do without football and quickly think, Come on, enjoy it; it's a fantastic job. Frankly, in England, as a manager, you live like a sportsman. That means you go to bed early, you don't drink and you don't go out, or you have no chance of doing your job properly. In the season you need to be focused every day, which I find the hardest part of the job in this country. When you would sometimes like to have a breather you can't, so it's physically very demanding.

Opposite: Arsène Wenger gestures during the Barclays Premiership match between Middlesbrough and Arsenal at The Riverside, Middlesbrough.

Left: Wenger organizing his team before the penalty shoot-out at the 2005 FA Cup final. Arsenal beat Manchester United 5–4 on penalties after a goalless match.

When you first took a look at the Arsenal team on paper, before you actually came here, did you think at that time that the defence would need to be replaced?

I thought they were a bit old, but I quickly changed my mind. Firstly, I was surprised how good they were and secondly, I was surprised by how intelligent they were because I had an image of players who were not serious. I discovered how different they were; the players were ready to think about every detail in the game, and were still as ambitious at 32 years of age. I was completely surprised and thought that with these guys you can go to war. There was something there that was really special, so I decided to keep them and was very lucky.

I was going to ask if you had to change the culture of the club and the players but from what you say you didn't have to very much, did you?

I did have to change the habits of the club; the culture was to win, but the players were receptive to change because they understood very quickly that they could extend their career. Remember at that time, the players didn't make the money they make today and most of them arrived at the age of 30 without having made big money. Players such as Dixon, Winterburn and Adams, I think, made their biggest income between 30 and 36.

What habits did you have to change?

Some different training and a different way of seeing the game sometimes, but the biggest part was there, so the main change was to more detailed stuff, like their diet. I remember when I went down to breakfast at the hotel everybody was on sausage, eggs and bacon. Now, if you go to any hotel and look at what people eat in the morning, it has changed completely. The consciousness of diet has altered throughout society in England in the last seven to eight years and we were just a little bit in front of everyone else.

What sort of relationship do you have with your players? Do you build friendships with them or are you the boss?

There is no friendship. I care about each of my players and I always try to have the right communication level with them. We are professionals and friendship is excluded because it's not possible to make the right decisions if you become friends. Friends for me mean support at any cost no matter what you do, and that's not possible in our job.

It sounds a fairly lonely role.

It is a very lonely role, maybe like every job when you have responsibilities, but you are rewarded with the success, the quality of your team's display and the knowledge that they feel happy.

If you are ever in the situation where you need advice who would you pick up the phone to?

I sometimes talk to friends in football, but my main advisors are my assistants, Pat Rice and Boro Primorac. When I am uncertain about what I would like to do I ask their opinion. They give me their frank and honest views, after which I make a decision. This game has one great quality in that it makes you humble because it changes so quickly. You may do well when you are 35 but when you are 15 or 20 years further into the job you have to continue to try and do it well for the next game.

Football is entertainment but when it gets to a level when it is war I feel we are going the wrong way

Thierry Henry is so influential that you always expect him to make a difference

Do you always have a rational, intelligent approach to the game? Or are you sometimes a shouter – no one ever sees you misbehave, or anything like that.

I try to be logical. I try to see where the problem comes from, and can sometimes become completely mad and completely crazy. In this job, which is highly exposed publicly, I've learnt over the years to be in control, because otherwise you could cause some damage which you could never repair.

But you've been involved in what one might call a verbal fracas at a distance with Alex Ferguson – what are your thoughts on that now?

Some of it is true and some of it has been exaggerated. People want to see what's happening with Manchester United and Arsenal, and what will happen between Ferguson and Wenger, but the interest should be with the quality of the game. Football is entertainment but when it gets to a level when it is war I feel we are going the wrong way.

After you were a coach in Monaco, you went to Japan didn't you? It seemed a strange move for somebody at a major club in Europe to go off to Japan.

It is a bit like that, but I took the job to be exposed to extreme situations. I had done ten years at the top level in France and felt it was time for me to move abroad. When the first club that came up was in Japan I decided to visit and liked the people that were in charge of the club. I went for two years and it was a great experience. I was 44 at the time and it gave me the distance away from friends and family, and time to think about my whole life. You still do your job but without outside influences. I feel it made me much stronger, much more able to cope and therefore was a good move, even though it seemed irrational. My friends thought I was killing my career.

Your most talented player of all, I think, is Henry. The criticism constantly levelled at him is that he doesn't perform in some of the biggest games – is there any truth in that?

Well no, first of all I must say that Thierry Henry is so influential in this team that you always expect him to make a difference. He is only a human and, if you look at his work within the Championship, it's amazing how many goals he's scored. He has one game where he is not making the difference and people immediately say he doesn't perform in the big games. I think that is not right, and not true.

How much, or how often, have you been tempted to leave Arsenal over the years?

Never, because I can tell you openly I've had many offers from many big clubs and I turned them all down for one simple reason: I never had the desire to leave this club. I would like to think I have an influence on the individual careers of the players, the results of the club, the points you can bring to a club, the training ground and the new stadium. I would like to build on what we have now and go to the end of what I feel is my job, and then put this club into the hands of a better manager who has all the possibilities to lead this club even further.

What about international management for you?

I've never been attracted by that. I don't feel at the moment that I want to get away from daily work. The interesting part of being a national coach is to do tournaments and the European Cup, but the rest is not very exciting anymore.

Opposite: *Arsène Wenger celebrates following Arsenal's victory in the 2005 FA Cup Final.*

Above: *Thierry Henry, newly-appointed Arsenal captain.*

WORLD CUP QUALIFYING

England book their place in Germany

Going into 2005 England were well placed in their World Cup qualifying group
with three wins and a draw from the opening four matches. The squandering of a two-goal lead
in Austria was the only blip thus far, and after the two spring 2005 fixtures,
Eriksson's men consolidated their position with six more points.

Northern Ireland provided dogged resistance at Old Trafford, frustrating England in the first half. The home side dominated possession and territory, but when they did penetrate the defence they found 'keeper Maik Taylor in prime form. Joe Cole made the breakthrough in the first minute after the break, latching onto a Tony Capaldi mistake and curling in a sweet 20-yarder. Owen added a second from close range, and when Chris Baird put through his own goal from Rooney's cross, the result was beyond doubt. A Lampard deflected shot rounded off a satisfying 4-0 win.

Gerrard eases fears

It was much the same story against Azerbaijan at St James's Park the following week. A string of chances went begging in a goalless first half, Azerbaijan 'keeper Kramarenko in inspired form just days after picking the ball out of his net eight times against Poland. Gerrard eased fears of a shock result by putting away Rooney's cross on 51 minutes, and Beckham ran onto a Lampard pass to double the score against Carlos Alberto's team.

Five months later, the World Cup season got off to a disastrous start. In the final warm up before crunch qualifiers in Wales and Northern Ireland, England crashed 4–1 in Copenhagen to Denmark, the country Eriksson's men had put out of the 2002 World Cup in the Second Round. It was an abysmal showing, England leaking three second-half goals in barely 10 minutes, with a Rooney strike providing scant consolation. It was the international side's heaviest defeat since going down by the same score to Wales in Wrexham in May 1980.

Opposite: Michael Owen scores the second goal during the qualifying match against Northern Ireland at Old Trafford.

Above: Frank Lampard celebrates his goal during the qualifier against Northern Ireland.

Left: A jubilant Steven Gerrard celebrates after scoring the opening goal during the England v Azerbaijan qualifying match at St James's Park.

If the World Cup should happen tomorrow then I know the 11 players I would play from how their season ended. It's very difficult to say who I'm going to pick in May 2006 because a lot of things can change – new players coming up; those players who were playing well last season not playing well this season – so it's very difficult.

Sven–Goran Eriksson

New role for Beckham

Back in World Cup mode on 4 September, a deflected Joe Cole shot beat Danny Coyne to give England all three points against Wales at the Millennium Stadium, Eriksson's side completing the double over their Group Six opponents. Beckham was imperious, revelling in his new role, playing in front of the back four. It was a position he said he had filled comfortably for Real, and it certainly suited his long-range passing game, which came into its own. Some pundits noted that the jury would remain out until he came up against sterner opposition, when the defensive duties required by that position would be more onerous.

Below: England's Joe Cole goes close to scoring a diving header during the qualifying match between Wales and England at the Millennium Stadium.

Right: Joe Cole celebrates scoring the only goal of the game against Wales with teammate Shaun Wright-Phillips.

Opposite left: Eriksson is stunned by England's first defeat in a qualifying game under his management.

Opposite right: Wayne Rooney is tackled by Chris Baird of Northern Ireland during the qualifier at Windsor Park.

BBC RADIO FIVE LIVE

England can be very good because they've got so many match winners, so many players who can turn a game. Michael Owen's goal scoring record, Wayne Rooney's talent, Gerrard, Beckham, Lampard – all scoring mid-fielders. They've got a lot of talent that other teams haven't. Winning World Cups – you've got to come to terms with players getting injured, having a good squad and having a little bit of luck.

Ryan Giggs
following England's 4–1 defeat by Denmark, and before the England v Wales qualifier

Sven's first defeat in a qualifier

Before the Wales game, manager John Toshack had commented on the gulf between the personnel on show at the Millennium Stadium: 'I don't think there are too many England players in the dressing rooms at Bristol City, Swansea and Coventry.' That point was equally applicable to the match at Windsor Park the following week, when England met a Northern Ireland side ranked 116 in the world. But it was Lawrie Sanchez's bargain basement outfit which came out on top, inflicting not only England's first defeat of the campaign, but the first reverse in any World Cup or European Championship qualifier during Eriksson's reign. Northern Ireland, who had gone four years without a victory in a competitive match, won twice in less than a week. A 2–0 win over Azerbaijan could hardly be counted a shock; taking all the points against England through a David Healy goal undoubtedly was. The Leeds United man's 74th-minute strike brought about England's first defeat in Belfast for 78 years.

BBC RADIO FIVE LIVE

Sven is contracted until 2008 and that's what we're working to. He's doing a significantly good job. We're on course for qualification, although we haven't qualified yet. His record in competitive games for England is better than any other previous England manager. He loves the job, he cares about the job. He's got a great set of England players.

Brian Barwick
chief executive of the FA

BBC RADIO FIVE LIVE

I think we worked as a team, we defended well and had some good attacks but we know we can play better football. I am excited because the big aim for us for two years has been to qualify for the World Cup - after the Northern Ireland game the critics began saying maybe not. So, of course, I am delighted. Now the aim is to prepare everything for the World Cup.

Sven–Goran Eriksson
following England's 1-0 win over
Austria at Old Trafford

England's place assured

For England fans defeat was bad enough, but it was made worse by an abject display, in particular changes in formation that seemed to bewilder the players as much as those watching. There were the inevitable calls for Eriksson's head, but the England coach vowed to fight on, win the last two matches and pip Poland for top spot in the group. At the very worst, a play-off place was already assured.

Wales were defeated 1–0 in Warsaw to make it two narrow defeats in a week; Toshack's men remained anchored at the bottom of Group Six, still without a win in eight qualifying games. 'Sack the Swede' rang round the terraces, and Eriksson's men did little to restore their dented pride in the penultimate qualifier, against Austria at Old Trafford. That at least yielded three points – courtesy of a Frank Lampard penalty – and assured England of a place in the finals as one of the best second-placed teams. The fact that England had made it to a World Cup with a game to spare for the first time since Mexico '86 did little to stem the tide of criticism, however. Much of it was directed at David Beckham, who became the 10th player to be sent off while wearing an England shirt, and the only man to feature in that list twice. The bookings may have been harsh, but the petulance brought memories of France '98 flooding back.

Having guided England to a third successive major championships, Eriksson was in upbeat mood, insisting that his side was one of 'four or five' who would go on to lift the trophy in Germany.

Wales managed to do what England couldn't: come away from Windsor Park with a win. Unfortunately, John Toshack's side first victory in the qualifiers came in their ninth match, leaving them vying with Azerbaijan for the Group Six wooden spoon. For both Wales and Northern Ireland thoughts were already turning towards Euro 2008.

False dawn for Scots

Scotland, meanwhile, had looked a rejuvenated side since Walter Smith took over from Berti Vogts. The Scots – and Kenny Miller in particular - enjoyed an excellent September, giving the Tartan Army renewed hope that they might have to keep June 2006 free after all. A Miller header earned a creditable home draw against Italy, and four days later he grabbed a brace in Norway to give Smith's side a 2-1 win, only their second of the campaign following the home victory over Moldova. Those four points left the Scots hanging onto the shirt-tails of Norway and Slovenia, the teams vying for second place behind Italy, with two games remaining. All the good work was then undone when the team crashed to a 1-0 home defeat at the hands of Belarus.

Brian Kerr's Republic of Ireland was faring much better in Group Four. A Thierry Henry goal gave France three points in Dublin, but that was the Republic's only reverse going into their final match, at home to Switzerland. Victory in that game would guarantee the Republic a play-off place, and even give Kerr's men a chance of qualifying as group winners if France slipped up in their home tie against Cyprus.

The campaign didn't start very well, but we've picked up since then. We had to show a little bit of improvement so that there is continuity. As far as qualifying is concerned, we know that we have to win the next three games, which is a very difficult task for any team.

Walter Smith

Above: *Scotland manager, Walter Smith, with assistant, Tommy Burns, during the qualifier between Norway and Scotland.*

Below: *Kenny Miller celebrates scoring the second goal for Scotland during the qualifier between Norway and Scotland in Norway.*

Opposite: *David Beckham talks to teammate Wayne Rooney after his booking during the qualifier against Northern Ireland at Windsor Park.*

Golf

THE OPEN

St Andrews double for Tiger

On 15 July 2005, the second day of the 134th Open, Jack Nicklaus bowed out of championship golf in style, birdieing the 18th at St Andrews for a round of 72 and an aggregate 147. The Golden Bear finished ahead of some illustrious names, including Funk, Price, Furyk, Love and Woosnam, not to mention his old sparring partner Tony Jacklin. David Duval and Ben Curtis, both recent winners of the Open, also trailed in the wake of the 65-year-old legend with 18 majors to his name. Two days later, the man widely thought capable of beating that phenomenal record left the Old Course with his second major of the year and 10th overall. Tiger Woods' victory at St Andrews in 2000 made him the youngest player ever to collect all four majors; his second victory at the Home of Golf put him third in the all-time list, just one short of Walter Hagen's career haul. It also meant that he matched Nicklaus's record of winning all the majors at least twice – and he had yet to celebrate his 30th birthday.

I am back in a position where I belong

Old Course lengthened

Since Woods' record 19-under victory in 2000, the Old Course had been lengthened to 7,279 yards, with five new championship tees. The extra 164 yards didn't faze Tiger. At the end of the first day he had a one-stroke lead over Mark Hensby after carding a 66 which included eight birdies. The Australian thus continued where he left off at the Masters and US Open, where he had enjoyed top-six finishes. A ten-strong group – including Goosen, Olazabal, Couples and Luke Donald – sat one stroke further behind on 4-under. Goosen hit seven birdies but suffered a double bogey at the 465-yard par-4 13th. 27-year-old Donald, playing with Nicklaus and Tom Watson, was one of the few to birdie that hole. For David Toms, the 2001 USPGA winner and one of the pre-tournament favourites, the Open finished early as he disqualified himself for striking a moving ball at the 17th, the famous Road Hole.

Monty makes his move

In the second round, Colin Montgomerie, who started the year ranked 81, launched his bid to capture that elusive first major, hoping to become the first European to win one of the sport's big four since Paul Lawrie's Open victory in 1999. Monty hit an eagle and seven birdies as he matched Woods' first-round score of 6-under. But that was only enough to peg the world No. 1 back by one stroke. Woods himself hit five birdies in his 67, and it could have been worse for the field as he drove the green at the par-4 5th, 9th, and 10th, and reached the 618-yard par-5 14th in two. The latter was one of the holes that had been extended, becoming the longest in Open history.

Woods thus led by four shots after 36 holes, and as he had converted a halfway lead into victory in five majors, it didn't bode well for the rest of the field.

Tiger misfires

Sandy Lyle, 20 years on from winning the 1985 Open at Sandwich, rolled back the years with a –5 on the second day, a fine performance after taking a seven at the 17th on day one to close on 74. He followed it up with a 69, which meant that for the middle 36 holes he stood two clear of Tiger, who misfired slightly in his third round. Woods did recover from two penalty shots on the front nine to return a 71, however. Monty, his playing partner, carded a 70, thanks to a 25-foot birdie at the 18th. That put the Scot on 9-under for the championship, three off the lead. He was joined by Goosen, the day's biggest mover with a 66, but it was Jose Maria Olazabal who was now leading the charge. He matched his opening round of 68 to go to 10-under and book his place alongside Tiger on the final day.

Opposite: Jack Nicklaus waves to the crowd as he stands on the Swilcan Bridge at what could be his last British Open.

Below: Colin Montgomerie holds the runners up award after the final round of the 134th Open.

> I think my record as a person, with my family – my kids and grandkids – is the most important thing to me. What I've done on the golf course is quite good but it doesn't mean anything if it's not right at home. I've got a great wife, great kids, 18 grandkids – that's the special part. The trophies are things that sit on the shelf, not something you share. They're symbolic – but the love that my family has shown for me and that we've shared is the most important thing by far.
>
> **Jack Nicklaus**
> after his final competitive appearance at the British Open

Monty within a stroke

I have to take positives from this. I'm back in a position where I felt I belonged back in the '90s which is great. I've felt over the last four years that things weren't going so well and I was dipping and it's nice to be back in this theatre. Number one or number two — there's never a disgrace in losing to by far the best player of our generation.

Colin Montgomerie

I really played well today. I hit it so well. It was probably one of the best ball striking rounds I've had all year — if not the best. To go out there and feel that comfortable with my golf swing, and hit it that well under so much pressure — I couldn't have asked for a better day ... One thing I can assure you is — I'm going to get better.

Tiger Woods
following his win at the British Open at St Andrews

This was such a hard-fought week, with the rain delays and everything. I didn't get off to the greatest of starts but all in all I'm very happy.

Tiger Woods
after his win at Augusta

Monty and Olazabal both applied what pressure they could over the last 18 holes. Monty went out in three to get within a stroke of Woods, and the Spaniard also narrowed the gap. But on the back nine it was they who faltered while Tiger stepped up a gear. The key moment was Olazabal's bogey five at the par-4 12th, while up ahead Monty almost simultaneously dropped a shot at 13. By the time Woods completed his round of 70 for an aggregate 274 – 14 under – the cushion was a comfortable five shots.

Monty's par gave him outright second place, his best result in a major since the play-off defeat by Ernie Els at the 1997 US Open.

His disappointment was tempered by a rise of 59 places in the rankings, back up to 22 and on course to fulfil his objective of a return to the top ten.

After his first win at the Old Course five years earlier, Woods had commented: 'If a golfer is to be remembered, he must win the Open at St Andrews'. In lifting the famous Claret Jug for a second time at the Home of Golf, Woods equalled Nicklaus's postwar record, cementing his place in the history books in the process.

Below: Tiger Woods looks at his name on the Claret Jug after winning the 134th Open at St Andrews.

THE MASTERS

Fourth green jacket for Tiger

Tiger Woods finally ended his barren streak by winning at Augusta in 2005, his fourth Masters win to put him equal-third with Gary Player and Ben Hogan on the all-time list of major winners.

During a two-year spell in which he had adjusted his swing, Woods had barely threatened to add to his haul of eight majors, prompting some to wonder if he would ever recapture his blistering early-career form. But his performance at the 2005 Masters – particularly a scintillating 65 in the third round – showed that Tiger was back to his best. In one 30-hole spell Woods made 16 birdies, and although he faltered from a seemingly impregnable position on the final day, he showed his mental strength in a play-off shoot-out with Chris DiMarco.

DiMarco sets the pace

It was DiMarco who made the early running. He opened with two 67s to put himself in prime position to claim his maiden victory in a major. Woods, by contrast, had a poor start, carding a 74 in a rain-affected first round that took two days to complete. And even though he followed it up with a 66, it still left him six shots adrift of 36-year-old DiMarco.

Woods continued his sparkling form on the third day. Having completed his held-over second round, he took just 31 shots to reach the turn in his third before play was halted. That included birdies on the 7th, 8th, and 9th, and he added four more when he resumed the next morning to equal Steve Pate's record, set on the same seven holes in 1999.

Two-horse race

DiMarco, meanwhile, was going backwards. His 74 meant that he now trailed Woods by three going into the final round as the Masters developed into a two-horse race.

A birdie at the first extended Woods' lead, and he was still three ahead at the turn. A bogey from Woods at the 10th, combined with DiMarco's birdie at the next, put the latter to within a shot of the lead, but that was undone when he in turn dropped one at the 12th. Back came DiMarco, whose excellent iron shot gave him a tap-in birdie at the 14th. But when Tiger chipped in from the back of the green at the 16th to put him two up with two to play, it appeared to be all over.

Play-off

Woods faltered, however, and two pars from DiMarco were enough to force a play-off. After 72 holes they were locked together on 12-under, seven clear of Goosen and Donald.

It seemed the momentum had swung back towards DiMarco, but Woods clinched his fourth Masters victory by rolling in a 15-foot downhill putt at the first extra hole.

Defending champion Phil Mickelson presented Woods with the famous green jacket, the world No.1 joining Arnold Palmer in second place in the all-time list of Augusta winners; only Jack Nicklaus, with six wins, now stood ahead of him. The Golden Bear's final Augusta victory, in 1986, had come 23 years after his first. Woods, by contrast, had needed just nine years to accumulate his four Masters titles.

Below: Tiger Woods smiles as he is presented with the green jacket by Phil Mickelson after Woods won the Masters.

US OPEN

First Kiwi major winner for 42 years

BBC RADIO FIVE LIVE

I knew it was probably going to be Ernie [Els] or Phil [Mickelson] to beat. I got off to a good start on the first hole which settled me down a little bit. Coming down the last, the key thing is hitting the fairway. I played that hole pretty aggressively the whole week... I wasn't going to 3 putt again. My main goal when I stood there was to 2 putt and get out of there – go and enjoy it!

Michael Campbell

Designed by Donald Ross in 1907, Pinehurst was extremely unforgiving. As Tiger Woods put it: 'You can putt off the green 50 yards and not feel like you hit a bad putt.' Lee Westwood said that pars were 'worth their weight in gold', which proved to be perfectly accurate as 36-year-old New Zealander Michael Campbell won with an even score over the four rounds.

Consistency vital

Consistency was the key. Phil Mickelson opened with an excellent 69 but had a nightmare on day two, when he carded 77 after missing a string of short putts. Davis Love III shot a superb five under for the last 45 holes, but a first round 77 – seven over par – proved the old adage that you can't win a tournament on day one, but you can lose it.

Like Love III, defending champion Retief Goosen also had three excellent rounds. He'd putted only 87 times in those 54 holes, with just six bogeys, and looked well on course to retain his title. Unfortunately, he saved his disaster for the final 18. Goosen began his Sunday round on 3 under, holding a three-stroke lead. His playing partner was the people's favourite, Californian Jason Gore, ranked 818 in the world. 46-year-old qualifier Olin Browne also went into the last round level, mainly thanks to the 67 which had left him tied for the lead with Rocco Mediate at the end of the first day. Michael Campbell was a stroke further back. It meant that the South African was five clear of the nearest big name, David Toms, and six ahead of Woods. With two US Opens already in the bank and a reputation for ice-coolness under pressure, most thought the world No. 5 was a shoo-in to add to his haul of majors.

Goosen finishes with an 81

But it all went disastrously wrong. Goosen went to the turn six over, and finished with an 81, which plummeted him outside the top ten in the final ranking. He and Gore – who shot an 84 – were left smiling in wry amusement as they played like novices for a combined 25 over on the day.

Woods, meanwhile, was on a charge. Birdies at 10, 11 and 15 brought him to 1-over for the championship, within two strokes of Campbell. Woods, who finished third at Pinehurst in '99, was looking a good bet to come through for his third US Open victory. But he had a bogey at the 492-yard par-4 16th, and when he three-putted at the short 17th –a hole that also cost him dear six years earlier – his chance had gone. Tiger did birdie the last for a 69 – one of only four sub-par rounds on the final day – but he finished two shots adrift of the winner.

Rehabilitation

Michael Campbell also carded a 69 to give him two rounds of 1-under and two of 1-over for his four days work. It was a heartwarming victory for a man who knew what it was like to snatch defeat from the jaws of victory. Campbell led the 1995 Open after 54 holes before having a 76-stroke nightmare on the final day. He then had a long battle against injury, and his form was so poor when he regained fitness that he lost his European tour card and thought his days as a pro were over.

Campbell's rehabilitation was completed at Pinehurst as he became the first New Zealander to win a major since Bob Charles' victory at the Open in 1963.

Left: Michael Campbell raises his putter as he pumps his fist after sinking a birdie putt on the 12th green.

US PGA

Second major for Mickelson

By common consensus, the solitary major against Phil Mickelson's name was a travesty for so talented a player. And although 'Lefty' had three tour victories in the bank in the early months of 2005, his form in the first three majors did nothing to suggest he was about to add to his tally at the 87th US PGA Championship at Baltusrol. But in a tense finale that spilled over into a fifth day because of an electrical storm, Mickelson held his nerve for a 72nd hole birdie which gave him the title by one shot.

Woods opens with 75

The US PGA Championship has been described as the 'minor major', yet 97 of the top hundred players convened in New Jersey with the aim of getting their hands on the Wanamaker Trophy and claim the final major honour of the year. The 7,392-yard par-70 Baltusrol course was thought to favour the big hitters like Woods. But in sweltering conditions everyone was able to hit long; hitting straight was now the key on a course known for its uncompromising rough. Woods was wayward in his opening round and paid the price with a five-over-par 75. Six men shared top spot on 67, including Mickelson and former Open champion Ben Curtis, while some 80 players were within five shots of the lead.

Chasing Armor's record

Lee Westwood carded successive 68s to put him four behind Mickelson at the halfway stage, while the unheralded Greg Owen was only one shot further back, his score boosted by an eagle at the final hole. Both were in the hunt to become the first European to win the PGA title since Tommy Armor in 1930.

Woods went into overdrive on day three, carding a 66 as a string of birdies made up for a hesitant start.

Monday's play

Monday's play lasted just short of an hour but it was enthralling stuff. Steve Elkington and Thomas Bjorn both had birdie chances at the 18th but both missed. They each finished with an aggregate 277, which ended Woods' hopes of being involved in a play-off.

That left Mickelson and Love, the final pairing. Love was out of contention, eventually joining Woods on 2-under for the tournament. Mickelson dropped a shot at the short 16th to go back to −3, level with Elkington and Bjorn. He went to the 18th

needing a birdie for victory, and guaranteed that with his third, a trademark flop shot out of the rough to within two feet of the pin. After finishing second or third in ten majors, Mickelson now had his second in as many seasons.

Above: *Phil Mickelson of the US celebrates his chip onto the 18th green during the final round of the PGA Championship at Baltusrol Golf Club.*

Horse Racing

THE GRAND NATIONAL

Hedgehunter romps home

Seeing Tony McCoy come to grief on Clan Royal at Becher's was like watching a drama unfold in slow motion. It shows that however outstanding a jockey you are – and McCoy is the greatest jump jockey – not everything works for you, and the Grand National has its own rules.

Carrie Ford did absolutely nothing wrong on Forest Gunner. The horse travelled beautifully and she looked every inch a Grand National jockey. It was a triumph for her and a sweet irony that while she finished fifth, Ginger McCain's Amberleigh House was only tenth.

Cornelius Lysaght

Right*: Ruby Walsh sails to a 14 length victory on Hedgehunter in the 166-year-old-race.*

Opposite*: Ruby Walsh's record in the race was a punter's delight: two wins and two fourth places from five attempts.*

The first John Smith's Grand National – and last before the bulldozers moved in to give Aintree a facelift – had quality and drama in equal measure. The three most recent winners – Bindaree (2002), Monty's Pass (2003) and Ginger McCain's defending champion Amberleigh House – were all bidding to win the race for a second time, a feat not achieved since McCain trained the legendary Red Rum to three victories between 1973 and 1977.

Hedgehunter's season geared to National

Of the 40 jockeys who lined up at the start, there were eight previous winners. These included Ruby Walsh, victorious with Papillon in 2000 and this year aboard the favourite, Hedgehunter. The Willie Mullins-trained horse had fallen at the final fence in 2004 and had spent the entire year gearing up for this year's race.

Walsh had notched his first Grand National success as a callow 20-year-old, at his first attempt. By contrast, champion jockey Tony McCoy was having his tenth crack at the race and still looking for his first win. His mount was Clan Royal, second in 2004 and thought by many – McCoy among them – to have a great chance of going one better this time round.

McCoy unseated

At the halfway mark McCoy and Clan Royal took up the running. For a time it looked as though the National was once again about to show its uncanny habit for producing winners whose name had a topical resonance. On the day of Prince Charles and Camilla Parker-Bowles' wedding, victory for Clan Royal in the world's premier steeplechase would have been apposite. But it wasn't to be. At Becher's second time round, disaster struck as a stray mount veered across McCoy's path. Clan Royal swerved and McCoy was unseated. Hedgehunter took the lead and was never headed. An unusually large group was in contention at the business end of the race – 21 would finish, the most since 1992. But the result was never in doubt. Hedgehunter stretched his lead on the run-in to romp home by 14 lengths. He became only the third horse in the past 25 years to win carrying more than 11 stone.

For Trevor Hemmings and Willie Mullins, Hedgehunter's owner and trainer respectively, it was a red-letter day. For multi-millionaire Hemmings, the owner of Blackpool Tower, it was victory at the 13th attempt, while Mullins had never before had a horse negotiate all 30 fences. The trainer immediately made his plans for Hedgehunter clear: 'The long-term plan is

to come back to Aintree for another National bid. We'll aim for that next year'

Ford equals record

28 years after Charlotte Brew became the first woman to ride in the National, Carrie Ford was widely tipped to make history by crossing the line first on Forest Gunner. In the event Ford rode a superb race to bring Forest Gunner home fifth, equalling the best ever performance by a woman. The much-hyped battle of the sexes obscured the fact that a part-timer with just a couple of outings under her belt during the season had beaten 35 of the 40-strong field, horses ridden by the cream of the professional ranks of male jockeys.

THE DERBY

Motivator brings romance To Epsom

The 226th running of the Derby saw 3–1 favourite Motivator romp home by five lengths,
yet this was anything but a run-of-the-mill victory. 2005 will go down as the year in which romance
came to Epsom as a syndicate with a bargain-price horse from a minnow stable took
on the big boys and won.

Dettori keen to break his Derby duck

It was billed as a wide open race, several horses in the 13-strong field having the credentials to win the turf's Blue Riband event. Kong won the Lingfield trial, edging Walk In The Park; Gypsy King got the decision in a photo-finish at the Dee Stakes; Hattan won the Chester Vase; and Godolphin colt Dubawi was an impressive winner over Oratorio in the Irish 2,000 Guineas.

Dante trial

The Dante Stakes at York was regarded as the most important bell-weather for Epsom. Sir Michael Stoute's North Light had completed the Dante-Derby double in 2004, and three weeks before Epsom 2005 Motivator – who cost just 75,000 guineas – also won at York. The horse's first outing since winning the Racing Post Trophy the previous October was an impressive one, Kieren Fallon bringing him home ahead of The Geezer.

Fallon's decision to become stable jockey to Aidan O'Brien meant that he was unable to ride the Michael Bell-trained colt at Epsom. Fallon, looking to become only the second jockey to complete a hat-trick of Derby wins, had his pick of the Ballydoyle crop and opted for the much-fancied Gypsy King, who would begin the race as second favourite.

Murtagh ban reduced

But the big story leading up to the race was who would ride Motivator. Just three days before the classic, Johnny Murtagh was successful in his appeal against a careless riding charge and saw his ban reduced from three days to two. That proved crucial, since one and two-day bans did not have to be served at premier meetings. That left the two-time Derby winner free to climb aboard the unbeaten favourite.

At the end of the race Murtagh's tally had risen to three and Motivator's record remained intact. Having sat on the shoulder of long-time leader Hattan, Murtagh let the horse go two furlongs from home. He later described his amazement at how much distance they managed to put between themselves and the chasing pack by the time they passed the post.

Opposite: John Murtagh riding the syndicate-owned Motivator wins his third Derby.
Above: Richard Hills on Eswarah wins The Vodafone Oaks at Epsom Racecourse.

The Oaks

Eswarah wins the Oaks

Eswarah, starting at 11–4 favourite, gave trainer Michael Jarvis his first Oaks success. Jockey Richard Hills kept his mount with the rest of the pack before taking up an outside position at Tattenham Corner in preparation for racing ahead in the final furlong. He managed to hold off a challenge from Something Exciting who finished in second place, half-a-length behind. Pictavia came in third a further three lengths behind. Eswarah followed in the footsteps of her dam Midway Lady who won the Oaks in 1986. However, three months later Eswarah was retired to stud by owner Sheikh Hamdam Al Maktoum when it was discovered that she had chipped a bone in her knee after an unusually poor performance in the Yorkshire Oaks.

BBC RADIO FIVE LIVE

He was always travelling really well and when I let him go at the two marker he just took off. I had a little peek round half a furlong down and I couldn't believe how far I was in front. He's a very, very high class horse. Once he got to the start, with his lad down there with him, as soon as he got down in the stalls he cooled off perfectly.

Johnny Murtagh
after winning his third
Derby on Motivator

The Grand National

1st	Hedgehunter
2nd	Royal Auclair
3rd	Simply Gifted
4th	It Takes Time
5th	Forest Gunner

The Derby

1st	Motivator
2nd	Walk In The Park
3rd	Dubawi

The Oaks

1st	Eswarah
2nd	Something Exciting
3rd	Pictavia

1,000 Guineas

1st	Virginia Waters
2nd	Maids Causeway
3rd	Vista Bella

2,000 Guineas

1st	Footstepsinthesand
2nd	Rebel Rebel
3rd	Kandidate

Cesarewitch Handicap (2004)

1st	Contact Dancer
2nd	Mr Ed
3rd	High Point

Irish Derby

1st	Hurricane Run
2nd	Scorpion
3rd	Shalapour

King George VI

1st	Azamour
2nd	Norse Dancer
3rd	Bago

Lincoln Heritage Handicap

1st	Stream of Gold
2nd	New Seeker
3rd	Common World

St Leger

1st	Scorpion
2nd	The Geezer
3rd	Yawqeet

L'Arc

1st	Hurricane Run
2nd	Westerner
3rd	Bago

Cheltenham Gold Cup

1st	Kicking King
2nd	Take the Stand
3rd	Sir Rembrandt

Hennessy Gold Cup

1st	Celestial Gold
2nd	Ollie Magern
3rd	Royal Auclair

1,000 Guineas
Virginia Waters completes the Classic double

As Virginia Waters galloped home to win the 1,000 guineas it gave trainer Aidan O'Brien and jockey Kieren Fallon a Classic double. The previous day Footstepsinthesand had won the 2,000 guineas, and with both horses owned by Michael Tabor and Sue Magnier, this was the first occasion in which the identical owner, trainer, jockey combination had completed the guineas double since 1942. After remaining towards the back of the field, Virginia Waters surged forward with less than two furlongs to go, beating Maids Causeway by two-and-a-half lengths, with Vista Bella finishing third.

2,000 Guineas
Footsteps sets a trail

Footstepsinthesand was the first horse home in the 2,000 Guineas at Newmarket. In the first Classic of the Flat season, the three-year-old, ridden by Kieren Fallon, raced up the hill, finally beating Rebel Rebel by one-and-a quarter lengths. Kandidate came in third, another three-quarters of a length back, while the favourite Dubawi tried to challenge but was eventually placed fifth. Trained in Ballydoyle, Footstepsinthesand is the son of Giant's Causeway and owned by Sue Magnier and Michael Tabor. This gave Fallon and trainer Aidan O'Brien their third Newmarket colts' Classic victory.

Cesarewitch Handicap (2004)
Contact Dancer makes the connection

Contact Dancer was successfully raced first past the post by jockey Royston Ffrench in the 2004 Cesarewitch Handicap at Newmarket. Trained by Mark Johnston, Contact Dancer pulled away from the pack during the final furlong, pushing joint favourite Mr Ed into second place by half a length. High Point came in third, with Quedex fourth. Familiar to success in this event, Ffrench had previously won the race on Inchcailloch in 1996. However, there was tragedy later in the day for trainer Mark Johnston when Mister Monet had to be put down after sustaining a triple fracture in the Champion Stakes.

Lincoln Heritage Handicap
Easy success at Lincoln for Stream of Gold

It was Stream of Gold who romped home three lengths ahead of New Seeker to win the Lincoln Heritage Handicap, making it to the front two furlongs after leaving the stalls. Ridden by Robert Winston and trained by Sir Michael Stoute, he surged up the stand rail on the straight mile at Doncaster. Winston, who with Stoute was celebrating their first Lincoln triumph, championed Stream of Gold who started as 5-1 favourite. Kieren Fallon came fourth, riding Resplendent One.

St Leger
Scorpion romps home

Frankie Dettori rode to victory on Scorpion in the St Leger at Doncaster. Beginning the race as odds-on favourite Dettori soon settled Scorpion in front, setting a moderate pace. Just before the final straight of this one-mile-six-furlong race the gallop was upped, and as they romped home, Dettori was able to hold off a late surge by The Geezer, leaving Tawqeet to finish third. Trained by Aidan O'Brien, the horse caused a few anxious moments as he jinked after running towards the rail but Dettori held him straight as they galloped home. Scorpion is owned by Sue Magnier and Michael Tabor.

King George VI and Queen Elizabeth Diamond Stakes
Success for Azamour

Azamour romped home to win the King George VI and Queen Elizabeth Diamond Stakes at Newmarket, breaking the track record in the process. Ridden by Mick Kinane, owned by the Aga Khan and trained by John Oxx, the 5–2 favourite came from behind to win 0.945 seconds faster than the previous record. Last year's winner Doyen had initially led the field while Azamour remained comfortably at the back before making his move in the straight. Norse Dancer and Bago made strong challenges in the closing stages but had to be content with second and third place. The race was run at Newbury because the Ascot course was being redeveloped.

Irish Derby
Fallon and Hurricane Run whirl home

Hurricane Run, the 4–5 favourite, romped home, giving jockey Kieren Fallon his first Irish Derby winner. Trained by Andre Fabre, the colt was purchased by John Magnier and Michael Tabor the previous weekend for an undisclosed sum that was into the millions. Sired by Montjeu, Hurricane Run beat Scorpion by half-a-length, forcing Shalapour into third position. Brahminy Kite initially set the pace with Scorpion settling into second position. Fallon, who was new to the horse, chose to run on the outside and made a final burst to narrowly win the race.

Hennessy Gold Cup
Celestial Gold shines

Six-year-old Celestial Gold triumphed in the Hennessy Gold Cup at Newbury when jockey Timmy Murphy chose to shadow the leaders during the race, making a final move with only three fences to go. Celestial Gold romped home, fending off a strong challenge from Ollie Magern who had led throughout but eventually had to settle for second place. Royal Auclair also made a last minute burst but finished in third position. The race gave Murphy his second Hennessy winner after a victory with Ever Blessed in 1999.

Cheltenham Gold Cup
Kicking King recovers to take Gold Cup

Kicking King was the first horse to storm home in the Blue Riband Cheltenham Gold Cup. Beginning the race as the 4–1 favourite and ridden by Barry Geraghty, this seven-year-old horse successfully beat Take The Stand into second place, while Sir Rembrandt, last year's runner-up, was placed third. Trainer Tom Taaffe is the son of Pat Taaffe who rode the legendary Arkle to produce a hat-trick of Gold Cup victories in the 1960s. Ironically, Kicking King, a previous winner of the King George VI, had been withdrawn two weeks before the race as Taaffe originally thought he was ill. Owner Conor Clarkson couldn't believe his fortune when the horse was re-instated only to romp home first, also giving Taaffe his first victory in this event. Three-time champion Best Mate had been pulled out after bursting a blood vessel, and it was initially Grey Abbey that made the running. Kicking King finally moved into second at the fourth last fence continuing to race ahead to win by five lengths.

Prix de l'Arc de Triomphe
Fallon achieves the treble

Fallon stormed ahead on Hurricane Run to win his first Prix de l'Arc de Triomphe at Longchamp four lengths ahead of Westerner, with last year's winner Bago coming in third. The win gave Fallon a Longchamp treble, after earlier successes that day with Rumpelstiltskin in the Prix Marcel Boussac and Horatio Nelson in the Prix Jean-Luc Lagardere. The 11–4 favourite was behind at the beginning of the race but manoeuvred to the front with a furlong to go. Andre Fabre trains three-year-old Hurricane Run and the win gave the French trainer his sixth Arc success.

> He's terrific. Not many horses can do it over the three distances; mile, mile-and-a-quarter, mile-and-a-half. He does it very easily. He had that race sewn up a long way out. When he gets to the front, he idles a bit. He never wins by far.
>
> **Mick Kinane**
> following his win in the King George VI and Queen Elizabeth Diamond Stakes

> It was so easy really. He's a really nice horse, with a bright future. I just had to steer the horse in the right direction and show him where the winning posts were and the race was over. I'm delighted to get that win for Sir Michael Stoute. It's on his CV now – and the same for myself!
>
> **Robert Winston**
> following his win in the Lincoln Heritage Handicap at Doncaster

Above: *Kieren Fallon and Hurricane Run return after landing the Prix De L'Arc de Triomphe.*

DES LYNAM MEETS

Frankie Dettori

The houswives' favourite jockey and racing superstar

How tough is your daily routine, your regime? I used to talk years ago to Lester Piggott and didn't hear much back from him, of course, but he used to survive on a glass of champagne and a cigar they always said.

I must say, it's not very easy when you have four children – the chocolate cupboard is always there to be picked at! I'm Italian, I love my food and I love a glass of wine but obviously if you do that you have to pay the price. On a regular basis I do between two and three miles every morning on a treadmill, wearing a ski suit, hat and gloves, and probably do half an hour in the sauna – if it's not seven, it will be six days a week. I'll be honest with you, if I do miss a couple of mornings, I don't feel right. This is my way of life and it sounds like torture, and obviously some days it is. But most of the times I do enjoy it.

You were champion jockey for the third time in 2004 but before that your last championship was as long ago as 1995. So there have been a lot of intervening years where you haven't been chasing the championship. Was that your decision, or perhaps you haven't been good enough? What's happened?

In '96, I broke my elbow; '97, I had a bad year; in 2000, I had a plane crash. Since 2000, I haven't been trying at all to win the Championship because my emotions were haywire after the plane crash. I thought, 'I want to give more time to my family because that's more important.' I was trying to do both, being a dad and being a jockey but I really didn't do either well. I guess it took me that long to get over it, and it wasn't until 2004 that I really had a lot of fire in my stomach – I just needed someone to push me. And it was Catherine, she said to me, 'Look, I know you're taking it easy, but you're only a pain in the backside when you're at home, you're in the way, you're grumpy when you see other people winning because you think it should be you riding, you're no good to anybody, we're all sick of seeing you in a bad mood. So just get out there and get to work.' And that was the push I needed because then I realized that I wasn't going to be missed by my family. They would rather see me happy, doing something that I love and being good at it, than being just in the way. I rolled my sleeves up and I gave it a go, and at the start I thought that 150 would be my target, and never in a million years did I think I would be fighting for the Championship.

As a professional, the thing that hurt me the most was I lost the respect of my colleagues, and to gain that back means a lot. It's like every team's got a captain who wears the armband. But the armband was ripped away from me and I lost it the last five years, and to get it back has been self-rewarding and great.

I can finally say this year that I've proved I'm out of it, and it's a great relief

You refer to the plane crash in the year 2000. A horrifying plane crash – you very nearly died. Ray Cochrane saved you, didn't he? And the pilot, sadly, did die in the crash. What memories do you have of that now, what did it do to you at the time?

What it did to me at the time, it messed my life up, it scared me to death. I really don't want to talk about the plane crash too much, it's not nice. But it's the afterthought really, because you come out of it, but obviously I was in pain, I was terrified, I was in shock. Then you ask yourself all these questions: 'Why did it happen to me? What if I died and left a wife and child? Do I want to ride? Why am I riding? What's the point?' You get all these things in your head and you're in a hole. The only thing that got me out of it was horseracing itself, that's the only thing I know and so I concentrated on rising again. But even so, when I got out of it I didn't know which role to play. Am I going to be a family man or am I going to stick with racing? That stayed with me a long time, it made me lazy, it made me complacent, it made me not my usual driving self. I can finally say this year I've proved that I'm out of it, and it's a great relief.

Above: Frankie Dettori and the Godolphin-trained Shamardal hold off the fast finishing Indesatched, ridden by Jamie Spencer.

Below: Frankie and his wife, Catherine, unveil his new range of men's grooming products.

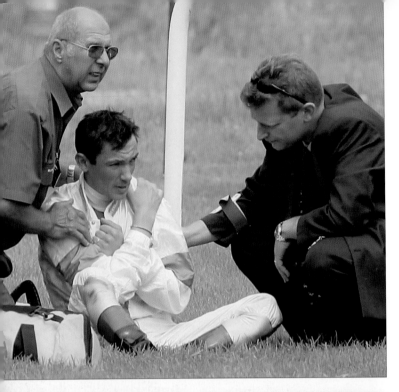

Were you depressed? Because you always seem such a happy-go-lucky guy. The public know you as smiling Frankie, full of fun and the rest of it. But it's interesting to hear that you had this element almost of despair.

Well, probably, it showed that I could not handle or make any sense of it and it wasn't depression as such, but absolutely your mind is twisted. I was looking for answers. But actually it was an accident, yet it took a while to get out of it.

You and Ray, I imagine, have a pretty special relationship don't you?

Absolutely, Ray saved my life. Even though I was the first one off the plane because I was nearest the door hatch, you know. I had a broken leg and I couldn't see where I was going because I had blood all over my face. He was conscious and the plane was full of fuel, so he dragged me away and when he went back for the pilot, the plane exploded. So I owe a lot of credit to him for his bravery and he saved my life. Ray's a very quiet person, he's not like me who likes to talk about things; we mentioned it once, but it's an experience we went through and it will be with us all our lives. As you know, now he's my racing manager and, like an old marriage, we're always shouting at each other. Tongue-in-cheek, obviously, but we always argue.

You've had so many successes in racing. You talk about your down period, but the rest of your career has been up. You've won so many Classics but the Derby has eluded you. Everybody refers to that. Is it hurtful that it's eluded you so far or is it an ambition to win it?

Well, it's an ambition. For starters, it's the only thing missing on my CV. I've won everything else twice, three times, four times. For me it's so important because it will be the last piece of the jigsaw. I can say that's it and I've completed everything that I can in my career, and that would be great for me. If I don't do it I'm not going to cry all my life and say that I haven't done it. As the years go by everybody has latched on to this and I'm carrying an enormous amount of pressure on Derby Day. First of all, because I feel like I want to win it more than any other race, and second, everybody wants me to win it. When I get to Derby Day, I feel more nervous than any other race in the world. Funny, I've been racing 18 years and I've won 2,500 races, and you think it's only a race, and I'm doing it every day, yet even so, I feel like a bag of nerves. Hopefully one day …

The jockey of yesteryear, the great Sir Gordon Richards, he won thousands of races and I think it was in 1953 he finally won the Derby?

Yes, he was 49 years old. I don't think I'll carry on until 49, but I hope that my life will be as much of a fairy tale as his and that one day I'll do it.

*Ray saved my life...
I was the first one off the
plane because I was nearest
the door hatch*

When I looked at the paper, I thought, This has got no chance

Most of us would see these thoroughbred horses and would be frightened to death to get on top of one of them; is there ever an occasion where you think, I don't fancy getting aboard this one?

Every horse is like a human being. Colts are like men: you can force your way with them and bully them a bit, and eventually come to terms. Fillies are like women: you can't argue with them, they always win. You've always got to treat them nice, give them a pat and feed them what they want to hear. Then you get all sorts. You get the guy who works in the shop, the lunatic, you get the football hooligan, you get the professor; all horses' characters are completely different, and I must say, in my time, I got on horses that I thought should be locked up in Strangeways, they're that mad.

When you won those seven races at Ascot in '96 it was a fantastic thing that had never been done before, and it's never been done since. When you got on the seventh one, that must have been the kind of pressure you feel on Derby Day?

That's what everybody thinks but, for me, when I looked at the paper, I thought, This has got no chance, the horse is out of form, it hasn't won a race all year. And I said to myself, 'I'm not going to let this race spoil the day, I'm the happiest man in the world, I've won six, I got the record.' So I went out there with that attitude, which I guess is probably what made me win it because I really did not feel any pressure at all, and I enjoyed the whole event.

Do you transmit your feelings to the horses? Is that what happens?

Yes, horses have a sixth sense. If you're negative, they won't do their best. You know when a jockey's on a high you just stick with them. When you go through a purple patch, horses feel you're positive.

Now, the famous dismount that you do when all is going well. Do you get that from your mother?

I'm very supple and I must have got that from my mother. But there was a jockey in America called Angel Cordero and he used to do it every time he won a big race. I was a big fan of his so when I had four winners in California on one day, I did it as a joke! I wish I hadn't because since that day, every time I win a race children, and everybody, want me to jump off. It's all done very tongue-in-cheek and if I don't think the horse is suitable enough to do it, I won't do it. Nevertheless, it's all a bit of fun so why not?

Horses have a sixth sense. If you're negative, they won't do their best

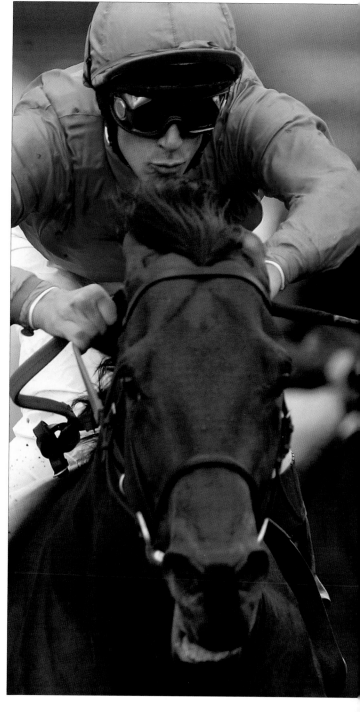

Opposite above: Paramedics attend Frankie Dettori after his fall from Celtic Mill during the Laurent Perrier Champagne Sprint Stakes at Sandown on 2 July 2005.

Opposite below: Marco-Pierre White and Frankie Dettori at the opening of their joint venture Frankie's Italian Bar and Grill.

Above: Frankie Dettori and the Godolphin-trained Dubawi winning the Irish 2000 Guineas race at The Curragh.

Motor Sport

FORMULA ONE

Spain hails its first F1 champion

2005 was the year in which the Schumacher-Ferrari stranglehold on the Formula One championship was finally broken. For the first time since Mika Hakkinen won the title for McLaren in 1999, Schumacher and Maranello were consigned to the also-rans. McLaren and Renault waged a year-long battle. By the time the destination of the title was settled – the 17th Round at Interlagos – these two teams had won every race bar one, and that was the shambolic USA GP in which Schumacher took a pyrrhic victory. It came down to a dogfight between Fernando Alonso and Kimi Raikkonen, and the greater consistency of the Renault proved crucial as the Iceman was bedevilled by ill luck. 24-year-old Alonso became F1's youngest ever champion, breaking the record set by Emerson Fittipaldi in 1972.

Flying start for Renault

Renault got off to a flying start in the record 19-race marathon, claiming first and third in Melbourne. The much-vaunted new R25 chassis showed its credentials immediately, though it was Giancarlo Fisichella who dominated from pole. Six points for Alonso was a fine return from 13th on the grid, while second-placed Rubens Barrichello showed that the 2004 Ferrari was still competitive as he, too, sliced through the pack from a midfield grid position. David Coulthard made a sensational start with the new Red Bull team. Fourth place gave a resounding answer to those who thought he should have called it a day after his nine-year association with McLaren came to an end. The pattern of Kimi Raikkonen's season was unveiled at the curtain-raiser: he started from pit lane after stalling on grid, picking up just one point for eighth place.

Hat-trick for Alonso

Three races later Alonso had 36 points to his name, having scored a maximum in Malaysia, Bahrain and San Marino. At Sepang it was his turn to win the race as he pleased from pole, finishing ahead of Jarno Trulli – giving the Toyota team its first podium – and the Williams of Nick Heidfeld. Raikkonen was in contention for third when he suffered a puncture, while DC was again in the points, finishing just ahead of Schumacher in sixth.

'We showed we are the team to beat,' said Alonso, and he backed that up by cruising to victory again in Bahrain. Apart from the service stops, Alonso was never headed. Trulli registered another eight points, showing that the bullish talk regarding the TF105 wasn't misplaced. Raikkonen rounded out the podium.

I am the youngest champion in Formula One and now I need to find new targets because this one is done. This is very important for me, my friends, my country and my family. It was always a dream to win the Formula One title. It's the maximum I have ever achieved in my life. It was a dream come true.

Fernando Alonso

Opposite: *Fernando Alonso becomes the world's youngest Formula One world champion after coming third in the Brazilian GP.*

Below: *Alonso during the San Marino GP.*

Opposite right: Kimi Raikkonen takes the chequered flag to win the Grand Prix of Canada in Montreal.

Opposite left: Kimi Raikkonen accelerates out of a curve during practice at the Grand Prix of Canada.

Above: Rubens Barrichello during practice for the San Marino GP.

Below: Fernando Alonso celebrates after victory in the San Marino GP.

New Ferrari ahead of schedule

Ferrari's lacklustre start to the campaign prompted the team to introduce the new car ahead of schedule. That decision seemed to be vindicated when Schumacher qualified second, but hydraulics failure ended his interest after 11 laps. It was the first time in four years that the seven-times world champion had retired with mechanical problems. Barrichello also failed to score, making it a miserable day for Maranello.

BAR, who finished second in the Constructors championship in 2004, was also struggling. Jenson Button suffered his third successive retirement, and things got even worse at Imola. Button finished third, then had those six points expunged and a two-race ban slapped on him as the BAR-Honda was found to be underweight. Button said his championship hopes had evaporated, though anyone thinking he couldn't wait to join forces with Williams in 2006 was to be proved wide of the mark.

Defensive race

The new Ferrari was up to speed at Imola, Schumacher back to his best as he stormed through from 13th on the grid to push Alonso all the way to the line. Alonso's brakes had gone, and in the latter stages he drove a superb defensive race to shut the Ferrari out. Pole-sitter Raikkonen was again the big loser, the McLaren limping out on lap nine having made the early running.

Barcelona saw the Renault's winning streak finally come to an end. Raikkonen won majestically from pole, his third career victory. Alonso was disappointed not to win in front of his home crowd, though second place meant that the Finn made only a tiny dent in his championship lead. Trulli fended off his Toyota teammate Ralf Schumacher to notch his third podium of the year. Michael Schumacher, a seven-times winner of the race, suffered his third retirement in five starts and now languished 34 points adrift of Alonso. Barrichello also finished out of points, leading Ross Brawn to comment that there was still much work to do with the new Ferrari.

I don't think anyone disputes the talents of Michael Schumacher and I think he's had a pretty horrible year. At the end of the day drivers have to be in the right car, with the right team at the right time. The worst thing that drivers can do is jump around trying to engineer themselves into what they think is going to be the team of the future. The best thing to do is to stay loyal to a team and let the team deliver to the driver a competitive car. We're definitely on a high now at McLaren. I think we'll be able to deliver a very competitive package next year and hopefully give Juan Pablo and Kimi every opportunity of winning the world championship.

Ron Dennis
talking to Mike Sewell

Kimi wins in Montreal

Imperious

Raikonnen made it back-to-back wins with another imperious performance in Monaco. A pile-up brought the safety car out for four laps. That didn't faze the Iceman, who streaked into the distance when it departed on lap 28. But Alonso was wrestling with tyre degradation and couldn't prevent both Williams from passing. It was second-placed Heidfeld's best-ever return, and Mark Webber's first podium.

Juan Pablo Montoya had to start from the back of the grid after being found guilty of an avoidable accident during qualifying; he did brilliantly to pick up four points for fifth.

Disaster for Iceman

The European GP at the Nurburgring was a disaster for Raikkonen, whose suspension failed when he was within sight of the flag. Victory was handed to Alonso, who gratefully stretched his championship lead to 32 points. Heidfeld, on pole for the first time in his career, left with eight points for the second race running. Barrichello gave Ferrari only their third podium in seven races.

David Coulthard had led the race briefly, the first time that Red Bull had been in front in a GP. A penalty for speeding in the pit lane stymied his chance of getting on the podium, though fourth was the new team's best effort to date.

Error-strewn

Montreal was a dramatic error-strewn race in which both Renaults and McLarens led. Raikkonen was in the right position at the end, though, and his day's work was made all the better as all his main rivals failed to finish.

Jenson Button, on pole for only the second time, crashed when running third and being chased hard by Michael Schumacher. He said afterwards that he would rather crash than cede a place. Montoya missed his chance of a first win for McLaren when he was black-flagged for ignoring a red light in the pit lane. Raikkonen crossed the line just over a second ahead of Schumacher, with Barrichello inheriting third from an unlucky Trulli, whose brakes failed in the latter stages.

I'm very happy to be on the podium. We have got so much information from this race, which is the first we have finished this year. I think we'll be strong in Barcelona. It's a different car, and I'm positive we can keep making these improvements.

Jenson Button
commenting after picking up third place at the San Marino Grand Prix

Schumacher's first win

Opposite: Fernando Alonso pulls away from his pit stop during the German Grand Prix at Hockenheim.

Above: American fans protest after all the teams with Michelin tyres retired after the warm up lap during the United States Grand Prix.

Below: Kimi Raikkonen leads Fernando Alonso into the first corner during the Spanish Grand Prix in Barcelona.

Farcical race

Schumacher went one better at Indianapolis, but his first win of the year came in farcical conditions. Just six cars competed – the Ferraris, Minardis and Jordans – as the 14 Michelin-shod cars all parked up after the formation lap. Tyres were the problem. Ralf Schumacher's big spill during practice was put down to the Michelins failing on the banked part of the circuit. Michelin had no other option for the teams using its rubber, and in any case the rules didn't allow teams to change tyres post-qualifying. The tyre company wanted a chicane added to the critical part of the track, but the FIA's response was that it could not be expected to alter the lay-out at the last minute to accommodate Michelin. With no guarantee of safety, the seven affected teams withdrew, leaving the race to the three Bridgestone-shod outfits.

What transpired was a hollow Ferrari procession in front of a crowd which left the principals in no doubt that they felt totally cheated. Jordan's Tiago Monteiro was one of the few who celebrated, after becoming the first Portuguese to get on an F1 podium.

Blown engine

Raikkonen's second place at Magny-Cours was an excellent return considering he had to drop ten places to 13th on the grid because of a blown engine during practice. Alonso's fifth victory came after the Spaniard lapped the entire field bar the two who joined him on the podium, the Iceman and Schumacher. It was the first time Renault had won their home race since Alain Prost's victory 22 years earlier. Fisichella looked to have fourth place sewn up but when his Renault stalled during the final pit stop it allowed Button to snatch his and BAR's first points of the year.

Raikkonen again fell foul of the replacement engine rule at Silverstone, which turned into a Renault-McLaren battle. The Finn had to settle for 12th on the grid, leaving teammate Montoya to grab the early lead. The field bunched after the safety car was deployed, the result of Takuma Sato's stranded BAR.

When racing resumed, Alonso tracked Montoya, with Button, who had qualified on the front row, a distant but comfortable third.

Maiden win at Silverstone

By mid-distance Montoya had established a six-second advantage over the championship leader, and although Alonso kept up the pressure, the Colombian never looked likely to let his maiden success for McLaren and fifth career win slip through his fingers.

Raikkonen once again did brilliantly to make the podium. His barnstorming late charge included setting the fastest lap on his very last circuit. However, having carved his way through to fourth, he did enjoy a slice of good fortune, capitalizing on Fisichella's stalled engine during the final round of pit stops. Jenson Button couldn't impose himself on the Renaults or McLarens but at least he was the best of the rest, finishing fifth, ahead of the two Ferraris.

Successive front rows for Button

All finally went well for Raikkonen at Hockenheim – in practice at least. He took pole, with Button again making the front row. It looked good for the Finn until the halfway mark, when he ground to a halt while leading comfortably. That left Alonso, Schumacher and Button as the 1, 2, 3, the BAR man being held up by Schumacher, whose soft-compound tyres were rapidly going off. Button executed a superb overtaking manoeuvre at the hairpin on lap 45, but by the time all the drivers had completed their second pit stops, 11 laps out, it was Montoya who was chasing Alonso. It was a marvellous effort by the Colombian from 20th on the grid, while Button took his first legitimate podium of the year.

I would very like to congratulate them. Fernando and the guys around him have done a very good job over the whole season. I have just met one of the mechanics [Jonathan Wheatley] from my time there. He is now the chief mechanic, and he was close to tears. It is really touching to see them after they have had to wait ten years to win the championship again. It was really nice and I am happy for them. They have done a good job.

Michael Schumacher

Schumacher relinquishes crown

I came from a country with no tradition in Formula One and I fought alone basically because I have not had any help from anybody all throughout my career. I arrived in Formula One thanks to the results in the previous categories. Now I think this title is the maximum I can achieve in my life and in my career and it's thanks to three or four people, not more than that.

Fernando Alonso

Opposite right: Fernando Alonso with the World Championship trophy.

Opposite left: Jenson Button in action during qualifying for the European Grand Prix.

Below: Ralf Schumacher and his brother Michael celebrate their third and second positions with winner Kimi Raikkonen after the Hungarian Grand Prix.

Faint hopes

Alonso held a 36-point advantage over Raikkonen going to Hungary, but the latter kept his faint hopes alive by reversing the outcome of the previous race: this time he walked away with maximum points, while Alonso left empty-handed. The Iceman did it the hard way too, for his DNF in Germany meant that he had the disadvantage of being first man out on the dusty Hungaroring circuit.

Raikkonen lined up fourth, and was soon up to second after a dramatic start which saw both Red Bulls out of the race. Alonso, meanwhile, had to pit for repairs to a damaged front wing after a bump with Ralf Schumacher. Despite his superior speed, Raikkonen was finding it difficult to pass Schumacher on a track regarded as second only to Monaco for the difficulty of overtaking. McLaren came up trumps in the final pit stop, though, the Finn running again in under six seconds. He emerged ahead of Schumacher, and Montoya's retirement gifted him victory. Schumacher took second, with the two Toyotas next. It was a bad day for Renault, only the third time that the championship leader had failed to score.

Turkish delight for Kimi

It was Turkish delight for Kimi when the F1 circus went to Istanbul for the first time. At the business end of the race, it looked like a nailed-on one-two for McLaren. But when Montoya ran wide on the penultimate lap, Alonso gleefully accepted second, limiting the ground conceded in the championship to just two points when it should have been four.

Schumacher officially had to relinquish his crown at Monza, where Ferrari again drew a blank. It was the first time in a decade that the team failed to score a point on its home patch. Montoya held off Alonso by 2.4 seconds on the fastest track on the F1 circuit, driving the final laps at up to 220mph, despite a disintegrating tyre. Raikkonen had the same problem. The Finn had been quickest in practice, but a third engine change in six races meant he had to start from 11th on the grid. He got up to second by lap 22 but dropped back after also suffering tyre wear which required an unscheduled wheel change. Raikkonen eventually finished fourth.

Kimi now trailed by 27 points with just 40 left on offer. He did all he could by winning at Spa, but when Montoya tangled with the lapped Williams of Antonio Pizzonia four laps out, it allowed Alonso to snatch second.

Worthy champion

Button to stay at BAR

Jenson Button finished third, just before the news broke that he had bought himself out of his Williams contract for 2006. In a major about-turn, Button now regarded BAR-Honda as offering him the best chance of realising his world championship ambitions. He paid a heavy price – thought to be between £10 and £20 million – and Eddie Jordan described Button as 'tainted goods' for reneging on the Williams deal. Button defended his actions as a simple business transaction.

To keep his hopes alive, Raikkonen needed a victory at Interlagos with Alonso nowhere to be seen on the podium. In the event neither part of the equation worked out. It was Raikkonen who made a mistake in qualifying, starting fifth on the grid while Alonso took pole. Ironically, Brazil saw McLaren score the one-two they had threatened on a number of occasions. But with Alonso secure in third place it came too late, and Montoya had no need to concede his third victory of the year.

Spain's had its first F1 champion, and it came just two years after Alonso became the youngest Grand Prix winner. He had had the advantage of the ultra-reliable MP4-20, and had undoubtedly enjoyed the rub of the green over Raikkonen. But 13 podiums and six wins in 16 starts – not counting the USA debacle – told its own story. Alonso was a worthy inheritor of Schumacher's crown, and at 24 looked set for a long and illustrious career at the top of the F1 tree.

 B|B|C RADIO FIVE LIVE

I think the qualities Alonso has are many. If you sort through them – at the top of the pile comes the ability to almost achieve a personal best every time you get in a car. It's this ability and self-confidence a driver has to say to himself, 'Here's my target, this is what I need to do'. And he goes out and does it – and he's probably never done it quite as well before. It's something you see in champions. I've seen it for sure in Ayrton, for sure in Michael and I can see it in Fernando.

Pat Simmons
executive director of engineering for Renault.

DES LYNAM MEETS

Bernie Ecclestone

The most powerful man in motor sport

Bernie, first and foremost, you are an aficionado and you love motor racing, but the average fan says it's become boring. What would you say to that?

I'd say rubbish, because, apart from Germany, all the attendance figures have been up everywhere in the world. Germany is down a little bit – 5 per cent something like that – possibly because in that country there's been a slight recession in general, so that could be the reason. I think it's the type of comment the newspapers or somebody will make as it's the current thing to say – we're still going to go although it's boring. If Ali was boxing again, you know full well he'll knock the other guy out in the second round anyway, so you may think it's going to be boring, but I'm still going. No, I believe people want to think it's predictable that Schumacher will win but want to watch in case someone beats him. As there's always that anticipation they want to be there to watch. Meanwhile, the rest of the race is still super down the field.

The tracks aren't capable of cars passing to a large extent – I'm thinking of Monaco, for example, you couldn't possibly pass anyone there.

Yes, difficult for sure. If the tyres are soft rubber and the rubber rolls off it's dangerous, so the drivers all stay in the one simple line, the racing line. In the rain, however, there is no line because those things don't happen to the tyres. So there are quite a few different issues and we're going to try and find a way to get harder tyres and just make it a bit more easier for people to be able to overtake.

Your Muhammad Ali analogy was an interesting one and I always think that Grand Prix racing is like Ali having a piece of metal in his glove in a sense because you get the best car and the best driver and they start in front.

Yes, you spend all day up until the race to find out which is the quickest car and then we put them in pole position, so why should they be overtaken, because they're the quickest? We know what's wrong but we don't know what's the right way yet.

We know what's wrong but we don't know what's the right way yet

I've often heard it said that if a guy wins a Grand Prix, in the next race he should start at the back and prove what a good driver he is.

What I'm trying to do at the moment is to have points for being the quickest, then have a ballot for the position on the starting grid. So maybe the guy that's been quickest in qualifying may find himself at the back of the grid, or maybe not, he could be lucky. Mathematically, they'll all be in with a chance of being in pole position, or at the back of the group. That would liven things up for sure, but then you get the drivers saying, It's not fair, as I'm quick and why should I be halfway down the field?' The difference is that the people who run the teams are all enthusiasts and they want to win, that's what they're there for.

Are you still as fascinated by Grand Prix racing as you have been all through the years?

Yes, it's the same and as far as I remember, it hasn't changed that much. If you look at other sports where there is a lot of changes of position, such as the motorbike 125 races where they change four times a lap, nobody watches them, so it's quite strange. I think people like the idea of saying can we catch the guy in front, rather than it's a certainty that we will.

When you were 16 though, how did you get into motor sport? I think you used to race yourself didn't you?

Yes absolutely. I left Suffolk when I was eight years old but started to race a little bit when I was about 15, before I had a licence. I went from racing motorcycles to racing cars, then owning teams and just progressed from there. I bought the Brabham team in 1970 and suddenly the guys said, 'Would you mind doing this, could you negotiate these things for us?' People relied on me, and thought I was going to do the right thing for them, which hopefully I did – it was getting people's confidence. Mr Ferrari was around and was a big supporter of Colin Chapman and me in those days.

Above: Bernie Ecclestone with Ron Dennis at the Hungarian Grand Prix.

Below: Bernie Ecclestone (c) with (l-r) David Coulthard, Michael Schumacher, Mika Hakkinen and Rubens Barrichello in Budapest, Hungary.

In those days we used to lose two or three top drivers a year

Are you ruthless?

No, more decisive – if I say I'll do something I'll do it, so you've got to be as good as your word and do what you say you're going to do. Providing you're fair and honest, you're half way there. Honestly I'm a pussycat really, I'm a real pushover – if you push hard, I mean!

Who have been your heroes, who have been the drivers you've been passionate about?

Well, a lot of the guys that drove for me. I was lucky to have a lot of nice men including Lauda, Graham Hill, Piquet and Patrese. I was attached to those guys, and one or two of them died. When they were killed, like Jochen Rindt, we were in a little business together – you got attached to those people. Nice guys.

How did you cope with it when he had the accident?

That was bad news. I stopped being involved at that time for a little while, which was a bit silly really and truly. It didn't bring him back, but don't forget in those days we used to lose two or three top drivers a year. It's only that things have become super safe now, and if and when there's an accident, like when we lost Senna, it's a big shock to everybody.

What about the real characters in Grand Prix Racing? I'm thinking years ago you had James Hunt and people like that, where are they right now?

I don't know what you can do, I don't know if there are any special tablets you can give these people to become characters! They make a lot of money and they're protected by sponsors so they don't have to be characters and say nice things. In the days that you're talking about, 15 or 20 years ago, a good half the field were characters but it doesn't happen any more. I mean I'd be upset if I was a driver and was interviewed by journalists. We have 800 journalists at a Grand Prix, and you have to listen to the same silly questions. Nobody asks anything original and you get fed up in the end.

What is it that makes the best drivers the best? How does it work?

Most guys that are world champions are quite together and bright, they know the way to win and want to win as well. You say, 'What do people do with the money; what is Schumacher racing for?' There is the chance that he may be hurt, and he's made an awful lot of money, but he is still determined to win. He doesn't want to be second, he wants to win.

Is Britain producing potential Grand Prix drivers? I think there are two on the pre-circuit aren't there?

If you're that good, like Button has proved he's good, he will be invited into a team immediately. If you're trying to come up through the ranks, the lower teams expect you to bring some sponsorship with you and it's not easy for these guys to do that. So some of the countries support their people much more than we do.

Button has proved he's good

Do you personally control motor sport as much as you have been deemed to have done over the last few years?

Not really, because we're now so democratic we have to listen to other people, which is both good and bad. If there are ten teams and ten people each thinking what's best for them they will never think of the big picture of F1, they will focus on what's in it for them in the next race.

With the sophistication of the machinery, will the cars get faster? Or will they not be allowed to get faster and always be restricted to a reasonable speed?

The federation is trying to slow the cars down. But I don't hold with that concept. I think F1 is all about having a lot of horsepower. The cars have got more than 900 horsepower now and I think that's what we should keep, but there are other ways of looking at it. Certainly the circuits need to keep changing to keep up with this so you have the run-off areas, and when you have longer run-off areas, the public is farther back which is also bad. I'm against regulations anyway. I think people should build a car and have a weight and an engine capacity and that's it, but it's probably not practical.

You mentioned circuits there, I'm always reading about Silverstone and that it may not have a Grand Prix in the future and you're going to sling them out or something. What is the truth of that, and what is the actual situation?

People come from all over the world to build new racetracks and when they come to London they ask if they can go to Silverstone. I say, 'Don't go there, it's like an old house. If you do go and look at it it's not what we want, go and look instead wherever they're building modern tracks.' You feel quite ashamed of the fact that that's all England's got to offer. Most of the teams are here, F1 sort of grew up in England and what have we got to offer – Silverstone with people getting stuck in the mud. We've put money into Silverstone, the government built the roads, and the owners of the circuit, the British Racing Drivers Club, have done virtually nothing except build a nice clubhouse for themselves that they treat as a gentlemen's club.

You had racing cars running around the centre of London recently. Surely nothing is going to happen with that is it? It wouldn't be safe.

We raced in Monaco, Detroit and Adelaide, and it would be okay but what we want Silverstone to do is just bring that circuit up to the twenty-first century.

You did race for a while. Would you have liked to be a Grand Prix driver?

Yes, I did for a while. I was in a lower formula and I won some races but had some accidents. Then after one of the accidents I decided to quit. I remember thinking to myself, I could be lying on my back for the rest of my life looking up at the sky, which I didn't like too much.

What are you going to do over the next ten years of your life?

Well I hope I'm going to survive ten years, that's the first thing, and if I do, I shall hopefully be able to continue what I'm doing. I'm happy with what I'm doing.

Opposite above: Bernie Ecclestone gets a pie in the face, courtesy of Michael Schumacher, at the Luxembourg Grand Prix in 1997.

Opposite below: During a visit to the Istanbul Speed Park in Kurtkoy, Bernie Ecclestone poses for the cameras.

Above: After the 2005 US Grand Prix fiasco Bernie Ecclestone arrives at FIA headquarters in Paris to attend a meeting along with other Formula One team managers and the FIA President Max Mosley.

MOTORCYCLING

Ferrari court seven-times champion Rossi

As the 2005 Moto GP season unfolded, the main talking point was not so much about the outcome – barring calamity, that was barely an issue by the halfway mark – but about how long Valentino Rossi would continue to dominate on two wheels before switching to four. As he closed in on his seventh world title, Michael Schumacher's star at Ferrari seemed to be on the wane, and rumours abounded that Rossi had tested for Maranello with a view to taking an F1 seat as early as 2007.

Arch-rivals

That was for the future, however. Before then, there was the small matter of securing a fifth successive Moto GP crown to add to the world titles Rossi had won at 125cc and 250cc.

Rossi had beaten arch-rival Sete Gibernau by 47 points in lifting the 2004 championship. When the riders reconvened in Jerez for the new campaign, it seemed the Spaniard would again provide the main threat. The fact that there was no love lost between the two added extra spice to the 17-race, eight-month battle.

After round one, home favourite Gibernau glowered at the champion in the paddock, following a last-corner incident which saw the two bikes touch. Gibernau ended up in the gravel; Rossi took the flag. Gibernau's Movistar Honda teammate Marco Melandri took third.

Appalling conditions

The next two races were run in appalling conditions. Gibernau crashed while leading in Portugal, Alex Barros holding off Rossi to give the Camel Honda team 25 points, the veteran Brazilian's first victory since 2002. Rossi qualified only sixth in China, but, like Schumacher, proved himself to be the Rainmaster. He won from Olivier Jacque, who had a superb ride as stand-in for the injured Kawasaki rider Alex Hoffmann. A former 250cc world champion, Jacque had made only sporadic wildcard Moto GP appearances in the previous 12 months, making his performance in Shanghai all the more impressive.

Last year was more of a surprise. This year, all the other riders want to beat me and try 100%. Capirossi played a cat-and-mouse game with me in three corners. I said to him: 'See you the next time.' Anyway, I'm champion for the seventh time.

Valentino Rossi

Opposite: Jubilant Valentino Rossi at the the Malaysian Grand Prix. Rossi claimed his seventh world championship title – his fifth in premier class – when he finished second.

Below: Valentino Rossi follows Spain's Sete Gibernau during the Grand Prix of Spain in Jerez.

Three-way battle

Round Four, Le Mans, witnessed a terrific three-way battle between Gibernau, Rossi and the Italian's Gauloises Yamaha teammate Colin Edwards. It was down to the big two at the business end of the race, however, and Rossi crossed the line 0.382 sec. ahead of his rival. Gibernau grudgingly accepted the winner's proffered hand in the warm-down lap. Edwards, the Texas Tornado, recorded his first podium for Yamaha.

Mugello saw another Rossi masterclass. From pole position he had an indifferent start, slipping to fourth, but within a lap he was back in front. Gibernau crashed out again, and it was left to Melandri and Max Biaggi to try and exert some pressure on the champion. Both had spells in the lead, but Rossi overtook when it mattered. Playfully, he overtook Biaggi at the very point on the circuit where Max's army of fans had congregated. It was undoubtedly a deliberate manoeuvre, since there was as much friction between the compatriots as existed between Rossi and Gibernau.

Local hero beaten

The circus moved to Catalunya for the second Spanish race of the season. Rossi tracked pole man and local hero Gibernau, overtaking him three laps from home. Melandri, the 22-year-old former 250cc world champion, came out on top in a dogfight for third, edging out Barros and Biaggi's Repsol Honda teammate Nicky Hayden.

Rossi made it six wins out of seven at Assen after a breathtaking high-speed duel round the fastest track on the Moto GP calendar. Rossi made a sluggish start from pole, and didn't carve his way through the field until after the halfway mark. But then he hit his stride, trading the lap record with Melandri in the latter stages. Rossi had the final word, setting a new fastest time on the final lap to take the flag 1.5 sec. ahead of Melandri, with Edwards third.

Rossi 100 points clear

American one-two

There were wild scenes at Laguna Seca as a fervent partisan crowd acknowledged an American one-two. Nicky Hayden led from start to finish, and for once not even 'The Doctor' could do anything about it. Rossi chased hard, as did Colin Edwards when he took over in second, but neither could catch the 23-year-old Kentuckian, who was overjoyed at his maiden victory in Moto GP.

There was more atrocious weather for the riders to contend with at Donington Park. In the conditions an accident-littered race was hardly surprising, and only 11 bikes went the distance. London-based Rossi regarded this as his second home Grand Prix and was determined to put on a show in his adopted country. The champion almost came to grief on several occasions, showing extraordinary balance and control to rescue the situation when he seemed destined to be parted from his machine.

He jousted with Barros and Kenny Roberts Jnr until six laps out, when he put the hammer down and disappeared into the distance. He gapped the field by eight seconds in just three laps before easing back to cross the line just over three seconds ahead of Roberts Jnr. Barros, riding in his 250th GP, added 16 points to his tally by taking third.

Rossi was now over 100 points clear in the championship, and he extended his lead with another maximum return at Germany's Sachsenring, a circuit he professed not to like. This race provided Moto GP with its first red flag of the year, following John Hopkins' spectacular high-side spill. A new 25-lap was ordered, the first five only counting towards a revamped grid line-up. Gibernau led on the last lap and looked like finally ending his barren spell. Victory would have been sweetened by the fact that Rossi had declared he wouldn't allow the Spaniard to win another race. In the event, Gibernau was unable to make the champion eat his words, for he gifted victory to his rival by running wide on the first corner of the final lap.

He got on pretty good. He took some time to get into it but in the end I think he handled it very impressively. I'd probably say he would come to a certain level which would be maybe competitive but to come to the final bit is usually the difficult bit.

Michael Schumacher
who was impressed by Valentino Rossi's Formula One driving skills

Opposite left: Valentino Rossi celebrates after winning the motorcycle Grand Prix of Spain in Jerez.

Opposite right: Italy's Marco Melandri in action during the Grand Prix of Catalunya at Montmelo in Barcelona.

Below: Nicky Hayden during the qualifying session of the Grand Prix of Catalunya.

Equals Hailwood's record

Rossi's 76th career win equalled Mike Hailwood's record, and The Doctor quickly unfurled a banner to broadcast the fact. With Melandri and Edwards back in seventh and eighth places, Rossi now held a chasm-like 120-point lead in the championship.

Brno, the venue for the Czech GP, witnessed another sparkling race-long duel between Rossi and Gibernau. But as so often during the season, luck was not with the Spanish ace, his bike failing him on the last lap. Loris Capirossi inherited second place, and went one better in the next race, Motegi.

The Ducati Marlboro rider was the star of the entire weekend in Japan. He took pole, Ducati's first of the year, while Rossi was a long way back on the fourth row. The champion did make it through to fourth place by lap four, but some way off the leading trio of Melandri, Capirossi and Biaggi.

Shock DNF for champion

At the halfway mark fans were left rubbing their eyes in disbelief as Rossi made a mistake which resulted in his first DNF of the year. He also took Melandri out, the Honda rider sustaining a nasty foot injury in the process.

Capirossi passed Biaggi six laps from home to win by 1.4 sec., with 2004 winner Makoto Tamada in third. It was a red-letter day for Bridgestone as well as Capirossi, as this was the first non-Michelin-shod bike to win in 2005.

Rossi would have sewn up the championship with either first or second place in Japan. Even so, he still enjoyed a healthy 112-point lead over Max Biaggi, the only man now with a mathematical chance of snatching the title. And just 13 points garnered from the remaining five races would remove even that remote possibility.

In fact, Rossi clinched his fifth successive Moto GP title – his seventh overall – in the next race, Sepang. Once again he showed his race-craft after an inauspicious qualifying run, battling for the lead with Capirossi after starting only seventh on the grid.

The Ducati man made it back-to-back poles and victories as Rossi eased off to take the second place which guaranteed him the crown. Carlos Checa was third, giving Ducati their best ever Moto GP finish. But the day belonged to Rossi, whose five premier–class championships on the spin equalled Mick Doohan's 1980s record. His second title since leaving Honda for Yamaha provided further confirmation, if any was needed, that the extraordinary run of success was down to the genius of the rider, not the hardware.

He is not obliged to race in Formula One. If he decides to, it is because he decides he is ready to win. He is very popular with Italians but we don't need popularity. We need a winning driver. If something comes of it, it will above all be his decision. If Ferrari and Rossi come together, it will be to win the world championship and not to put on a show that we do not need.

Luca Di Montezemolo
Ferrari chairman

Opposite above: *Italian Loris Capirossi of Ducati kisses his trophy at the podium after winning the Malaysian Motorcycle Grand Prix in Sepang.*

Opposite below: *Valentino Rossi takes a corner in Sepang.*

Left: *Yamaha's Valentino Rossi before a free practice session for the Qatar Grand Prix World Championships in Doha.*

ROWING

Five-medal haul for Brits

Andy Hodge, Alex Partridge, Peter Reed and Steve Williams won Great Britain's first gold medal in the men's four at the World Rowing Championships at Gifu, Japan. In oppressive heat, they beat the Dutch and Canadians to win the coxless four in a time of six minutes 11.59 seconds.

Twenty-four hours later the women scored another victory in the quadruple sculls. Katherine Grainger, Frances Houghton, Rebecca Romero and Sarah Winckless pipped Germany to the finishing line by 0.34 seconds to win in a time of 6 minutes 9.59 seconds, bringing home Britain's second gold medal of the tournament.

A further bronze medal was won in the women's lightweight quadruple sculls. Tanya Brady, Lorna Norris, Hester Goodsell and Naomi Hoogesteger achieved a time of 6 minutes 22.49 seconds while 19-year-old Zac Purchase went on to win silver in the lightweight single scull in 7 minutes 23.10 seconds. Adaptive (disability) four also won gold battling against very windy conditions.

At the end of the tournament Italy won the Team trophy leading the medals tables with ten medals, including two golds.

We decided to row how we have for the last three months and dominate from the start. We took a second out of the second boat in the third 500m, and from there we walked away — game over.

Alex Partridge

We played every one of our strength cards in the final — it's just massively satisfying that we got it right.

Katherine Grainger

We are looking to win four medals in the championships.

David Tanner
Team manager

British Results

Men's coxless fours	1st	6 mins 11.59 secs
Women's quadruple sculls	1st	6 mins 9.59 secs
Adaptive (disability) four	1st	8 mins 12.07 secs
Men's lightweight single scull	2nd	7 mins 23.10 secs
Women's lightweight quadruple sculls	3rd	6 mins 22.49 secs

Above: Rowers of British four, (l-r) Alex Partridge, Andrew Triggs Hodge, Peter Reed, and Steve Williams acknowledge their victory during the award ceremony.

Opposite above: Great Britain's Zac Purchase in action prior to his lightweight single sculls semi-final during the 2005 Rowing World Cup.

Opposite below and left: The exhausted but elated quadruple sculls team: Katherine Grainger, Frances Houghton, Sarah Winckless, and Rebecca Romero.

THE BOAT RACE

Third fastest time as Oxford triumph

The heaviest-ever boat crew

The Oxford crew came home six seconds ahead of Cambridge in a finishing time of 16 minutes 42 seconds, the third-fastest time on record and a two-length win. It was Oxford that made the stronger start and although Cambridge did recover, they were still left to chase Oxford throughout the course. This victory for the Dark Blues made up for their controversial defeat last year when both sides clashed on the Fulham bend. The heaviest-ever boat crew on record were delighted with their success – Cambridge had won the toss choosing the Middlesex station which gave them an initial advantage. However, the better technique from the Oxford crew soon showed. Both crews contained four Olympians and were claimed to be the best ever, in terms of quality.

Isis and Goldie

This was the 151st race in an event that began in 1829 after letters were exchanged between two friends at each university and Cambridge challenged Oxford to a rowing race. It is still a tradition that the losers challenge the winning team the following year. Each year from September onwards coaches work to select the final team to row in the 'Blue Boat' while those who do not make it race in the reserve boat – 'Isis' for Oxford and 'Goldie' for Cambridge. These boats compete against each other 30 minutes before the main race. The current course has been used since 1845 and begins in Putney, finishing just before Chiswick Road Bridge, a distance of 4 miles and 375 yards. The current record for the course stands at 16 minutes 19 seconds – set by Cambridge in 1998.

BOAT RACE CREWS

	Oxford	Cambridge
Bow	Robin Bourne-Taylor	Luke Walton
2	Barney Williams	Thomas Edwards
3	Peter Reed	Henry Adams
4	Joseph Von Maltzahn	Steffen Buschbacher
5	Christopher Liwski	Sebastian Schulte
6	Michael Blomquist	Matthias Kleinz
7	Jason Flickinger	Tom James
Stroke	Andrew Triggs Hodge	Bernd Heidicker
Cox	Acer Nethercott	Peter Rudge

Left: The victorious Oxford crew after the 151st University Boat Race.

Opposite and right: The Oxford team pull away to win in the third-fastest time in the history of the event.

Rugby

THE SIX NATIONS

Dragon roars as Wales claim first Grand Slam since 1978

The 2005 RBS Six Nations Championship looked to be the most open for years. Ireland, with a team that had been together for some time and at the height of its powers, were probably slight favourites; Bernard Laporte's France side had won the Grand Slam in 2002 and 2004; Wales, wooden spoonists in 2003, were resurgent under Mike Ruddock; and England, under new coach Andy Robinson, were still smarting after finishing third in 2004, their worst performance for a decade.

Monster kick

The reigning world champions quickly found that reputation mattered naught. Retirements and injuries meant that this was a team in transition, and it fell at the first hurdle, the Millennium Stadium. The twinkle-toed Shane Williams scored the only try of the match, helping Wales to an 8–3 half-time lead. Charlie Hodgson's third successful penalty put England in front 9–8 for the first time in the match with six minutes to go. But Gavin Henson, making his Six Nations debut, provided the most memorable moments: a couple of bone-crunching tackles on the teenage Newcastle centre Mathew Tait; and a monster injury-time penalty which snatched victory for the home side. It was England's seventh defeat in 12 games since lifting the William Webb Ellis Trophy – and worse was to come.

Eddie O'Sullivan's Ireland won at the Stadio Flaminio, but only after a spirited performance by Italy, who were in contention for long periods. They were only 8–6 behind at half-time, and that in spite of the fact that

Orquera squandered three penalty opportunities. Brian O'Driscoll didn't get on the scoresheet but two pieces of magic created tries for Geordan Murphy and Peter Stringer. Denis Hickie went over late on to make the scoreline more comfortable, while prop Leandro Castrogiovanni's injury-time consolation try was no more than Italy deserved.

Williams fumes at sin-binning

Scotland, bottom of the heap in 2004, came close to recording a major shock in Paris. Chris Paterson's third successful penalty put the Scots 9–0 ahead early in the second half. The home side levelled in the dying minutes with two penalties and a dropped goal from Yann Delaigue. Scotland's Aussie coach Matt Williams was fuming at the sin-binning of Jon Petrie for deliberate offside, and with his team down to 14 men, centre Damien Traille scored a charge-down try in injury-time.

France, Wales and Ireland kept their Grand Slam hopes alive in the second round of matches. Ireland recorded their highest ever score at Murrayfield, even without the services of O'Driscoll and D'Arcy. Locks Paul O'Connell – captaining the side in O'Driscoll's absence – and Malcolm O'Kelly were imperious, and both scored tries. Ireland went over five times in all, grinding out good field position and regularly turning over possession deep in Scotland's territory. Scotland's seventh successive defeat gave Matt Williams little cause for celebration on the anniversary of his appointment as coach.

Opposite: Gareth Thomas (l) and Michael Owen hold aloft the trophy after winning the Grand Slam by beating Ireland in the RBS Six Nations at the Millennium Stadium in Cardiff.

Left: Dwayne Peel, the Welsh scrum half, celebrates victory at the final whistle which brought his country their first championship for 11 years and their first Grand Slam since 1978.

Above: Gavin Henson, on his Six Nations debut, produced a monster injury-time penalty which snatched a crucial victory for Wales against England.

BBC RADIO FIVE LIVE

No team goes into a Six Nations game thinking they're going to lose. You can't afford to have that mental application. It's very much look at yourselves, look at where your strengths are. There's no question that Wales are a better side and if Wales are on their day and we're not, Wales will win; but on the flip side of that, if England are on their day and Wales don't turn up, then England will win! It's very simple.
I can't see anybody winning a Grand Slam.

Matt Dawson

ENGLAND v IRELAND

England could have won that match. With the retirements and injuries, there was always the risk that this was going to be a season in transition and that's the way it panned out. I think what was really important to them today was a big performance and I think they can hold their heads high. It was on a different level to the way they've played in earlier games.

Hugo MacNeill

First away win in four years

Wales went one better than Ireland, running in six tries against Italy. It was their first away victory for four years, and sweet revenge for the loss in Rome on their 2003 visit.

Had Charlie Hodgson and Olly Barkley had their kicking boots on, England might have notched an equally comfortable score against France. Tries from Lewsey and Barkley – the latter's first international touchdown – gave England a comfortable 17–6 half-time advantage. But six penalties failed to find their mark, while the opposition's scrum-half Dmitri Yachvili showed the England pair how it was done. He popped six over to give France an 18–17 lead. Hodgson also missed an injury-time dropped goal attempt that had the Twickenham crowd yearning for a speedy Jonny Wilkinson recovery. France were hardly impressive in recording their first win on English soil since 1997, but had come up against a side in even worse form.

England slump to third defeat

By the end of the third round of matches, only Ireland and Wales remained as Grand Slam contenders. Ireland inflicted yet another defeat on England at Lansdowne Road. The visitors were on top for long periods but couldn't convert superiority into points. Ronan O'Gara kicked superbly out of defence to relieve the pressure, and also helped himself to 14 points, converting O'Driscoll's brilliant try and putting two penalties and two dropped goals between the posts. He thus notched 500 points on his 50th international appearance. Andy Robinson felt aggrieved at two disallowed tries: Cueto was ruled offside after gathering Hodgson's crossfield kick, and the referee was unconvinced by a claimed touchdown under a pile of forwards.

France v Wales was one of the matches of the tournament. Laporte's men stunned the visitors with early tries by Rougerie and Yachvili, but two Stephen Jones penalties took Wales into the break facing only a nine-point deficit. A brace of tries from flanker Martyn Williams turned the match on its head in a blistering five-minute spell. Wales were now 18–15 up. The mercurial Michelak levelled with a dropped goal before six points from Jones' boot sealed victory. It meant three wins out of four trips to the French capital, the only blot being a broken thumb sustained by full back and captain Gareth Thomas.

Paterson boot ends run of defeats

Scotland entertained Italy in a match that was already looking like the battle to avoid the wooden spoon. Scotland came out on top in a dour match, Chris Paterson's six-out-of-six penalty haul enough to end Scotland's run of six home defeats on the spin, their worst run for 50 years. John Kirwan's side had the consolation of scoring the game's only try, courtesy of Andrea Masi.

Any hopes that Scotland would go from strength to strength were ended a fortnight later, when a rampant Wales put the result beyond doubt in the first quarter. There were tries from Ryan Jones, Rhys Williams and Shane Williams, Stephen Jones slotting the conversions and adding a penalty for good measure. When Rhys Williams went over for his second touchdown after 49 minutes, Wales led 43–3. Scotland restored a modicum of pride with tries from Andy Craig, Rory Lamont and Chris Paterson, but it was all too little, too late.

Pelous joins the centurions' club

Ireland lost the chance of a Grand Slam winner-take-all showdown with their Celtic cousins when they suffered a home defeat at the hands of the French. Winger Christophe Dominici scored two tries, with 21-year-old Toulouse centre Benoit Baby also going over on his full debut. Baby was named man-of-the-match, while his captain, Fabien Pelous, became only the fifth player to reach 100 caps, following in the footsteps of Leonard, Sella, Gregan and Campese. Ronan O'Gara also reached a landmark, becoming his country's record points-scorer, and a typical piece of brilliance from O'Driscoll gave his side a late try, but Ireland had seen their hopes of a first Grand Slam for 57 years evaporate. However, there was still much to play for: back-to-back Triple Crowns and a first championship since 1985.

Under new captain Martin Corry, England thrashed Italy 39–7. Sale winger Mark Cueto grabbed a hat-trick, while Hodgson's four missed kicks didn't prove crucial against modest opposition. That same weekend saw Jonny Wilkinson injured in his comeback match for Newcastle, ending all hopes that he could yet play a part in the championship.

I was there [1978]; I saw the passion, I saw the romance of it and suddenly we've got a little bit of that back. Hopefully we can do our bit now, and if we do, it'll be in the memory of people like JPR, Phil Bennett, JJ, Gareth and all of the boys because they're the ones who have inspired me as a coach, and a lot of people around me … and what we're trying to get the players to do is express themselves in that way.

Mike Ruddock

Opposite: Harry Ellis of England runs for the line as he scores in the corner during the match between England and Scotland, recording his first international try.

Above: *England's Danny Grewcock wins a lineout ball during the match against Scotland. England won the Calcutta Cup 43–22.*

Wales stand on the threshold of a first Grand Slam for 27 years. The dragon is breathing fire once more!

Cueto the top try-scorer

Apart from the Calcutta Cup, all that rested on the England-Scotland clash in the final round of matches was fourth place in the table. England came out on top, running in seven tries. Jamie Noon notched a hat-trick, while Cueto's touchdown made him the tournament's top try-scorer. Harry Ellis also recorded his first international try before being replaced by Matt Dawson. Three wins from Matt Williams' 17 games in charge – and those coming against Samoa, Japan and Italy – meant that his days as Scotland coach were numbered.

Meanwhile, Wales, Ireland and France all carried hopes of winning the title into their last games. The mathematics were complex, but Wales had it in their own hands, knowing that a win or draw against Ireland would be enough.

France did all they could, running in seven tries against Italy, a rout which ended a miserable series for the Italians and precipitated the termination of Kirwan's contract the following month. France now had four wins and eight points on the board; an Ireland victory in Cardiff and it would all come down to points difference. History suggested that was a likely outcome: Wales hadn't beaten Ireland in Cardiff since 1983, and the Irish went into the match on a five-match winning streak between the two sides. But Mike Ruddock's men chose the ideal moment to break that run.

First championship since 1994

Prop forward Gethin Jenkins was the unlikely scorer of the first half's only try, charging down O'Gara's kick and showing neat footwork to hack the ball over the line. Confidence drained from the Ireland stand-off, who was eventually replaced by David Humphreys. When full back Kevin

Morgan finished off a move begun by a coruscating break from Tom Shanklin on the hour mark, Wales held a 29-6 lead. Tries from Marcus Horan and Geordan Murphy reduced the arrears but Wales never looked like surrendering the lead which brought them their first championship for 11 years and first Grand Slam since 1978.

Opposite: The waiting is over as the triumphant Wales team salute the crowd after completing their first Grand Slam since 1978 following a 32–20 victory over Ireland.

Below: Dwayne Peel of Wales makes a break during the match against France at the Stade De France in Paris.

Results

5/6 February

France	16	-	9	Scotland
Wales	11	-	9	England
Italy	17	-	28	Ireland

12/13 February

Italy	8	-	38	Wales
Scotland	13	-	40	Ireland
England	17	-	18	France

26/27 February

Scotland	18	-	10	Italy
France	18	-	24	Wales
Ireland	19	-	13	England

12/13 March

Ireland	19	-	26	France
England	39	-	7	Italy
Scotland	22	-	46	Wales

19 March

Italy	13	-	56	France
Wales	32	-	20	Ireland
England	43	-	22	Scotland

Final Table

	P	W	D	L	T(tries)	F	A	Pts
Wales	5	5	0	0	17	151	77	10
France	5	4	0	1	13	134	82	8
Ireland	5	3	0	2	12	126	101	6
England	5	2	0	3	16	121	77	4
Scotland	5	1	0	4	8	84	155	2
Italy	5	0	0	5	5	55	179	0

 BBC RADIO FIVE LIVE

The whole rugby world is looking at Wales and saying, 'Hey, this is wonderful — wonderful for the game! We love the style you're playing, we love Gavin Henson and Shane Williams; it's wonderful!' Throughout Wales every pressman, every journalist has gone bananas!

JJ Williams

Wales stand on the threshold of a first Grand Slam for 27 years. The dragon is breathing fire once more!

Mark Pougatch

THE BRITISH LIONS TOUR

Blackwash for Lions

As the Lions departed for the antipodes, coach Clive Woodward hailed his 45-strong squad as the best-prepared group of players to leave the country's shores in the 117-year history of touring sides from the British Isles. Hopes were high that the class of 2005 might emulate the legendary 1971 Lions, the only side in 12 visits to New Zealand to come away with a series win.

The final warm-up match, a 25–25 draw against Argentina at the Millennium Stadium, was noteworthy for Jonny Wilkinson's seven successful kicks, suggesting a timely return to fitness and form for the England fly half after a nightmare 18 months since his boot won the World Cup in such dramatic style. There would be a spate of injuries, however. Iain Balshaw's failure to recover from a thigh strain opened the door for Mark Cueto, while Malcolm O'Kelly's tour was over before a ball was kicked. Wasps' Simon Shaw was drafted in to replace the Irish lock, increasing the English contingent to 22. That raised some eyebrows – notably Welsh ones – as England's form since the glories of November 2003 had been distinctly underwhelming.

Dallaglio's tour ends after 25 minutes

The Lions opened their 11-match tour with a 34–20 victory over Bay Of Plenty. Josh Lewsey went over twice in the first six minutes, and Cueto touched down to give the Lions a 17–0 lead inside a quarter of an hour. The opposition replied with two tries to level by half-time, but that paled into insignificance compared with the loss of Lawrence Dallaglio, stretchered off with a broken ankle after 25 minutes. For the Wasps No. 8 it was an agonizing case of deja-vu, his 2001 Lions trip to Australia having also ended prematurely. The team finished strongly, Shanklin, Peel and D'Arcy making it a six-try haul, while O'Gara's return of just two successful kicks from six didn't prove costly. Llanelli flanker Simon Easterby was hastily diverted from his trip to Japan with Ireland, but the loss of the inspirational pack leader was a huge blow to the tourists.

'Fourth Test' brings first defeat

The Lions struggled in the first half against Taranaki, and were somewhat fortunate to trail just 7–6 at the break. As the home side faded – their cause not helped by the sin-binning of hooker Andrew Hore – the Lions cut loose. They took the lead with Martin Corry's 49th minute try, winger Shane Horgan rounded off a slick move to touch down, and Geordan Murphy went over twice in the last five minutes. Charlie Hodgson, with four penalties, two conversions and some good tactical kicking, had a good day at the office.

The third match brought the first defeat. The clash with the New Zealand Maori was dubbed 'the fourth Test', despite the fact that they had never beaten the Lions in seven previous attempts. The Lions defended well – and needed to – but barely threatened their opponents' line until the mercurial Brian O'Driscoll, the tour captain, scored in the dying seconds. Stephen Jones converted, adding to his two first-half penalties, but Woodward said he had no complaints as the Maori dominated the rucks and mauls.

Opposite: British and Irish Lions captain Brian O'Driscoll (r) looks over to the New Zealand All Blacks during the national anthems before the first Test match, played in Christchurch, 25 June 2005. The All Blacks defeated the British and Irish Lions 21–3 to take a 1–0 lead in the three Test series.

Above: Daniel Carter, the All Black standoff, chips past Josh Lewsey to score his first try during the second Test match at the Westpac stadium in Wellington.

Nothing quite matches the challenge of a Lions Tour to a great rugby power like New Zealand. If we win the Test series that will be, in my view, an outstanding achievement to match any other – and I mean any other.

I know it'll be hard, but I believe we can win. We have tremendous respect for New Zealand. Rugby means more to the people there than any other country on earth. It is an integral part of their culture and their daily life. They have great coaches, great players, great support and I do not underestimate the challenge.

Rugby is changing fast and I believe that we are at the cutting edge of that change.

History! Historic is exactly what a win would be. Since 1888 we've only won six out of 35 Test matches, winning only one series in 11 attempts.

Sir Clive Woodward
following his announcement
of squad for the Lions Tour

Wilkinson enters the fray

The Lions got back on course with a 23–6 win over a depleted Wellington side, a game which saw Wilkinson enter the fray. He converted Gethin Jenkins' injury-time try at the end of the first half, and Gareth Thomas' chip and follow-up on the stroke of full-time. He added three penalties to make it five out of seven. Both the difficult conditions and personnel changes militated against a cohesive, fluid performance.

Next up was Otago, who had beaten the '93 Lions. None of their All Blacks featured this time, so a shock was always unlikely. Even so, the Lions didn't take the lead until the 55th minute, Ryan Jones going over to cap a great debut at No. 8. Will Greenwood had scored a try at the end of the first half, and Shane Williams made it a hat-trick for the Lions seven minutes from the end as they once again finished more strongly than their opponents.

Henson omitted from Test squad

The announcement of the line-up to face Southland on 21 June was eagerly awaited, since Woodward made it clear that those selected would not be in contention for a squad place for the first Test four days later. The biggest surprise was the omission of Wales' Six Nations hero Gavin Henson, who was the stand-out player in a disappointing performance. His two tries were the difference between the sides, but for the first encounter with the All Blacks Woodward eschewed youth and form in favour of experience and loyalty to those who had served him well in the past. There were no Scots in the side, the first time since 1959 there had been no representation from north of the border.

BBC RADIO **FIVE LIVE**

Brian O'Driscoll is an inspirational player. He is a magnificent centre, the best in the world at the moment so he can lead by example, but he's also got to draw the best out of all the other players, and that means blending four countries into one in a very short space of time.

Ian Robertson

Above right: Richie McCaw, the All Blacks flank forward, is held by Julian White and Lewis Moody (r) during the second Test match.

Right: Gavin Henson and Jonny Wilkinson talking tactics. For the second Test in Wellington Woodward brought in seven new faces and made four positional changes, including Wilkinson back at No. 10.

I have no doubt whatsoever it was a spear tackle that has ended my tour

First Test: Christchurch

In the first minute of the first Test the Lions lost their talismanic captain Brian O'Driscoll, who suffered a dislocated shoulder following a spear tackle in the midst of a ruck. The perpetrators, hooker Keven Mealamu and captain Tana Umaga, went unpunished, incensing Clive Woodward, who focused on a cynical and dangerous piece of foul play, perhaps by way of taking the eye off an inept, lacklustre performance. To make matters worse, Danny Grewcock was handed a two-month suspension for biting Mealamu's finger, an incident that was picked up.

In the game itself the Lions were second best in all departments, including the lineout and scrum, where the tourists were expected to hold sway. Shane Byrne looked as though he had never been introduced to his jumpers at the lineout, and with no momentum from the pack, there was no platform for the backs to make inroads into the All Blacks' defence. Forwards coach Andy Robinson offered no excuses for a poor display in which New Zealand got to grips much better with the appalling conditions.

With the help of some desperate defence, and two interventions by the video referee which went their way, the Lions managed to keep the deficit to just 11–0 at the break. Ali Williams went over on the half-hour mark, and the man who'd kept the great Andrew Mehrtens out of the side, new golden boy Dan Carter, added two penalties. Minutes into the second half it was over as a contest. A third Carter penalty was quickly followed by a superb Sitiveni Sivivatu try. The latest Pacific Island sensation, Sivivatu – a cousin of Joe Rokocoko – beat the despairing attempts of Lewsey and Robinson to end a sparkling move. The Lions' only consolation was a Wilkinson penalty midway through the half. Woodward had opted to keep the Welsh half-back pairing of Dwayne Peel and Stephen Jones, playing Wilkinson at inside centre. The Lions failed to get even the basics right against an irresistible black tide, and former New Zealand coach Laurie Mains wasted little time in calling this the worst Lions team he had seen. Woodward's problems increased with the loss of flanker Richard Hill, who sustained knee ligament damage during a first-half tackle on Williams.

Above right: Tana Umaga of New Zealand is stopped by Lewis Moody and Ryan Jones of the Lions during the second Test match.

 BBC RADIO **FIVE LIVE**

I have no doubt whatsoever it was a spear tackle that has ended my tour. To have worked so hard to get this only to have it taken away so quickly is very disappointing. It was beyond the rules and regulations of the game. My real disappointment is with Tana Umaga who never came up as a captain to see how I was. I could see it happening as soon as I was in the air; it could have been worse had I landed on my head.

Even now it's difficult to talk of; the realization is I only had one minute to captain the Lions. It's hard to take.

Brian O'Driscoll

Seven changes for the second Test

In posting 109 points against Manawatu in the next tour match the Lions recorded their second biggest win ever, the 2001 side having racked up 116 against Western Australia's President's XV. The opposition was second rate, boasting only one full-time professional, but even so, it was a clinical performance. 11 players shared the 17-try haul, with Shane Williams going over five times. That put the Welsh flyer joint-second on the all-time list behind two illustrious wingers of yesteryear, David Duckham and JJ Williams, on the 1971 and 1974 tours respectively.

For the second Test in Wellington Woodward brought in seven new faces and made four positional changes, including Wilkinson back at No. 10. In the first encounter too many had failed his famous TCUP test – Thinking Correctly Under Pressure. There he had opted for experience; now he was picking the form men.

Second Test: Wellington

It began well, centre and new captain Gareth Thomas scoring a try after two minutes, converted by Wilkinson for a 7-0 lead. It was a huge fillip, the team having barely threatened the try line in the entire 80 minutes a week earlier. But while the Lions would play better than in the first match, they would ship twice as many points in a record defeat.

The chief architect was 23-year-old Carter, now acknowledged as the best fly half in world rugby. He scored two penalties, then went on a searing 50-metre run in a stunning counter-attacking move which ended in a try for Umaga. He also set up Sivivatu's second try in as many weeks, but a stalwart defensive display kept the deficit down to eight points at the break, 13–21. A ten-point blitz by Carter early in the second half took the game away from the Lions. Carter scored a penalty, then followed his own grubber kick for a touchdown, which he duly converted.

Simon Easterby scored in the corner after a ruck in the 73rd minute to reduce the arrears to 18–34, but tries from Carter and Richie McCaw in the last five minutes completed the rout. Carter's personal haul was 33 points – two tries, four conversions and five penalties, and he was involved in the All Blacks' other three scores.

Woodward described it as 'a great match'. The harsh reality was the Lions were turned over 16 times and fell off 20 tackles. One of the few crumbs of comfort was a shoulder injury for Carter, who would miss the final encounter.

Above left: *Chris Jack of New Zealand wins a lineout ball during the second Test match in Wellington.*

Opposite: *Julian White, the Lions' prop, is held by Greg Somerville during the third Test match at Eden Park.*

After the hype surrounding him [Sir Clive] after the World Cup people are taking the opportunity to knock him ... But it's a collective thing. There are so many things that go into making these tours a success. You can't pin the blame, or the success, on one person. It's a team effort. He has a huge array of coaches around him and the critical mass of players did not step up to the mark and live up to their own expectations. That's got to come into the mix too. It's a collective responsibility.

Philip de Glanville

The better team won in the end

Midweek side maintains unbeaten record

Ian McGeechan's midweek side completed its fixtures unbeaten, rounding off with a 17–13 win over a dangerous Auckland side that had beaten the Lions in 1983 and 1993. Charlie Hodgson's early penalty put him on 53 points for the tour; he would be the Lions' highest points-scorer. When he departed through injury, the Lions lost a measure of control in an error-strewn game. Cueto played himself into the Test side with a fine match. He beat three men to set up the ruck from which Martyn Williams scored the Lions' only try of the game.

Third Test: Auckland

With the series already lost, the Lions were playing for pride in the final Test at Eden Park – and trying to avoid the 'blackwash' that the 1966 and 1983 tourists suffered. Another backs shake-up meant that Dwayne Peel was the only man to play in all three internationals in the same position. It made little difference. Even without Carter, and even playing for 20 minutes with a man short after the sin-binning of Umaga and Collins, the All Blacks comfortably wrapped up a 3–0 series win. They brushed aside an early reverse – two Stephen Jones penalties in the first ten minutes – to notch five more tries, making it 12 in total in the three matches. Two of those, from Smith and Williams, put New Zealand 14–6 ahead when Umaga was off the field for killing the ball at a ruck. The captain returned to go over twice, either side of half-time, effectively ending the contest. A maul took Moody over the line on the hour to make it 31–19, but the fact that two of the Lions' three Test tries came from forward drives was a telling statistic. Rico Gear pounced on a Greenwood error to score in the dying seconds, and Luke McAlister – the All Blacks' third-string fly half – popped over his fifth conversion.

Below: Sir Clive Woodward, the Lions' head coach (l), with team manager Bill Beaumont, as they leave the pitch after losing the third Test match 38–19 at Eden Park.

Opposite: Victorious All Blacks' captain Tana Umaga lifts the DHL Lions Series Trophy after the third Test.

Inquest

As the dust settled on a disappointing tour, the inquest began. Was the squad too large and unwieldy? Some mooted that a smaller party geared only to Test match success might have produced better results. But that called into question the midweek fixtures, whose continuation was integral to the very ethos of Lions rugby. All Blacks coach Graham Henry – who led the 2001 Lions tour – had a simpler explanation: that the game had moved on since the 2003 World Cup. As Sir Clive Woodward switched footballing codes to become technical director at Southampton, the only incontrovertible fact was the unique nature of the Lions brand. Next port of call in the four-yearly jamboree: South Africa 2009.

This is a fantastic group of players. We gave everything but New Zealand's skill levels are above ours and I think the better team won in the end.

The Lions are different. It's not like coaching a national team when you can build things and build things – you have to try and do something special in a few weeks.

There are not many things I would change. We've lost, and I accept that. I have had my go at it. The biggest thing I've had to learn is to start with the Test side from day one. I'd also try and squeeze a few more games in.

Sir Clive Woodward

Results

International Matches:

New Zealand 21-3 Lions
(Jade Stadium, Christchurch, 25 June 2005)

New Zealand 48-18 Lions
(Westpac Stadium, Wellington, 2 July 2005)

New Zealand 38-19 Lions
(Eden Park, Auckland, 9 July 2005)

New Zealand Maori 19-13 Lions
(Waikato Stadium, Hamilton, 11 June 2005)

Wellington 6-23 Lions
(Westpac Stadium, Wellington, 15 June 2005)

Otago 19-30 Lions
(Carisbrook, Dunedin, 18 June 2005)

Southland 16-26 Lions
(Rugby Park Stadium, Invercargill, 21 June 2005)

Tour Matches:

Bay Of Plenty 20-34 Lions
(Rotorua International Stadium, 4 June 2005)

Taranaki 14-36 Lions
(Yarrow Stadium, New Plymouth, 8 June 2005)

Manawatu 6-109 Lions
(Arena Manawatu, Palmerston North, 28 June 2005)

Auckland 13-17 Lions
(Eden Park, Auckland, 5 July 2005)

DES LYNAM MEETS

Clive Woodward

I could have played football but ended up playing rugby

Despite all that you've achieved in rugby, your first love was football, wasn't it?

That's right. I didn't play rugby until I was 15. York City's my team. I spent years standing on the terraces at Bootham Crescent watching the likes of Ted MacDougall and Phil Boyer.

Did you play yourself in those days?

Absolutely. In fact, it was one of the reasons why I was sent to boarding school. The football was going very well but I'd given up on the academic side completely. My dad panicked and took one of the benefits of being an air force officer by having his son sent away to school. And there they only played rugby.

So you were thrown into rugby, as it were?

When I first played the game I really didn't like it because I was quite small and it's tough, even at schoolboy level. But to survive at any typical boarding school you have to be good at sport so I persevered, and after a year or so I got used to the game and really liked it.

How good do you think you could have been as a soccer player?

You never know, and that's the kind of thing you do regret. I could see why my parents did it. The headmaster was saying that this guy is a potential university student, but all he does is play football. So my dad took the decision to get me away from the round ball. I rebelled for a time but then realized you couldn't beat the system. So I started playing rugby and eventually became pretty good. But I still look back and think 'What if…?'

What were the first signs of you being good at rugby?

When you play at school you pick the game up quickly. I think most talented kids could probably go into various sports in their early teens, and I was no different. I could have played football and ended up playing rugby. But I enjoyed all sports: cricket, tennis, golf.

What position did you play?

I started as a scrum-half because I was tiny. It was a classic situation that small kids played scrum-half, the big kids prop forward and second row, and the kids that couldn't play were stuck on the wing. By the age of 18 I was a lot taller, and when I left school I started playing fly-half and centre.

I was quite quick, I represented Wales at 400m. I think in most sports if you've got pace you've got a chance

You played centre for England, so you must have been pretty speedy?

Yes, I was quite quick. I represented Wales at 400m – that's where my school was. I think in most sports if you've got pace you've got a chance.

You played for some top clubs, but then you went to Australia and played there for several years.

Yes. Obviously I loved playing for England, but you've got to remember in those days it was an amateur game. When I could see the England side dropping off, I had to make a decision. I'd worked for Xerox since leaving university, and one day I got a call saying there was a job with the company going in Sydney. I thought it was a no-brainer. I could work and play rugby as well. I stayed there five years, and had a fantastic time. Australia's just a wonderful place to live and the sport is brilliant; it's the only country I'd live in outside England.

Was that your entree into coaching, playing in Australia, watching them coach there and the way they played the game?

I always had it in the back of my mind to go into coaching eventually. I did a Sports Science degree at Loughborough and a year's teaching training, so obviously I loved the teaching and coaching side. But rugby was an amateur sport, so you played – and coached – for fun. I played for the first couple of years in Australia, but gave up when I was 30, which in Australian terms is very old! That's when I started dabbling in coaching.

And when you came back, you started coaching here?

Yes. I came back in 1990, and the game went professional in 1996. I started off at Henley, but it was always just for fun. I set up my own finance company, and that was my daytime job; coaching rugby was pure enjoyment.

How did the England job come about?

The coaching went pretty well, first at Henley, then with London Irish and Bath. Every side I coached seemed to do pretty well, and I was also coaching the England U-21s when the game went professional.

That was a very contentious issue wasn't it?

Hugely contentious, and it was very much pushed by the southern hemisphere teams, who saw that the game had to go professional because there was so much underhand dealing going on.

There was so much finance involved in it, wasn't there, and that money had to go somewhere, so it might as well have gone to the players?

Correct. When I played for England there was always a full house at Twickenham. There was a lot of revenue, and to take the sport to a new level the game had to go professional, but there's no doubt the people at Twickenham were caught unawares. It was a year before they decided to appoint a full-time coach. There was no process of applying for the job. How, or why, I got it I don't really know. I literally got a phone call one day and was summoned to Twickenham and they offered it to me. It was a huge decision to give up a successful business career, and all my business instincts told me it wasn't the right move. But it was one of those jobs that you just knew you wouldn't be offered again so I had to accept.

Were you dealing with professional players straight away?

Most of the top players had been snapped up by the clubs. In the southern hemisphere the unions signed the players, but here the RFU wasn't ready, so the club owners stepped in. By the time I became coach in September 1997, the Johnsons, Dallaglios and their ilk were all full-time professionals, which was great. When it was an amateur game, there was always an excuse. I think England were the great amateur team. Once the game went professional, England had the opportunity to become the great professional side – which I think is what we ended up achieving.

Once the game went professional, England had the opportunity to become the great professional side – which I think is what we ended up achieving

Above: Clive Woodward fields questions from the media over the team's heavy defeat by the All Blacks in the second Test match in Wellington. The All Blacks thumped the Lions 48–18 to take a 2–0 lead in the three-match series.

Opposite: *Woodward points out the spear tackle on Lions captain Brian O'Driscoll by New Zealand All Blacks captain Tana Umaga and Keven Mealamu, during a press conference.*

How much better are the players today than they were, say, five years before it turned pro?

Oh, hugely. If you see these guys stripped, they are just massive, and that can only happen by being a full-time athlete. Although rugby's a team game, I try to get across to the players that they have to train like individual Olympic athletes, setting new standards in terms of speed, fitness, power and skills. If you can train 15 people to become individual world champions, then mould them into a team, you have half a chance. So it's like breaking up the team first, because sometimes players can hide behind the team. We tried to blow that away, create huge peer-group pressure 24 hours a day, seven days a week. Then you chuck them all onto the pitch together. That gives you the chance of doing something special.

What do you say to the traditionalists who bemoan such a professional attitude, those who say that rugby used to be such a social game for everybody?

I've never seen it in better health. Rugby's expanding all over the world because of world cups and the way the game's played. You could sell out some of the club matches ten times over, and the international game is powering ahead. If rugby had stayed amateur, I think it would have just dropped away. Obviously, football is the number one sport, but rugby is fighting its corner. It's also moving into new areas around the world which haven't traditionally embraced the game.

You brought a very professional attitude to the coaching, didn't you?

I hope so. That came from my Loughborough background. Seb Coe was a contemporary of mine there, so I could see first hand what goes into making a champion. Rugby is a pretty specialist sport, so I started to employ specialists on the medical side, the nutrition side, and brought in specialist coaches.

You had a big disappointment in '99, didn't you?

A huge one. I'd been there less than two years and we lost in the quarter-finals. There was the normal vitriol which follows defeat in any sport, and calls for my head. Fortunately, one or two people at Twickenham believed in what I was doing and backed me. And then, between 1999 and 2003, came the most successful period in the history of English rugby, and not just the World Cup win. In that time we started beating New Zealand, Australia and South Africa regularly, home and away. That was the biggest turnaround because we'd always got smashed by those teams. England arrived at the World Cup as the number one ranked side in the world, and favourites to win it. Before then we seemed to be happy with fourth or fifth favourites. I didn't want that, I wanted to go as the team everyone had to beat.

How did the World Cup victory change your life?

I'm not sure it did really. It was certainly a huge relief, because all of us knew we ought to win the tournament. For us *not* to win it someone was going to have to play badly, or I was going to have to make a mistake on selection, or during the game. That's pressure. So when we actually won it – and let's face it we won it by an inch – the relief was huge. I'm not sure how I'd have coped if we'd lost.

We had the best team by a long way and still only just sneaked over the line

Perhaps it would have changed your life had you not won it.

That's probably true. Before 2003 I thought only football could attract 40,000 England supporters to a tournament halfway round the world. And when I came back I was staggered by the reaction in the country. I knew that if we were to do it all again, it meant making changes, setting new levels. The RFU couldn't understand because we'd just won the ultimate prize. But we had the best team by a long way and still only just sneaked over the line with Jonny's drop-goal in injury time. I said if we didn't make changes, we'd lose in 2007. That brought me into immediate conflict with the administrators.

And that's why you left?

Yes. They clearly weren't going to change. So I thought about it for six or seven months, finished the season and decided it was time to move on. It was the right decision because I couldn't do the job if I was exploding inside, thinking the system wasn't right. You just can't deliver as a coach in those circumstances.

Had you stayed, do you think you'd have found good enough players to win it again?

They've got the players now! The big question mark is the structure, how we're doing compared to our major rivals. The southern hemisphere teams have full control of their players, whereas we're doing it a different way. Wales and Ireland have also contracted most of their players, so they're catching up and will provide stiff competition too. France, like England, are going a different route, and I think that's why they've never won a World Cup. So I think England need to move on, but they definitely have the players.

Would you like to manage a club in the long run?

I'm not sure yet. To me it's just a fantastic opportunity. I know I've got to learn the coaching side, then I'll decide in a couple of years time whether I think I can take the ultimate step – that's assuming anyone will give me a job! I'll know pretty quickly whether it's something I can do, and if it doesn't work out maybe I'll go back to rugby union, or do something totally different.

It'll be interesting to see you having a crack at football.

I'm really looking forward to it. Football is a great game for kids because it teaches balance. I can't think of any of the great rugby union backs that I played with who weren't great footballers. Kids can also learn a lot by playing rugby as well, because of the physical side of the game. I think kids should play football one term and rugby the next till they're 13 or 14, then let them decide which game they want to play.

ZURICH PREMIERSHIP

Wasps triumph in showpiece final

The final season of Zurich's sponsorship of the English Premiership had a familiar ring to it. The teams who had dominated English rugby for the past six years finished first and second, and for the third successive season the team which topped the table lost out in the showpiece final. Leicester did the double over Wasps in the Heineken Cup, and a mere fortnight before the final ran out 45–10 victors at Welford Road; a 17–17 draw in the other league clash was Wasps' best effort in four meetings with their arch-rivals.

Left: Wasps' captain Lawrence Dallaglio shakes hands with Martin Johnson, captain of Leicester Tigers, after Wasps' convincing 39–14 victory in the Zurich Premiership final.

Above: Josh Lewsey (r) of Wasps skips over a tackle from Leicester's Martin Corry (l) during the Zurich Premiership final at Twickenham.

Opposite: Lawrence Dallaglio holds up the trophy with his team after beating Leicester Tigers in the Zurich Premiership final.

But as in the previous two campaigns, Wasps again proved themselves masters on the big occasion. Warren Gatland – in his final season with the London side before returning to New Zealand – led his men to a 43–22 victory over Sale in the semi-final, then set his sights on a hat-trick of Zurich Premiership titles in the Twickenham showdown. Wasps had beaten Gloucester in the 2003 final and Bath in 2004, both via the play-offs, and repeated the trick against the shell-shocked Tigers, spoiling Martin

Johnson's farewell party. Leicester were 13–0 down inside ten minutes and never recovered. Wasps outscored their rivals three tries to one, Tom Voyce, Mark van Gisbergen and Rob Hoadley all going over the whitewash. It was a red-letter day for the Kiwi full back van Gisbergen, who becomes available for England in the 2005–06 season. He added three conversions and five penalties for a personal haul of 26 points, Wasps eventually running out 39–14 winners.

Harlequins relegated

Relegated Harlequins made two key signings at the end of a disappointing season. Former Leicester and England forward Dean Richards (below) was appointed coach, while legendary All Blacks fly half Andrew Mehrtens (right) joined the playing staff. In July 'Quins and London Broncos announced that they were rationalizing their resources under a single umbrella club, a deal which paralleled that done by Leeds' Union and League sides in 1998. The Broncos would henceforward be known as Harlequins Rugby League, playing their matches at the renamed Twickenham Stoop.

Zurich Premiership Final Table

	P	W	D	L	BP	P
Leicester	22	15	3	4	12	78
Wasps	22	15	1	6	11	73
Sale	22	13	0	9	8	60
Bath	22	12	2	8	6	58
Saracens	22	12	2	8	5	57
Gloucester	22	10	1	11	5	47
Newcastle	22	9	2	11	7	47
Leeds	22	9	0	13	7	43
Worcester	22	9	0	13	6	42
London Irish	22	8	0	14	8	40
Northampton	22	8	0	14	8	40
Harlequins	22	6	1	15	12	38

HEINEKEN CUP

Mercurial fly half Frederic Michalak was the hero in Toulouse's dramatic win over Stade Francais in the 2005 Heineken Cup final, staged at Murrayfield. Toulouse trailed their Parisian rivals for almost the entire 80 minutes before a Michalak penalty took the game into extra-time. He then landed a penalty and a dropped goal to give Toulouse an 18–12 win and a record third victory in the competition.

Officials say that they will investigate scenes that marred the after-match performance when the Toulouse coach, Guy Noves, was escorted from the pitch after trying to help a club official join in the celebrations! Toulouse became the first side to win the Heineken Cup three times after a nail-biting victory over French rivals Stade Francais at Murrayfield.

Left: *Toulouse's captain Fabien Pelous holds up the Heineken Cup after Toulouse defeated Stade Francais.*

Above: *Frederic Michalak of Toulouse kicks a penalty during the Heineken Cup final.*

POWERGEN CUP

Bath 12 Leeds 20

Leeds flirted perilously with relegation in 2004–05, propping up the Zurich Premiership table in April in a campaign that would see them lose 13 of their 22 league fixtures. But the Tykes saved their best form for the cup, reaching their first Twickenham final when tries from Chris Bell and David Doherty helped them to a 15–6 win over London Irish in the semis.

There they met cup kings Bath, ten-time winners of the competition between 1984 and 1996. The West Country club made it to their first final in nine years with a thrilling extra-time victory over Gloucester at Kingsholm. The game looked set for a dropped goal shoot-out when an Andy Williams kick-and-chase try broke the deadlock in the final minute of overtime.

Bath went into clash with Leeds as overwhelming favourites. The record books showed that when Bath reached a cup final, they departed with the trophy, although in their previous visit to Twickenham, the 2004 Premiership play-off, they had gone down to Wasps.

Leeds were hampered by the loss of England star Iain Balshaw and Phil Christophers in the first half, Balshaw's thigh injury eventually costing him a place on the Lions tour. Even so, the underdogs barked to great effect, stunning Bath with a 20-point blitz in the first 40 minutes. There were tries from Chris Bell, who pounced on a Gordon Ross chip, and a 70-metre interception touchdown from South African winger Andre Snyman. Ross converted both and added two penalties to give the Tykes a 20–9 half-time lead from which Bath never recovered.

Leeds still had to avoid the drop for their famous victory to earn them a Heineken Cup place, eventually pulling clear to end the season five points ahead of relegated Harlequins.

Below: Leeds celebrate after winning the Powergen Cup final.

Opposite left: Tom Biggs and Chris Bell of Leeds take down Joe Maddock of Bath.

Opposite right: A dejected looking Iain Balshaw of Leeds sits on the sidelines after injuring his leg.

Quarter-finals:

Sale	23-24	Bath
Gloucester	21-0	Bristol
Northampton	19-24	Leeds
Saracens	15-21	London Irish

Semi-finals:

Leeds	15-6	London Irish
Gloucester	19-24	Bath

Final:

Bath	12-20	Leeds

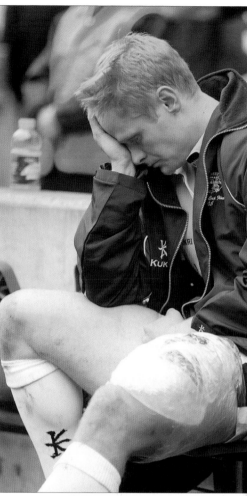

Farrell crosses over

In March 2005 Andy Farrell became the latest high-profile rugby star to cross codes. The 29-year-old Wigan and Great Britain captain joined Saracens and was set to be fast-tracked into the England set-up, with the 2007 World Cup the ultimate objective.

I'm relieved that the medical people finally found out what the problem was and that we have got the operation out of the way. Now I can set my mind on the rehabilitation needed to get myself fully fit again.

Andy Farrell
Saracens former Rugby League star faces fighting his way back to fitness after an operation on his damaged toe.

RUGBY SUPER LEAGUE

Saints march on despite Millward's exit

For the first two-thirds of the season the form sides were Leeds Rhinos – the 2004 Grand Final winners – and St Helens. Saints recovered from the shock of losing coach Ian Millward mid-season to hold off both their Yorkshire rivals and the team which finished the campaign on a storming run, Bradford Bulls. Brian Noble's side claimed eight wins on the spin, including a 32–18 victory over Saints on the last day of the regular season. That was Daniel Anderson's first taste of defeat since taking over at Knowsley Road; it was also a result which confirmed third place for the Bulls.

Bulls gunning for fifth Grand Final appearance

A fifth successive appearance in the Grand Final was still on the cards for Brian Noble's men, but this time they would have to do it the hard way; in the four previous campaigns the Bulls had reached the showpiece having ended the regular season in either first or second place.

Warrington, boosted at the tail-end of the campaign by the arrival of the world's best player, scrum half Andrew Johns, clinched their play-off place with superb victories over Leeds and Hull. In their final match Warrington scored a great 30–16 win in the Challenge Cup winners' back yard, but that result was reversed when the two teams met a week later at the Halliwell Jones Stadium in the first eliminator. A Nathan Blacklock hat-trick rocked Warrington, and a superb try by Johns was nothing more than a consolation as John Kear's men piled on the agony in the last quarter. Final score: Warrington 6–40 Hull FC.

Worst season for two decades

In their last league match London Broncos thrashed relegated Widnes Vikings 68–10 to secure the final play-off place, the Broncos edging out Wigan Warriors on points difference. Wigan had enjoyed a good run-in – five wins in their last six – but it wasn't enough to prevent 2005 going down as the Lancashire club's worst year in two decades; not since 1984 had Wigan finished outside the top six.

Opposite: Willie Talau (c) of St Helens is congratulated on his try by Paul Wellens (l) during the Engage Super League match between St Helens and London Broncos at Knowsley Road.

Right: Paul Deacon of Bradford breaks through Kirk Yeaman of Hull's tackle during the Engage Super League match between Bradford Bulls and Hull FC at the Odsal Stadium.

Swansong for Broncos

The Broncos reached the play-offs for only the second time in the club's history, a remarkable achievement at the end of a season overshadowed by massive debts and winding-up orders. It was the final flourish after 25 years on the Rugby League stage, for the Broncos' name was about to disappear, the club reappearing as Harlequins RL in 2006, playing at The Stoop. The wheels came off against the in-form Bulls at the first play-off hurdle, Lesley Vainikolo and Iestyn Harris both scoring twice in the Bulls' 44–22 victory. Even so, the Broncos had acquitted themselves admirably in their final outing before their proud name was consigned to the history books.

We all know what a player like Sean [Long] can do but Saints have got some very good youngsters to call on. It can be harder to defend against these younger ones. You know what to expect from Sean but some of these youngsters are an unknown quantity, which makes life difficult.

Kevin Sinfield

insisting that St Helens will be a very tough proposition in the play-off battle

POWERGEN CHALLENGE CUP

Hull break big four stranglehold

Since Halifax's 1987 victory, only one name outside Rugby League's Big Four had appeared on the Challenge Cup. Sheffield Eagles were rank outsiders in 1998 when they faced mighty Wigan, the team which had dominated the sport for over a decade. Eagles coach John Kear masterminded that shock, and he repeated the trick in 2005 with Hull FC.

Kear had steered Hull to an impressive top four spot in Super League, but few would have backed them to go all the way in the Challenge Cup, particularly since Bradford Bulls, St Helens and Leeds were all to stand in the way of the club's first success in the competition since their victory over Widnes in the 1982 final.

Hull weather erupting Volcano

The Bulls, Hull's fifth round victims, were rocked by a four-try blitz that saw them trail 20–0. Brian Noble's men staged a marvellous fightback after the break, including two tries from Lesley Vainikolo. But not even an eruption by the Volcano could spoil Hull's day as they ran out 26–24 winners.

Leeds and Saints cruised into the last eight, with routine wins over SM Pia and York City Knights respectively. Saints, winners of five trophies in as many seasons, were also in the news for all the wrong reasons. Coach Ian Millward was suspended for 'gross misconduct', alleged swearing incidents which were eventually upheld. His exit from Knowsley Road paved the way for the arrival of former New Zealand national team coach Daniel Anderson. The script then took a mouth-watering turn as Millward moved to Saints' bitter rivals Wigan, where former star player Denis Betts was having a difficult time. Almost inevitably, the Challenge Cup draw threw them together, the stand-out tie of the last eight and a repeat of the 2004 final. In fact, the game failed to live up to the billing as Saints put 75 points on a team struggling for form.

Opposite: Hull celebrate their win after the Powergen Challenge Cup final against Leeds Rhinos at the Millennium Stadium.

Left: Ewan Dowes of Hull FC is tackled during the Powergen Challenge Cup fifth round match between Hull FC and the Bradford Bulls at the KC Stadium.

Fairytale run for Toulouse

In beating Salford in the fifth round, London Broncos had notched up their first win on the road against Super League opposition. The Rhinos proved to be a much tougher nut to crack in the quarters, the Broncos going down 32–12. Hull had a brief respite from top-class opposition as they eased past Leigh Centurions, who would be relegated from Super League long before the end of the season with their 'points for' column still in single figures. Meanwhile, Toulouse were providing the competition with a David-and-Goliath sub-plot, the French outfit overcoming Widnes to become the first team from that country to reach the last four of a Challenge Cup.

When the semi-final draw kept Saints and Leeds apart, they looked odds-on to meet at the Millennium Stadium on 27 August. Leeds duly booked their place, courtesy of a 56–18 victory over Toulouse. But it was by no means a stroll for the Super League leaders and reigning world champions, who had been widely tipped to rack up a record Challenge Cup score over a team made up mostly of part-timers. As it was, Wigan's 71–10 hammering of Bradford in the 1992 semi-final still stood at the end of an absorbing 80-minute contest, one which the Rhinos only ran away with in the latter stages.

Leeds reach 20th final

Coached by former Wales international Justin Morgan, Toulouse were in inspired form, taking a shock lead in the second minute through Adrien Viala. When Chris McKenna levelled the score and Rob Burrow converted, most expected Leeds to shrug off their early jitters. But Toulouse skipper James Wynne held off two Leeds tacklers to restore the French side's advantage, and even when they shipped two more tries, through Gareth Ellis and Danny McGuire, Toulouse refused to fold. Sebastien Raguin, a parking attendant by trade, scored a terrific solo try, and his side trailed just 22–18 at the break. Unsurprisingly, the part-timers faded in the second half while the Rhinos, no doubt spurred on by some harsh words from coach Tony Smith, went on to score 34 unanswered points after the break. Leeds ran in ten tries in all to reach their 20th Challenge Cup final, but Toulouse won all the plaudits for an extraordinary first-half performance.

Below: Mark Smith of Widnes Vikings scores a try during the Powergen Challenge Cup quarter-final match between Toulouse Olympique XIII and Widnes Vikings at the Stade des Minimes.

My back was tightening up and I had stomach cramp. All I could remember was the Don Fox incident. I've no idea how that got in my mind so I thought I'd get it over and done with. I looked at the clock when Cooky scored and there were only three minutes left. Once I'd kicked the goal there were only a few seconds so I knew we were almost home. It didn't dawn on me that I'd just sealed the cup and I don't think it will for a while to come.

Danny Brough

First cup win over Saints for 69 years

First cup win over Saints for 69 years

The other semi was always going to be a much closer affair, Saints and Hull standing second and third in Super League at the time. Saints were hot favourites, though. A fifth successive semi-final appearance made this a routine day out for the fans; Hull, on the other hand, hadn't got this far for five years and were bidding to reach the final for the first time since 1985. History was also on Saints' side: they hadn't lost a Challenge Cup tie to Hull since 1936.

But John Kear, no respecter of reputations, did it again. Hull took an 8–2 half-time lead, Shayne McMenemy going over after a great slip pass from man-of-the-match Paul Cooke. When Jamie Lyon pounced on a Sean Long bomb that the Hull defence failed to deal with, it looked as though the comeback kings were going to produce one of their famous turnarounds. Paul Sculthorpe's conversion tied the scores but Cooke added a penalty and a superb runaround try from a great offload by McMenemy, and the latter then went over the whitewash for his second score of the match. Hull suddenly held a 22–8 lead, a considerable amount of daylight even for the star-studded holders. Former Brisbane Broncos star Motu Tony and Richard Horne added the final nails in Saints' coffin in the last ten minutes. Horne's try was created by a piece of Stephen Kearney magic, the 32-year-old Kiwi in his final season with Hull.

Above: John Kear, coach of Hull, celebrates his team's win during the Powergen Challenge Cup semi-final between Hull FC and St Helens at the Galpharm Stadium.

Below: Motu Tony of Hull following his try during the Powergen Challenge Cup semi-final match.

I've let myself down and I've let the team down. The ankle's been well all week and in the warm-up everything seemed fine. In hindsight, it might not have been the best thing to do. When you have that decision to make, it's not easy to pull out. It just got worse as the game went on. Full credit to Hull, they capitalized on some of things that we couldn't do. I think the better side won. They achieved the dream they've been after.

Keith Senior

History and form-book favour Rhinos

In simply reaching the final Hull had achieved no mean feat, the first team outside the Big Four to reach the showpiece since London Broncos in 1999. Both history and the form book suggested that Kear's men would have to be content with the runners-up spot. Hull had won only three of the 15 Challenge Cup meetings between the sides, and Leeds had come out on top on the two occasions they had met in the final, albeit way back in 1910 and 1923. More ominous for the Millennium Stadium clash, Leeds had won both home and away in 2005 and were unbeaten in ten head-to-head meetings. Hull also suffered a late blow when full-back Shaun Briscoe went down with appendicitis just days before the match.

Tony Smith had a less clear cut injury worry as centre Keith Senior – a member of Kear's victorious Eagles side in 1998 – was struggling with an ankle injury. In the end Senior took the field, a decision he was later to regret as he limped out of the action at half-time.

Most dramatic final ever

When the Rhinos drew first blood through a Marc Calderwood penalty try and Kevin Sinfield conversion, few would have believed this would be probably the most dramatic final in the competition's 108-year history. Hull levelled through Motu Tony, who went over in the corner after gathering Shayne McMenemy's crossfield kick, palmed on by Richard Whiting. Scrum half Danny Brough added the conversion in what was to be a faultless kicking display. The former York City Knights player had taken a pay cut to swap his building and plumbing work for a full-time playing contract. Less than a year later he would take possession of a Challenge Cup winners medal and play a crucial role in the victory.

Suicidal error from Bai

Five minutes after the break Brough added another two points after Gareth Raynor scored from an assist by stand-in full back Nathan Blacklock. Man of the match Kevin Sinfield sent prop Danny Ward over, then kicked Leeds level at 12–12. Hull restored their advantage when Whiting gleefully pounced on Marcus Bai's mind-boggling decision to offload in his in-goal area. And Brough then struck a sweet left-footed drop goal, only one point but such a crucial one in the final analysis.

On 65 minutes Marc Calderwood's coruscating break from a scrum gave him his 103rd try in 138 games for Leeds. Sinfield converted, and just three minutes later Bai made amends for his earlier aberration, taking a high ball and touching down under the posts. It was now 24–19 to the favourites, the first time the Rhinos had led since the ninth minute.

Brough casts aside Fox memories

But Hull had the final word. In the 77th minute Paul Cooke, fed by Horne, sold a lovely dummy and gave a clenched fist salute before dropping on the ball under the sticks. Brough had an easy kick to give Hull a one-point lead, though memories went back to Don Fox's famous Wembley miss for Wakefield in 1968. Brough made no such mistake. Kevin Sinfield's last-gasp drop goal effort was charged down, and the bloodied Leeds skipper had to be content with picking up the Lance Todd Trophy.

Hull had their hands on the cup for the first time since 1982, and only the third time in the club's history. John Kear, the Challenge Cup king with the Midas touch, became the first coach since Alex Murphy in the 1970s to win the trophy with two different clubs.

Opposite: Paul Cooke of Hull celebrates scoring the winning try during the Powergen Challenge Cup final. between Hull FC and Leeds Rhinos at the Millennium Stadium.

Left: Richard Swain, the Hull captain, raises the trophy after his side win the Powergen Challenge Cup final.

RESULTS

Fifth Round

Hull	26-24	Bradford Bulls
Leeds	70-0	SM Pia
St Helens	62-0	York City Knights
Wigan	16-10	UTC
Toulouse	32-18	Doncaster Dragons
Barrow Raiders	8-50	Widnes Vikings
Leigh Centurions	40-20	Halifax
Salford	12-26	London Broncos

Quarter-finals

Leeds Rhinos	32-12	London Broncos
St Helens	75-10	Wigan
Toulouse	40-24	Widnes
Hull FC	46-14	Leigh Centurions

Semi-finals

Leeds Rhinos	56-18	Toulouse
Hull FC	34-8	St Helens

Final

Leeds Rhinos	24-25	Hull FC

BBC RADIO FIVE LIVE

We're just delighted that the players have hung in there. I thought that it was reward for the self-belief. It was like a boxing match. Both teams were out on the ropes. We felt that if we could get the right field positions, something would come for us – and it did for Paul Cooke and it's a marvellous feeling. To know that you've put out Wakefield, Bradford, Leeds – it's absolutely sensational!

John Kear

Hull coach, following their last minute win in the Challenge Cup against Leeds Rhinos

SNOOKER

Qualifier Murphy defies 150–1 odds

The 30th and last world final to be sponsored by Embassy provided shocks and drama in abundance, producing a new champion and snooker superstar. Insiders had long known all about Shaun Murphy's potential, yet the 22-year-old from Rotherham had never won a match at the Crucible, had to play two qualifiers just to get to Sheffield and went into the tournament as a 150–1 outsider.

Williams makes 147

Murphy's first-round victory over Chris Small was overshadowed by events elsewhere. There was Mark Williams' 147 against Robert Milkins, the sixth Crucible maximum earning the former title-holder a cool £161,000. Reigning champion Ronnie O'Sullivan edged the impressive Stephen Maguire 10–9, a match that was billed as a possible first-round shock. But the biggest cheer was for Paul Hunter, recently diagnosed as suffering from bowel cancer. He went down to Michael Holt but the very fact that he decided to participate was an extraordinary achievement.

Champions fall by wayside

Three former champions – Higgins, Doherty and Williams – all bowed out in the second round, as did Jimmy White, beaten 13–5 by Matthew Stevens. Shaun Murphy had accounted for Higgins, and in the quarters came up against 47-year-old Steve Davis, whom he had once trailed after as a starry-eyed young autograph hunter. Murphy blitzed his hero 13–4.

The last eight saw two giants crash out: seven-time champion Stephen Hendry, Stevens' latest victim, and the Rocket himself. O'Sullivan showed flashes of brilliance in going 8–2 up against Peter Ebdon but wasn't at ease with himself, his composure further unsettled by his opponent's pedestrian play. Ebdon ground out an attritional victory, while O'Sullivan said it was a relief as much as a disappointment and spoke of taking a year out of the game.

The other quarter-final matched Alan McManus and Ian McCulloch. The 33-year-old 'Lancashire Hot Pot' had already put out the 2004 runner-up Graham Dott and two-time champion Mark Williams. His superb form continued with a 13–8 win.

He's only 22, plays the game really fast and hits the ball hard. He's got a fantastic future. I came here to win but I didn't do that. I'll be back. I will win the World Snooker Championship before my career ends.

Matthew Stevens

Opposite: Shaun Murphy, the lowest-ranked finalist since Terry Griffiths, on his way to the World title.

Below: Peter Ebdon in action during his first-round match against Quinten Hann.

Favourite Stevens forges ahead

Two qualifiers reach semis

Of the semi-finalists, Ebdon was the only man who had lifted the trophy. Stevens also had a proven Crucible pedigree, but few would have predicted that two qualifiers would make it to the last four. Ebdon was up against Murphy, while Stevens, reaching the semis for the fifth time in six years, took on McCulloch.

Ebdon and McCulloch made the early running, but both matches were locked at 12–12 after three sessions. Murphy, fearless with his long potting and scoring very heavily, reeled off five frames to win 17–12. It meant that a third former champion had fallen at his hands. Meanwhile, Stevens came within three pots of grabbing a share of Williams' maximum break prize. Despite the missed blue, he went 14–13 ahead and clinched the match 17–14.

The final thus pitted Stevens, world No. 6, against Murphy, 42 places below him and the lowest-ranked finalist since Terry Griffiths in 1979. It was now certain that a new name would be added to the 78-year-old trophy. Stevens, the bookies' favourite, opened up a four-frame lead in the second session. Murphy, who had never played a match longer than 19 frames, was in uncharted water but hit back brilliantly on the second day. He levelled the match at 11–11, a sparkling run which included a 137 total clearance, his tenth century of the championship. His 11th ton came in the first frame of the final session and he also took the next to go in front for the first time since the opening frame. It was Stevens playing catch-up, and he took frame 32 to make it 16–16; it was now best of three for the coveted title and the £250,000 prize.

Second youngest champion

Murphy took the two frames he required with breaks of 97 and 83, becoming the second youngest world champion in history. Hendry had been 21 when he claimed the crown for the first time; many were predicting that Murphy could go on to have a similar impact on the game.

This means so much to me and it is something I have dreamed about since I was eight years old and first started to pick up a cue.

I knew that I had the capability to win. It wasn't anything more than that. I kept believing and going for my shots... I was very fortunate. I was quite happy in myself. I hadn't played very well in either of the first two sessions, but I felt that was because I was really nervous. It was my first final – let alone the Embassy World Final and I had all these things to contend with – the whole razzmatazz of playing in the final and still having to play a competitive match of snooker. It was very, very difficul t... I said to my friends, 'Maybe tomorrow will be my day. Today hasn't been'... Looks like I was right!

Shaun Murphy

Opposite: *Matthew Stevens in action during the final against Shaun Murphy.*

Left: *A dream come true: World Embassy Snooker champion Shaun Murphy.*

Nine world records fall

British swimmers came away from the 11th FINA World Championships in Montreal after securing three bronze medals. A determined David Davies fought a hard battle against the Americans in the 1500 metres freestyle, a distance for which he currently holds the British and European record, clocking up a time of 14 minutes 48.11 seconds. Meanwhile, teammate Liam Tancock broke his British record achieving a time of 25.02 seconds in the 50 metres backstroke. In the women's races Caitlin McClatchey won her bronze in the 400 metres freestyle in a time of 4 minutes 7.25 seconds, an event for which she currently holds the British record.

During the Championships nine world records were smashed and Australian Grant Hackett and Kirsty Coventry from Zimbabwe eventually emerged as the top swimmers of the meet. Hackett won three gold, a silver and a bronze, setting a new world record in the 800 metres freestyle, while Coventry came away with two gold and two silver medals.

World Championships

British Results

David Davies	1500m freestyle	Bronze	14 minutes 48.11 seconds
Liam Tancock	50m backstroke	Bronze	25.02 seconds
Caitlin McClatchey	400m freestyle	Bronze	4 minutes 7.25 seconds

Below left: Grant Hackett 1st (c) of Australia stands with David Davies 3rd (r) and Larsen Jensen 2nd of the USA following the 1500m freestyle.

Below right: Caitlin McClatchey after receiving the silver medal in the 400m freestyle final.

Opposite: Britain's Liam Tancock starts in a heat of the 50m Backstroke.

It's pretty awesome for my first world championships. All the big boys were there and hopefully I have put my mark down on world swimming.

Liam Tancock

I am delighted with my bronze medal and my time because my aim was to go under 14 minutes 50 seconds, which is a big milestone in 1500 metre swimming.

David Davies

Tennis

WIMBLEDON

Hat-trick for flawless Federer

On the eve of the Wimbledon championship, four-times Grand Slam winner Roger Federer was named Laureus World Sportsman of the Year. Despite having failed to add to his haul of majors thus far in 2005, Federer remained the most feared player on the men's circuit, particularly at SW19, where he had been unbeaten since 2002. Two weeks later, that view was fully justified as the Swiss dropped just one set en route to his third successive title, at times playing sublime tennis.

Second-round defeat for Henman

Neither Greg Rusedski nor Tim Henman had to concern themselves with finding a way to beat the Federal Express; both went out in Round Two. Henman, four times a Wimbledon semi-finalist and seeded six this time round, fought back from a two-set deficit to beat Finland's Jarkko Nieminen in his opening match. Next time out he crashed to Dmitry Tursunov, a player ranked outside the top 150, losing 8–6 in the fifth.

Henman bemoaned the use of a different kind of grass at the All England Club, and heavier balls, a combination which he felt had made the game slower. That wasn't to the advantage of the serve-volleyers; but it was good for base-liners – and for longer rallies, which made for better television.

Whether or not there was a commercial conspiracy at work, it was the first time in a decade that Henman hadn't been the last Brit to go out of the tournament, and there was the usual outpouring from the doom-mongers suggesting that the man who had carried the nation's hopes for so long had missed his chance of ever being crowned Wimbledon champion.

 BBC RADIO FIVE LIVE

Not being able to finish it off and come out with a win is disappointing. I have to give him a lot of credit. I didn't think he could serve that consistently for so long a period of time and that was a big, big factor. There is no comparison between today's match and the way I played in the first round. I knew that I had to pick up my game. The guy was hitting aces, hitting the line, hitting unreturnable serves. You sit here now and feel somewhat numb – but what can you do? I would think about it [quitting Wimbledon] if all of you who were ninth best in the world quit with me – but there wouldn't be many of you left would there?

Tim Henman
following his defeat by
Dmitry Tursunov in the second round

Opposite: Roger Federer holds the winner's trophy.

Left: Tim Henman in his match with Dmitry Tursunov.

Murray throws away two-set lead

Rusedski rues decision

Rusedski fared no better. He went out at the same stage to No. 11 seed Joachim Johansson, the four-set defeat including two tie-breaks. The players were consulted over the murky Centre Court conditions, and Rusedski must have been left ruing his decision to carry on.

That left junior sensation Andrew Murray to fly the flag in the men's draw. The 18-year-old, who hailed from Dunblane but had been based at a Barcelona academy for three years, opened with a straight-sets win over the Swiss George Bastl. That set up a clash with Czech Radek Stepanek, the 14th seed. It was Murray's first appearance on a show court, only his sixth match on the ATP tour and he was up against an opponent ranked 299 places above him. Yet the Scot blasted his opponent off the court, 6–4 6–4 6–4, the biggest scalp of his career thus far.

That set up a third-round Centre Court encounter with the 2002 beaten finalist David Nalbandian. Murray went two sets up, standing on the verge of a place in last 16. He wasn't able to close the match out, losing in five, but the first Thursday of the 2005 championship seemed to many to be the day on which the mantle passed from the old guard to the new. After the tournament the Scot's ranking rocketed from 312 to 213, and a maiden win on the Challenger tour a month later pushed him up to 164. John McEnroe was among those luminaries who were hugely impressed with Murray's game and temperament, the three-times champion predicting that he would soon break into the top 50.

Nadal fails to reproduce clay-court form

Neither of the 2005 Grand Slam winners progressed very far. Rafael Nadal, the man who had taken Roland Garros by storm the previous month, was seeded four on the strength of his extraordinary clay-court record. His only excursion onto the grass, in 2003, had ended in a third-round defeat at the hands of Paradorn Srichiphan. In the event it transpired Nadal was not yet ready to make the transition as he failed to find a way past Luxembourg's Gilles Muller in Round Two.

Australian Open champion Marat Safin, seeded 5, had threatened never to return to Wimbledon after his first-round exit in 2004. Safin did somewhat better this time, though a third-round defeat against Feliciano Lopez wasn't about to kindle a love affair with grass.

In the last 16 Lopez put out the dangerous Mario Ancic, the last man to beat Federer at Wimbledon, back in 2002. He became the first Spaniard to reach a Wimbledon quarter-final for 33 years, but there he found Lleyton Hewitt too hot to handle.

Left: Greg Rusedski serves to Joachim Johansson during the third day of Wimbledon.

Hewitt fumes at seeding

Hewitt, the world No. 2, was less than happy at being seeded three at Wimbledon. It meant that in the semis he would have to face Federer, who had got the better of him on seven successive occasions in the past two years. Hewitt duly got the chance to make it eighth time lucky after the Swiss beat Chile's Fernando Gonzalez in the last eight. Gonzalez was the only man not to have dropped a set in reaching the quarters, yet he had little answer to the reigning champion, who was in imperious form. Federer won 7–5 6–2 7–6.

In the other half of the draw, No. 2 seed Andy Roddick needed five sets to put out Sebastien Grosjean in their quarter-final clash.

Grosjean drew first blood, taking a set off the big-serving American for the first time in three years. Roddick took a two-sets-to-one advantage, then faltered in the fourth before closing out the match to reach his third successive Wimbledon semi-final.

Roddick's opponent in the last four was Sweden's Thomas Johannson. The 12th seed celebrated reaching his first Wimbledon quarter-final with a straight sets win over David Nalbandian. 30-year-old Johannson, the 2002 Australian Open champion, was the oldest man to reach the last eight, and then became the first Swede to make it to the semis since Stefan Edberg 12 years earlier.

The way Murray played those first two sets was incredible. To go out on Centre Court and produce that type of tennis speaks volumes for his tennis and his ability to handle big occasions. It's frustrating at the end when it's not tennis issues that lose you the match. The tennis is there and that's the nice part about it. The other part of it – the fitness side – you can work on and solve. To go and see a kid like that go and produce it against a guy like Nalbandian was inspiring.

Mark Petchey

Above: Judy Murray (r) and Mark Petchey, mother and coach of Andrew Murray cheer him on has he plays Radek Stepanek of the Czech Republic.

Left: Andrew Murray on court.

Rain delay

Johannson was bullish about his chances of reaching the final, but went out to Roddick in a rain-affected marathon. Resuming after a delay at 6–5, Roddick let two set points slip away and Johannson capitalized, taking the opening set on a tie-break. The American cruised through the second to level, but the last two sets both went to breakers, and both to the American, who thus booked his place in his third Grand Slam final and second successive appearance in the Wimbledon showpiece.

Earlier in the year, Federer had fallen at the semi-final hurdle at both the Australian and the French. There was no mistake this time as he bludgeoned Hewitt into three-set submission in the last four here, setting up a final that vindicated the seedings and featured the same protagonists as the previous year. Hewitt's early break proved to be a false dawn as the world No. 1 beat the man ranked just below him in straight sets. The Australian had not only lost for the eighth time running to Federer, but had failed to even capture a set in their previous five meetings.

21st consecutive final victory

Roddick's record against Federer offered him little more encouragement. He went into the match having won just one of their nine matches, and three sets later the record books were amended to read 9–1 in favour of the Swiss. Federer's 6–2 7–6 6–4 win was his 21st consecutive victory in a final, this one bringing him his fifth Grand Slam title. Federer said afterwards that he played the game of his life in the 101-minute demolition job. It was near-flawless tennis. One of the many highlights was a full-blooded Roddick smash, from which Federer hit a winner.

One dropped set in seven matches – against Nicolas Kiefer – was the only blot on the landscape as Federer became only the third player of the open era to notch a hat-trick of Wimbledon victories, following in the footsteps of Borg and Sampras. He was also closing in on Borg's record of 41 consecutive wins at Wimbledon. The bookmakers wasted no time in making him red-hot favourite to make it four Wimbledon titles in a row, and few would have backed against the 23-year-old eclipsing Borg's record of five consecutive titles, achieved between 1976 and 1980.

As for Roddick, his post-match comment showed that he was struggling to think of a way of beating his arch-rival: 'Maybe I'll just punch him or something.'

I'm very impressed with Federer. He seems to be able to raise his game all the time. The thing I was disappointed with in that game was that I expected Hewitt to come in with a different game plan – he just didn't attack. In the third set he was really going to go for it and he played the better tennis. He started hitting winners, he started coming forward. He's a very good volleyer, he's quick around the net. That's the sort of play he should be doing.

Pat Cash
talking to Des Lynam

The feeling is hard to explain – it hasn't sunk in yet! During the entire match I felt that this is almost unreal – I am in another Wimbledon final, but still couldn't believe it. Then I was about to win. Once it happens, all you want to do is lie down and then enjoy that one little moment that you get where you're just exhausted and proud. It's just an incredible feeling that goes through your whole body. People were telling me – if you win this then you equal Borg. Three wins anyhow would be great and now that they're in a row – I'm speechless because Borg and Sampras were heroes and idols. It's because of them I started to play tennis and now, to be alongside them, to look at the board and see the three names underneath each other – it's just a real thrill.

Roger Federer

Opposite: Lleyton Hewitt of Australia sits down at the change of ends as fans show their support during his match against Justin Gimelstob of the USA.

Left: Andy Roddick of the USA in action against Sebastien Grosjean of France during the ninth day.

Venus back on top

As in the men's competition, the Ladies' Singles semi-finals featured three of the top four seeds. The player missing from the line-up was Serena Williams, but the last four did include a Williams, Venus recapturing the kind of form that won her back-to-back titles in 2000 and 2001. Seeded only 14 in this year's tournament, Venus put out reigning champion Maria Sharapova in the semis, then defeated top seed Lindsay Davenport in the longest women's final in Wimbledon history.

Shock exit for French champion

2001 runner-up Justine Henin-Hardenne was the early big-name casualty. Although seeded only seven, the newly crowned French Open champion was widely tipped to add a Wimbledon crown to her Grand Slam collection. A first-round defeat at the hands of Greece's Elena Daniilidou meant that the fans didn't have long to enjoy one of the sweetest backhands in the game.

On the first Thursday, Jane O'Donoghue had the dubious honour of being the last of the seven British wildcard entries to bow out of the 2005 championship. She was the only one of that number to make it through to the second round, where she took just three games off 14th seed Nathalie Dechy.

Venus exacts revenge on Craybas

No. 4 seed Serena Williams surprisingly went out to unsung compatriot Jill Craybas in Round Three. Williams had had injury problems which had kept her out of the French, but had made a late decision to compete at SW19. She struggled through her first two matches, against indifferent opposition, and was again out-of-sorts in the defeat by Craybas, an unseeded player she would normally have dispatched with ease.

Had she beaten Craybas, Serena would have set up the latest family showdown with sister Venus. As things transpired, it was left to Venus to avenge her sister's defeat, which she did with gusto: Craybas took only two games as Venus booked her place in the last eight to face Mary Pierce.

Pierce was showing some of the best form of her life, having come to SW19 on the back of reaching the final at Roland Garros. She was featuring in only her second Wimbledon quarter-final, nine years after her first appearance in the last eight. Williams, by contrast, had limped out of the French Open in the third round to 15-year-old Bulgarian sensation Sesil Karatancheva. But here the ferocious serve and punishing ground strokes were back with a vengeance, as was the winning smile as the victories kept coming. Williams romped through the first set in just 21 minutes, Pierce failing to register a game. The second couldn't have been more different. Pierce failed to convert any of her five set points, and Williams took the match courtesy of a 12–10 scoreline in a thrilling tie-break. In this kind of form it was barely conceivable that Williams' only title of the year had come on clay in Istanbul. As for the vanquished Pierce, there would be the consolation of a victory in the mixed doubles with Mahesh Bhupathi.

More Grand Slam agony for Clijsters

Yet another big gun of the women's game had to go out at the last 16 stage, as Kim Clijsters took on top seed Lindsay Davenport. The Belgian, beaten in four Grand Slam finals, had won the traditional warm-up tournament at Eastbourne and looked to have put behind her the horrendous injury problems which kept her sidelined for most of 2004. Davenport, meanwhile, was contesting her 12th Wimbledon. Champion in 1999, runner-up in 2000, Davenport hadn't won a major for five years, yet was displaying the kind of form which suggested she could end that drought at the All England Club in 2005. She broke Clijsters three times in the first set, and although she let slip a match point in the second – which the Belgian took on a tie-break – Davenport was always in control in the decider.

Opposite: Venus Williams returns a backhand to Nicole Pratt of Australia during their second round match at the 119th Wimbledon Tennis Championships.

Below: Eastbourne winner Kim Clijsters hits a shot to the UK's Katie O'Brien during their first round match.

Davenport puts out US Open champion

That victory set up a quarter-final encounter with Svetlana Kuznetsova, the reigning US Open champion and No. 5 seed. Kuznetsova was in contention until the first-set tie-break, where she was steamrollered 7–1, and the result was never in doubt thereafter. Davenport took the second 6–3.

No. 2 seed Maria Sharapova showed that her 2004 victory was no flash in the pan; nor was she any the less determined to defend her title, despite the extraordinary level of off-court attention she had received over the previous 12 months. Her 7–6 6–3 victory over Nadia Petrova in the quarter-finals was her 22nd consecutive victory on grass. The first set against her fellow Russian was a tight, serve-dominated affair, lasting almost an hour. Petrova's best chance of a break came when she was 3–5 down in the second set. But the defending champion held her nerve and served out to set up a semi-final clash with Williams.

Mauresmo squanders lead

Many were wondering whether this would be Amelie Mauresmo's year. The No. 3 seed needed barely an hour to beat Anastasia

Myskina in the last eight. Myskina, the 2004 French Open champion, was in uncharted Wimbledon waters and it showed, Mauresmo extending her head-to-head record over the Russian to 6–1.

Mauresmo, the only one of the last four not to have won a Grand Slam, had picked up the tag of the nearly-woman of women's tennis; or, more unkindly, a choker. Her third successive appearance in a Wimbledon semi-final did nothing to dispel that view.

Her match against Davenport told an all too familiar tale. In what was the players' first meeting on grass, Mauresmo squandered a set and 4–3 advantage with a break. Davenport fought back to level in a breaker, and the 1999 champion then gained the initiative. She was 5–3 up in the third when the rain came, and they had to come back the following day. It was a brief return to the court, lasting just eight points. Mauresmo served out to make it 5–4, but Davenport also held to love to reach the final for the third time.

Defending champion beaten

Meanwhile, the Venus bandwagon rolled on. It had been four long years since Williams' last Grand Slam victory, and the 25-year-old

Wimbledon Results:

Men's singles

Roger Federer SUI bts Andy Roddick USA
6-2 7-6 6-4

Ladies Singles

Venus Williams USA bts Lindsay Davenport USA
7-6 9-7

Men's Doubles

Stephen Huss (Aus) and Wesley Moodie (RSA)
Bt
Bob Bryan USA and Mike Bryan USA (2)
7-6 6-3 6-7 6-3

Ladies Doubles

Cara Black ZIM and Liezel Huber RSA (2)
Bt
Svetlana Kuznetsova RUS and Amelie Mauresmo FRA
6-2 6-1

Mixed Doubles

Mahesh Bhupati IND and Mary Pierce FRA
Bt
Paul Hanley AUS and Tatiana Perebiynis UKR
6-4 6-2

Defending champion beaten

former champion had dropped out of the top ten. Her semi-final opponent, 18-year-old Maria Sharapova, had hammered her in their last two meetings. Yet this was to be the fortnight when Williams rediscovered the form which had brought her two singles titles.

The battle between two of the game's biggest grunters was hotly contested, the first set going to a tie-break after each player dropped serve once. Williams took it 7–2, and then cruised through the second set, breaking the holder three times to close out the match 7–6 6–1. Venus thus eliminated the woman who, as a 17-year-old underdog, had prevented Serena from completing a hat-trick in the previous year's final.

Repeat of 2000 final

The final was thus a repeat of the 2000 showpiece, when Williams had beaten Davenport in straight sets. Venus's fifth appearance maintained a remarkable family record: a Williams had featured in the final in every year of the century thus far.

Although Davenport was seeded 13 places higher, it was Williams who went into the match as slight favourite. It was the world No. 1 who drew first blood, however, taking a 5–2 lead with two breaks. Williams pulled one back before Davenport closed the set out 6–4.

Davenport had a chance to serve for the match at 6–5 in the second, but Williams broke back to love, then took the breaker 7–4. Despite suffering a back problem which required treatment, Davenport was also out of the blocks quickest in the deciding set. She led 4–2 and 40–15, but Williams hit back to take the set and the match 9–7, though she later conceded she had enjoyed a slice of good fortune in mishitting a backhand winner when matchpoint down.

Williams said she always felt it was her destiny to stand at the pinnacle of the women's game once again. She certainly fought her way back to the top in spectacular style: her third Wimbledon title came after an enthralling 2 hr. 45 min. marathon, the longest women's final in the history of the championship.

Left: Defending champion Maria Sharapova in action against Sesil Karatancheva of Bulgaria during the fourth day of Wimbledon.

Above: Top seed Lindsay Davenport hits a shot to Alina Jidkova from Russia during their first round match at Wimbledon.

AUSTRALIAN OPEN

Safin ends Hewitt's Melbourne dream

No Australian had won a men's singles title in the country's home Grand Slam since Mark Edmonson's victory in 1976. In the centenary of the championship, Lleyton Hewitt seemed destined to give home fans a long-overdue win.

Seeded three, the Adelaide-born former world number one had overcome rising star Rafael Nadal in five sets to reach the last eight, where his match against David Nalbandian also went the distance. In the semis he faced Andy Roddick, the man who had accounted for Greg Rusedski in the second round. Tim Henman had fared only marginally better, going down to Nikolay Davydenko in straight sets in Round Three. It was a bitter disappointment for the British number one, seeded seven, who had beaten Davydenko in their previous two meetings.

The Hewitt-Roddick semi went the Australian's way in four sets, though two of those were tie-breaks in which the American had held mini-breaks.

'Don't ask me for advice'

Federer, the defending champion, beat four-times Australian champion Andre Agassi to reach the semis. 'He does everything well and a lot of things great,' said Agassi afterwards. 'I suggest his next opponent doesn't come to me for advice.'

The next opponent trying to derail the Federal Express was No. 4 seed Marat Safin, who had lost seven times to the world number one. But Safin celebrated his 25th birthday with a five-set victory. The Russian came within a point of defeat in the fourth-set breaker, while Federer, who was not at his best, saved six match-points before succumbing on the seventh, Safin taking the final set 9–7 in a four-and-a-half-hour thriller. It was Federer's first defeat in 27 matches.

Seven-game run proves decisive

In the final, Safin made a string of errors as Hewitt raced through the first set 6–1. But the Russian, who had lost in two of the previous three Melbourne finals, reeled off the next three sets to give him the second major of his career. The turning point came when Safin trailed 4–1 in the third. He reeled off seven straight games to take that set and go a decisive break up in the fourth.

Final score: Safin beat Hewitt 1–6 6–3 6–4 6–4.

Grunting is not ladylike, but the whole art of sport is not necessarily ladylike. When you see them fearsomely in competition like that, you're not looking for ladylike femininity. You're not looking for the wave of the fan or the waft of the parasol. You're looking for the strength, the sinew, the determination, the desire to win, to triumph, to quash their opponent, trample them into the dirt and then stand above them grunting!

Jonathan Ross

Grand Slam No. 7 for Serena

British number one Elena Baltacha went into the Australian Open ranked 185 in the world. Victories over two higher-ranked players – Slovenia's Katarina Srebotnik and Stephanie Cohen-Aloro of France – pushed her into the top 130 and made her the first British woman to reach the third round in Melbourne since Clare Wood in 1991. The glory run ended there, 21-year-old Baltacha going down to Italy's No. 15 seed Silvia Farina Elia.

Match-points saved

Of the main title contenders, Serena Williams, seeded seven, was showing the kind of form which had brought her six Grand Slams. Her last victory in a major had been Wimbledon 2003, and in the semi-final she came up against the woman who had wrested that title from her, Maria Sharapova. The 23-year-old former world number one had to save three match-points as the Russian twice served for the match, at 5–4 in the second set and the same score in the third. Serena survived those nervy moments to win the decider 8–6.

In the final she faced Lindsay Davenport, world number one and top seed, despite the fact that she hadn't won a slam since her victory in Melbourne in 2000. Davenport had been an unconvincing winner over 19th seed Nathalie Dechy in the semis, losing the first set and coming within two points of defeat in the second-set tie break. She recovered to take that, and won the deciding set 6–4.

Reversal of fortune

The final witnessed a remarkable reversal of fortune. Williams lost the first set 2–6, and to make her plight worse sustained a rib injury which required lengthy treatment. But from that point on she played inspirational tennis, while Davenport's game deserted her. Williams lost just three of the next 15 games, a love set in the decider giving Serena her second Australian title.

Final score: Williams beat Davenport 2–6 6–3.

Opposite: Marat Safin (l) of Russia and runner-up Lleyton Hewitt (r) of Australia pose following the men's final which Safin won by three sets to one.

Left: Serena Williams (l) of the US poses with runner-up and compatriot Lindsay Davenport while holding their respective awards following the women's singles final.

Above: Serena Williams reaches for a return against Lindsay Davenport in the women's singles final.

251

FRENCH OPEN

Nadal the new clay-court king

BBC RADIO FIVE LIVE

My coach, my uncle, my family – they always say the important thing is to fight, fight and never give up. I want to improve. I like to play on grass a lot. I know it's not my best surface – it's a little bit fast. I need to improve some things in my game to play better on grass and the fast courts. I want to improve my serve and volley and for that I need to play one or two tournaments before Wimbledon.

Rafael Nadal
following his victory over Mariano Puerta

Tim Henman had reached the last four on the clay at Roland Garros in 2004, but expectations of another lengthy run were dashed when the British number one fell to Peru's Luis Horna in the second round. Henman at least did better than Greg Rusedski and Andre Agassi, who were both first-round losers. Agassi, the No. 6 seed, suffered a recurrence of a long-standing back injury in his match against Jarkko Nieminen, and his 17th visit to the French Open ended with a love fifth set.

No. 2 seed Andy Roddick was another early casualty. He held a two-set advantage in his second-round match with Argentine Jose Acacuso, ranked 62 in the world, but he too went out in five.

Five clay-court titles

Rafael Nadal was the favourite to lift the title in what was his first visit to Roland Garros and only the sixth Grand Slam of his career. The Spanish prodigy had already won five clay-court titles in 2005, and went into the tournament on a 17-match unbeaten run.

A nephew of footballer Miguel Nadal, the famous 'Beast of Barcelona', he had already shown himself to be a great showman as well as fierce competitor, with his penchant for bandanas, sleeveless fluorescent tops and three-quarter length pantaloons.

Least favourite surface

Nadal, seeded four, won his way through to face top seed Roger Federer in the semis, which most commentators felt was the de facto final. Federer, who had never been beyond the quarters on his least favourite surface, had not dropped a set thus far; Nadal had let just one set slip en route to the last four.

The left-hander from Majorca celebrated his 19th birthday with a superb four-set victory over the world's best player: 6–3 4–6 6–4 7–5. It was only the third defeat of the season for Federer, one which meant he would have to wait at least one more year to add to his haul the only Grand Slam that had so far proved elusive.

Puerta back after drugs suspension

The other semi featured two unlikely players, Nikolay Davydenko, the 12th seed, and Mariano Puerta, neither of whom had reached the last four of a Grand Slam before. The unseeded Argentine, who had recently served a nine-month suspension for failing a drugs test, came through in five sets.

Puerta's fairytale return continued when he took the first set of the final on a tie-break. But Nadal powered his way to the next three sets to take the title. He became the first player since Mats Wilander to win the French at the first attempt, and the youngest winner of a grand slam since Michael Chang, who won at Roland Garros as a 17-year-old in 1989.

Men's Singles Final: Nadal beat Puerta 6–7 6–3 6–1 7–5.

No fairytale ending for Pierce

Justine Henin-Hardenne, the 2003 French Open champion, had dropped out of the world top 10 after a seven-month lay-off through illness and injury. She returned to the circuit just two months before the 2005 tournament got under way, and was immediately back in the winning groove. Seeded 10, the 23-year-old was most people's favourite to claim her second title at Roland Garros.

Williams beaten by teenage sensation

As Henin-Hardenne made sure-footed progress to the latter stages, other big names tumbled. Venus Williams crashed to 15-year-old Bulgarian Sesil Karatantcheva in the third round. Williams lost her serve nine times as she went down 6–3 1–6 1–6 to the 2004 junior champion, making her first appearance in the senior competition. Amelie Mauresmo also fell to a teenager at the same stage, Serbia's Ana Ivanovic putting out the No. 3 seed in three sets. Mauresmo's poor run in her home slam thus continued.

Defending champion Anastasia Myskina fared even worse, beaten in the first round by Maria Sanchez Lorenzo, a player ranked 109 in the world. It was the first time the holder had fallen at the first hurdle.

Pierce reaches her third final

Top seed Lindsay Davenport struggled in reaching the quarters, taken to three sets in every match. It was barely a surprise when a rejuvenated Mary Pierce got the better of her, 6–3 6–2. Pierce, a finalist in 1994 and champion in 2000, then thrilled the home fans by thrashing Elena Likhovtseva in the semis, her 6–1 6–1 victory coming in less than an hour.

Standing between Pierce and a second French title was Henin-Hardenne, who put out second seed Maria Sharapova in the quarters, then eased past Nadia Petrova 6–2 6–3 in the last four.

Inconsolable

For 30-year-old Pierce, the final was a match too far. What should have been a fascinating duel between one of the best servers in the women's game – Henin-Hardenne – and one of best returners disintegrated into a one-sided affair. The Belgian cruised to a 6–1 6–1 victory, leaving Pierce shell-shocked and inconsolable. Henin-Hardenne's 24th consecutive victory since returning from injury took her back up to number seven in the rankings; it also gave her momentum going to Wimbledon, the only Grand Slam she had yet to add to her tally.

Women's Singles Final: Henin-Hardenne beat Pierce 6–1 6–1.

Rafael Nadal has proved that when he has some time he is defensively outstanding. He can run down a lot of balls. He plays with a lot of desire. He's the best player in the world right now on a clay court. When it comes to grass courts, things happen a lot faster. The ball can skid on a grass court. You have to make decisions more quickly. You have to just react – and some players like a little bit more time to think about it. So a guy like Roger Federer, in the last couple of years, has shown why the game just comes naturally to him on this surface.

John McEnroe

Opposite: Rafael Nadal celebrates winning a point against Argentinian Mariano Puerta during the final.

Below: Belgian Justine Henin-Hardenne (l) and Mary Pierce of France (r) hold their trophies after their women's final.

US OPEN

Federer spoils Agassi's 20th party

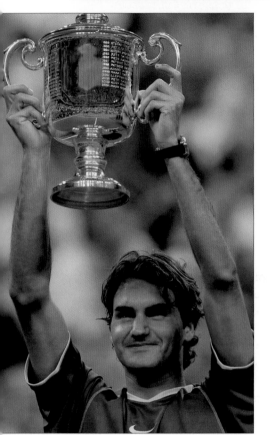

Following his Wimbledon heroics, Andy Murray became the youngest Briton ever to qualify for a Grand Slam when he made it through to the main draw at Flushing Meadows. The Scot had won the junior title in New York in 2004; a year later he was scalp-hunting in the senior division. Andre Pavel was his first-round victim, an excellent five-set win over a former top 30 player. His next opponent, Arnaud Clement, halted his progress in a thriller. Murray came back from two sets down to level against the veteran Frenchman before running out of steam in the fifth. Even so, it had been another step up the ladder, and yet another tournament in which he outshone Henman and Rusedski, who both limped out at the first hurdle.

Blake's inspired form
Henman, semi-finalist in 2004 and seeded 12, suffered a straight-sets defeat against Spain's Fernando Verdasco, his cause not helped by a niggling back injury. Rusedski went into the tournament in excellent form, and with a real chance of reclaiming the British No 1 spot. 25-year-old wildcard entry James Blake ended that hope. The lightning-quick New Yorker, who had never been beyond the third round in a Grand Slam, also beat No. 2 seed Rafael Nadal in an inspired run to the quarters, where he came up against Andre Agassi. Blake took a two-set lead against the two-time champion but lost in a final-set tie-break, a result Agassi described as the best of his career.

Roddick stunned
2003 champion Andy Roddick suffered a shock first-round defeat – all tie-breaks – at the hands of Luxembourg's Gilles Muller. That made top seed and title holder champion Roger Federer an even hotter favourite. Fabrice Santoro and Nicolas Kiefer both gave the Swiss something to think about, but he moved into overdrive against Nalbandian in the last eight. Federer lost just seven games in a 1 hr. 40 min. blitz to set up a semi-final clash with Hewitt, the man he had beaten in the previous year's final. It meant that Federer had reached the semis in six of the last seven Grand Slam events.

Hewitt's nemesis
Federer became Hewitt's nemesis for the ninth successive time, a three-sets-to-one victory taking him through to meet Agassi in the final. Agassi, competing in his 20th US Open, reached his sixth final with a five-set win over unseeded Robby Ginepri. At 35 he became the oldest Grand Slam finalist since 39-year-old Ken Rosewall was demolished by Jimmy Connors in the 1974 Wimbledon final.

Agassi couldn't notch his third US victory, however. He took the second set to square the match and went a break up in the third. But from there it was all downhill. Federer breezed through the third-set tie-break 7–1, then raced through the fourth 6–1 to land his sixth Grand Slam title. That put him just two behind Agassi, a man 12 years his senior. Sampras's 14 majors was still a long way off, though after the match Agassi – who had fought toe-to-toe so often with Pistol Pete – said Federer was the best player he'd ever faced.

Men's Singles Final: Federer beat Agassi 6–3 2–6 7–6(7-1) 6–1.

Clijsters Breaks Grand Slam duck

The top dozen seeds all made untroubled progress through the first two rounds, with the exception of reigning champion Svetlana Kuznetsova, who went out to unseeded fellow Russian Ekaterina Bychkova on day one. A 3–6 2–6 defeat, against a player barely in the top hundred, meant that the woefully out of form Kuznetsova became the first US champion to fall at the first hurdle.

Revenge for Pierce

Round Four saw Mary Pierce gain her revenge over Justine Henin-Hardenne for the humiliating defeat the Belgian had handed her at Roland Garros. Pierce was seeded 12, five places below Henin-Hardenne, but reached the quarter-final with a straight-sets victory, her first win over the Belgian in five attempts.

At the same stage, Venus came out on top in the latest Williams sisters battle. Serena, who had been struggling with injury since Wimbledon, fought a close first set, which her sister took on a tie-break. The second set was easier for Venus as Serena began to tire.

Williams found No. 4 seed Kim Clijsters too hot to handle in the last eight, however. The first two sets were shared, following a string of service breaks, but Clijsters ran away with the decider to set up a semi against top seed Maria Sharapova.

Davenport beaten

Mary Pierce and Elena Dementieva contested the other semi, after beating higher-ranked players in the last eight. Pierce enjoyed a straight-sets win over close friend Amelie Mauresmo in an all-French affair. It was the first time in six years that Pierce had got the better of Mauresmo.

Dementieva began like a train against second seed Lindsay Davenport, taking the opening set 6–1. Davenport upped her game in the second set to level, and both players had chances to take control of the decider before Dementieva clinched victory on a tie-break.

Accusations of gamesmanship

Dementieva failed to reach the final for the second year running, despite taking the first set off Mary Pierce. The Russian was clearly annoyed as Pierce took a 12-minute injury break. It was within the rules but Dementieva's body language suggested she thought there was an element of gamesmanship, particularly as Pierce seemed sprightly enough round the court in taking the next two sets 6–2 6–2 to win the match.

Clijsters beat Sharapova in the other semi, after squandering five match-points. Clijsters was a set and 6–5 up, and had the top seed at 0–40. Sharapova bounced back and won the breaker, but Clijsters took the third set 6–3.

Deja-vu for Pierce

The Belgian had lost in four Grand Slam finals, but there was never much doubt that she would finally break her duck at Flushing Meadows. Clijsters broke Pierce five times in a comprehensive 6–3 6–1 victory. For Pierce it was a case of deja-vu; as at Roland Garros, she had played superbly until the final, where she underperformed against a Belgian playing at the top of her game.

Women's Singles Final: Clijsters beat Pierce 6–3 6–1.

I have a good feeling for the game and I sense when there's a big moment and I think I play them pretty well. When I play a shot I almost see what the opponent is going to do on the next one and then I can work out what I'm going to do. I'm not that far ahead – maybe one or two shots.

Andrew Murray

Opposite: *Roger Federer holds up the championship trophy after defeating Andre Agassi to take his sixth Grand Slam title.*

Left: *Kim Clijsters holds her trophy after defeating Mary Pierce of France (l) in the final.*

LONDON 2012

This is just the most fantastic opportunity to do everything we ever dreamed of in British sport.

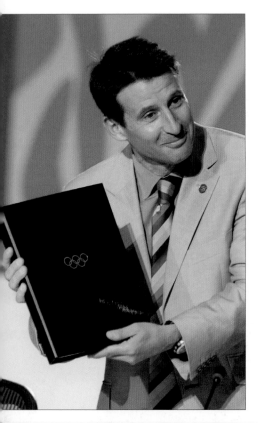

BBC RADIO **FIVE LIVE**

Today we are showing London, the UK and the world that preparations for the 2012 Olympic and Paralympic Games are under way. The passion and commitment we put into the bid is now carrying through to delivering what will be the greatest Olympics ever.

Ken Livingstone

This is just the most fantastic opportunity to do everything we ever dreamed of in British sport

Lord Sebastian Coe

After months of tension and speculation Jacques Rogge, President of the International Olympic Committee finally announced that the 2012 Olympic Games will be held in London. The capital won by 54 votes to 50 after a two-way contest with Paris at the IOC meeting in Singapore. Bids from Moscow, New York and Madrid had been eliminated in previous rounds and Paris was the clear favourite but Lord Sebastian Coe, bid chairman, pulled out all the stops with his final impressive and persuasive presentation. With the announcement of the first Olympics to be held in Britain since 1948, the news swept across the nation. Supporters who gathered in Trafalgar Square and Stratford, the site of the new Olympic park, could not contain their delight as they celebrated the news and messages of congratulations soon poured in including those from the Queen and Prime Minister, Tony Blair, who had made a whistle stop visit to Singapore to support the bid team.

Left: *Sebastian Coe holds the Host City contract during a press conference after London won the vote to stage the 2012 Olympic Games at the Raffle City Convention Centre on July 6, 2005 in Singapore.*
Below: *Londoners celebrate in Trafalgar Square as the announcement is made.*